An Introduction to Multilingualism

OXFORD TEXTBOOKS IN LINGUISTICS

PUBLISHED

The Grammar of Words
An Introduction to Linguistic Morphology
THIRD EDITION
by Geert Booij

A Practical Introduction to Phonetics
SECOND EDITION
by J. C. Catford

An Introduction to Multilingualism
Language in a Changing World
by Florian Coulmas

Meaning in Use
*An Introduction to Semantics and
Pragmatics*
THIRD EDITION
by Alan Cruse

Natural Language Syntax
by Peter W. Culicover

Principles and Parameters
An Introduction to Syntactic Theory
by Peter W. Culicover

A Semantic Approach to English Grammar
by R. M. W. Dixon

Semantic Analysis
A Practical Introduction
by Cliff Goddard

Pragmatics
SECOND EDITION
by Yan Huang

Compositional Semantics
*An Introduction to the Syntax/Semantics
Interface*
by Pauline Jacobson

The History of Languages
An Introduction
by Tore Janson

The Lexicon
An Introduction
by Elisabetta Ježek

A Functional Discourse Grammar for
English
by Evelien Keizer

Diachronic Syntax
by Ian Roberts

Cognitive Grammar
An Introduction
by John R. Taylor

Linguistic Categorization
THIRD EDITION
by John R. Taylor

IN PREPARATION

Translation
Theory and Practice
by Kirsten Malmkjaer

Grammaticalization
by Heiko Narrog and Bernd Heine

Speech Acts and Sentence Types in English
by Peter Siemund

Linguistic Typology
Theory, Method, Data
by Jae Jung Song

Cognitive Grammar
An Introduction
2ND EDITION
by John R. Taylor

An Introduction to Multilingualism

Language in a Changing World

FLORIAN COULMAS

OXFORD

UNIVERSITY PRESS

OXFORD

UNIVERSITY PRESS

Great Clarendon Street, Oxford, OX2 6DP,
United Kingdom

Oxford University Press is a department of the University of Oxford.
It furthers the University's objective of excellence in research, scholarship,
and education by publishing worldwide. Oxford is a registered trade mark of
Oxford University Press in the UK and in certain other countries

Published in the United States of America by Oxford University Press
198 Madison Avenue, New York, NY 10016, United States of America

British Library Cataloguing in Publication Data
Data available

Library of Congress Control Number: 2017939644

ISBN 978-0-19-879110-2 (Hbk)
ISBN 978-0-19-879111-9 (Pbk)

Printed and bound by
CPI Group (UK) Ltd, Croydon, CR0 4YY

Contents

CONTENTS

Preface

The global transformations that mark our age include, among others, rapid urbanization, forced displacement of people by war and armed conflict, labour migration from south to north, demographic ageing, and the intensified spread of digital technologies. While these developments work as transformative forces each in their own right, there is also interactivity between them. For instance, mobile telephony allows refugees and migrants to communicate with people in their homeland much more than would have been possible a generation ago. Similarly, more students take part in study abroad programmes and labour markets have become more international and permeable.

Both increasing multilingualism and growing medial and scholarly occupation with it are effects of these developments, which, however, is not to say that something that used to be small is now big. While multilingualism can be understood as an outgrowth of the said trends, it is at the same time itself undergoing transformations as one aspect of the ever-changing system of the world's languages.

Multilingualism cannot be understood as a phenomenon that waxes and wanes with changing circumstances, while staying substantially what it is. Just like multilingualism in 2017 London is not the same as multilingualism in 2017 Kolkata, the multilingualism of today's Western European cities is not what it was a hundred years ago in the same cities.

Multilingualism is not only an observable objective fact, but a condition that is subject to evaluations, policies, and ideologies that shape our perception as well as the reality we create. It is not in any way my intention to advocate unconditional cultural relativism; there are many facts that can be positively established about the coexistence and interaction of multiple languages. But it is necessary to stress that, regardless of whether it is examined as an individual, societal, or political condition, multilingualism is a phenomenon about which every age produces its own truths. Wherever possible it should be conceptualized as a process rather than a state of affairs.

This book is about change. While writing it, it became clear to me that change is what most prominently characterizes multilingualism today. One conspicuous change is that, because the number of people who live with two or more languages in their everyday lives—estimated at constituting more than half the world's population—is still increasing, and that, therefore, multilingualism is today less frequently seen as a rare phenomenon than used to be the case. This book examines the many faces of multilingualism and the reasons why they keep changing.

Many colleagues have helped me to develop this perspective, and some of them have actively contributed to the enterprise. As the reader will find out in Chapter 2, they have a say on the matter, which I gratefully acknowledge here.

F. C.
Venice, February 2017

List of figures and tables

Figures

Tables

Introduction

Multilingualism is a wide canvas, too wide to be painted by the brush of a single discipline. More able hands from a variety of fields are needed to sketch the outlines and fill in the details of the intricate mosaic of linguistic forms of expression the human mind has produced and to shed light on their functions for the formation of society. Language is a crucial part of human nature, and the multiplicity of languages is part of the human condition. What Oscar Wilde supposedly once quipped about Britain and the USA, that they were divided by a common language, could be said about humanity at large, and Elias Canetti, who lived a life with several languages, called the fact that there are different languages 'the most sinister fact of the world' (Canetti 1993: 18). We are all endowed with language, in the plural, however. United by the faculty of language, a common trait that distinguishes us from other animals, we employ different languages that segregate us more rigidly than almost anything else does. Thus, commenting on the fact that a shared common language is pre-eminently considered the normal basis of nationality, Max Weber (1978: 359) called his time 'the age of language conflicts', a characterization that has hardly lost its aptness in our time.

Because language unites and separates, it is not just linguists who take a serious interest in it, but several scientific disciplines, ranging from the natural sciences, including physical anthropology, to the social sciences, including cultural anthropology, psychology, cognitive science, on to economics, and political science. They all have their specific concerns and look at language from the point of view and by means of the tools of their field. They all produce valuable knowledge about this most human of human properties. However, the apparent commonality of the object of research notwithstanding, the walls that divide scientific disciplines sometimes prove as hard to scale as language boundaries, if not more so.

For example, I have often noticed that sociologists and linguists rarely talk to each other, and when they talk about language among themselves, it is hard to recognize that they are talking about the same phenomenon, for their concepts of 'language' are quite different. In the event that sociologists take issue with language, they tend to take languages as a given, something that has an independent existence. They may use terms such as 'mother tongue' and 'native speaker' as a matter of course, while linguists may feel compelled to define these terms or try to avoid them altogether. Social scientists have little interest in structure, language change, or the coming into existence of new languages. To linguists, on the other hand, the question is of major interest how languages, dialects, and other varieties are related to each other in terms of structure, vocabulary, and pronunciation. Sociologists think that writing is important; linguists usually do not. To linguists all languages are, in principle, equal, that is, equally promising for gaining insights about the architecture of language, whereas sociologists are more interested in the inequality of languages, their prestige, level of cultivation, whether they are used for political or religious purposes, and so on. Psychologists study the acquisition, disorder, and loss of language. Educationalists take issue with measuring the distance between languages in order to improve foreign language teaching and learning. Political scientists are intrigued by the fact that words can be loaded and used more or less skilfully in election campaigns, to inform, or misinform, or manipulate people. Schoolteachers know whether *you may turn on the TV* or *turn the TV on* and generally how to use prepositions correctly. Linguists, by contrast, have serious difficulties with the very notion of correctness. And so on.

Many other questions about language as a natural faculty of Homo sapiens, on the one hand, and a cultural product of distinct groups, on the other, have been studied in the past and continue to be researched today. Because language is so central to human life, various disciplines and theories are concerned with it, and I have mentioned only some. By focusing on particular aspects of language they unravel the mysteries of how children acquire language, how language connects us to the world, how it binds communities together, and allows us to absorb and communicate knowledge. In one way or another, they all contribute to our understanding of language and languages. Both the singular and the plural of 'language' seem to be equally important, certainly, if we look at the world today and that of former times. For all we know, the multiplicity of languages has accompanied the human race as long as the most sophisticated scientific tools can look back into the prehistory of the mind. Each and every language is worth studying, but just as people do not live as monads, languages are not isolated from one another. The coexistence of languages is, therefore, a field of study in its own right, which, however, relies on the insights of many other disciplines, some of which I have mentioned above.

This book describes and explores the consequences of the multiplicity of languages from various points of view. It begins with an overview of the geographic distribution of languages on the planet and then presents a summary account of the complex history interlinking states and languages. Against the background of a discussion about language and power, it offers an account of the world language system as it exists today and from there goes on to examine various explanations grounded in history and political philosophy for where, when, and why multilingualism came to be regarded as a problem, that is, under conditions of the assumed or mandated dominance of a single language.

Subsequent chapters examine the reality of multilingualism with regard to polyglot individuals, international institutions, super-diverse cities, multiethnic countries, and the seemingly borderless cyberspace.

The final part of the book takes up theoretical issues centred upon the integrity of linguistic systems and social systems, raising questions about drawing boundaries, inclusion and exclusion, incorporation and segregation, approval and prohibition. In the light of the examples expounded in the following chapters it will become clear that nowadays multilingualism is not an exotic occurrence, but that it is rather common, and therefore presents a serious challenge for both linguistic and social theory.

1

The polyphonic world

1.1 Numbers

Pashto, Urdu, Hindi, Nepali, Sinhalese, Dzongkha, Brunei, Armenian, Turkish, Georgian, Persian, Kazakh, Kyrgyz, Tajik, Uzbek, Turkmen, Mongolian, Lao, Khmer, Vietnamese, Thai, Burmese, Indonesian, Malaysian, Tetun, Arabic, Filipino, Iban, Hebrew, Mandarin, Tamil, Japanese, Korean. Γ Afrikaans, Bari, Chokwe, Dyrema, Eleme, Fulfulde, Gbaya, Hausa, Idakho-Isukha-Tiriki, Jowulu, Kunda, Loko, Mama, Nupe, Ogbia, Pangwa, Pulaar, Qimant, Ronga, Serer, Swahili, Tetela, Urdu, Viduna, Wanji, Wolof, Xhosa, Yoruba, Zimba. Γ Fijian, Samoan, Nauruan, Palauan, Tok Pisin, Hiri Motu, Ekari, Makasai, Māori, Arrernte, Kala Lagaw Ya, Tongan, Xaracuu, Rukai, Puyuma, Skou, Bislama, Tahitian. Γ Inuit, Micmac, Navaho, Nahuatl, Yucatec Maya, Sranan, Quiché, Aymara, Apalaí, Bororo, Guaraní, Pomeranian, Quechua, Mapudungun, Aymara. Γ Spanish, English, Portuguese, Russian, German.

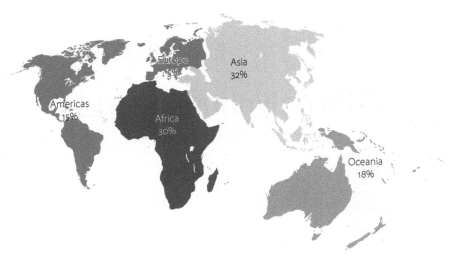

Figure 1.1 Percentage of number of languages spoken on the five continents.

Source: Data from *Ethnologue* 2013. This source is used here in spite of the fact that the organization behind the *Ethnologue*'s database, the Summer Institute of Linguistics (SIL), pursues a Christian missionary agenda and, partly because of that, uses a classification system that is beset with some problems, as Kamusella (2012) has demonstrated. The International Organization for Standardization also provides a list of the world's languages, from Afar to Zazaki (ISO 639-3), but since the organization invited SIL to develop the list, it is just as well to refer to Ethnologue.

The first paragraph of this chapter that you just read, if you have read it, contains the same information as the map in Figure 1.1, although this is perhaps not immediately apparent. It lists 100 languages representing 100 per cent of the multitude of languages known to be used today somewhere on our planet. The enumeration is divided into five sections by the Greek letter Γ gamma, short for γλῶσσα (*glossa*) 'language'. The five sections are of variable length, the first one encompassing 32 languages, representing 32 per cent of the world's languages, the second 30 languages, representing 30 per cent of the same stock, and so on. The five sections thus refer to the five continents, but the languages in each section are not listed on the basis of the same ordering principle. The first section, includes one language each of 32 Asian countries. In Africa, the second section, the multitude of languages extends from A to Z. Oceania, in the third section, includes very old languages that developed in relative isolation for a long time as well as some very young languages that came into existence in the language-richest country on earth, Papua New Guinea, as if they had not enough already. The fourth section registers fifteen languages that are indigenous to the Americas, with one and a half exceptions (which?). And finally, the five languages given for Europe are ordered for number of native speakers.

The map in Figure 1.1 looks slightly different than world maps based on the Mercator projection[1] which are likely what the reader is most familiar with. This is because I have adjusted the size of the continents to reflect the percentage of languages found on each. Africa, which accounts for 20 per cent of the land area on planet earth, therefore, is larger than usual, occupying 32 per cent of the surface. Asia is quite close to its conventional size, since the difference between percentage of landmass and share of the world's languages is just 3 per cent. Europe has 7 per cent land area, but only 5 per cent of languages and is therefore slightly smaller, whereas Oceania is considerably bigger. The Americas look small, because the percentage of languages, 15, is noticeably less than the 28 per cent of land-mass. Two other features of the map, which are obvious, but still warrant comment are that Australia, New Zealand, and the Pacific islands are lumped together as Oceania, and that Antarctica is not shown. As for the former, this is because the spoken languages of Australia and the Pacifics are often dealt with together; and for the purpose at hand, Antarctica is irrelevant because no language has a permanent footing there, all settle-ments being temporary only (cf. also Figure 1.5 below).

In passing it may also be noted that the map is Eurocentric, as most world maps are, which is just to remind us of the inescapability of a point of view. The world map is a good metaphor of the inevitable bias of our considerations; for it represents the globe on a flat surface, which, as mathematician Carl Friedrich Gauss (1777–1855) proved in his 'remarkable theorem' (*Theorema Egregium*) almost 200 years ago, is not possible without distortion. We cannot avoid the bias, but we can try to be aware of it. A European point of view informs all social sciences, subtly or openly, even though we are living in the age of global networks and global-everything. When talking about language, ridding ourselves of biases and prejudices is extra difficult, because languages arouse emotions and almost everyone has opinions about language; about the 'beauty' and 'ugliness' of certain pronunciations; about some languages being harsh and aggressive and others poetic and sweet; worse, some lan-guages not being languages at all but barbaric gibberish. When dealing

---

[1] This projection is so called for the Flemish cartographer Gerardus Mercator (1512–1594). It has been used for nautical purposes since the seventeenth century and, reflecting the European expansion, thus became something like the world standard of world maps.

with the multiplicity of the world's languages, questions of liking and loathing should best be set aside.

The map in Figure 1.1 reflects the geographic distribution of languages. Dividing the world population—7 billion, give or take a few hundred million—by the number of known languages—7,000, give or take a few hundred—$7^9/7,000$, is a simple calculation that gives us a neat round number: one million Γ. Had the world been designed by a mathematician, this would be the average number of speakers per language with little variance, but if indeed a mathematician (mathematical laws) had been involved in its creation, the Platonic order of the universe has been all messed up by human intervention. The average number of speakers per language says nothing about the real world, for the size of language groups varies widely, testifying to the migration and settlement of humans from their earliest dwellings in Africa to cover all continents where they shaped their own ways of speaking. In the course of history, some languages expanded, others stayed small, and many fell by the wayside. The distribution of languages across continents thus contains implicit stories about population dynamics, expansion, conquest, and growth propelled by advances of civilization. Several interesting facts can be inferred by examining the speaker populations of the world's languages. A rough numerical grouping is given in Table 1.1.

There are 134 languages with fewer than 10 speakers constituting some 2 per cent of all languages, and so on. On the whole, there are

Table 1.1 Number of languages by number of native speakers and their percentage of the languages of the world.

Language group size	Number	Percentage
<10	134	2
≤100	340	5.1
≤1000	1054	15.9
≤10K	1984	29.9
≤100K	1798	27.1
≤1M	928	14
≤10M	308	4.7
≤100M	77	1.2
>100M	8	0.1

Source: Ethnologue 2013.

Table 1.2 The top twelve languages by number of native speakers.

Language	Number of native speakers in millions
Chinese	982
Hindi	460
English	375
Spanish	330
Portuguese	216
Bengali	215
Arabic	206
Russian	165
Japanese	127
German	105
French	79
Korean	78

Data source: statista.com/statistics/266808/

many languages with few speakers and few languages with many speakers. Table 1.2 lists in descending order the twelve languages with the most native speakers. Twelve of some 7,000. Taken together their speakers account for almost half the world population, 47.6 per cent, to be exact, although striving for exactitude must be a futile endeavour here. Every figure cited in the table can be contested. Are there really 982 million native speakers of Chinese, rather than 981 million or 983 million? Not to mention the millions of Chinese babies that will be born before this book goes to press and who will grow up to be native speakers of Chinese. And what Chinese? We will come to that. At this point, suffice it to note that data on languages collected through censuses—and there are few other ways—are fraught with problems. They depend on the design of questionnaires, the purposes of the agencies that commission and execute the census, the understanding of respondents and their willingness to respond. All international comparative statistics are faced with similar difficulties which, however, in regards to language are compounded by often politically sensitive issues of language proficiency. The figures (absolute numbers even more so than percentages) must therefore be used with caution. For the purpose at hand, the order of magnitude is what counts: Less than a dozen languages, however defined, with more than 100 million speakers and more than 4,000 languages with fewer than 100,000 speakers. Many ramifications of this disproportion for the social and political existence of languages will occupy us in subsequent chapters.

Numbers do not tell us everything and cannot always be trusted, but even if they suggest a higher degree of precision than in fact can be established, they often allow us to see relationships that would otherwise be hidden. My above speculation that no mathematician was involved in the creation of the world, especially not when it comes to the distribution of languages, may have been rash. Dieter Wunderlich (2015: 37) has pointed out that if we transform Table 1.1 into a bar graph it looks surprisingly like a Gaussian normal distribution of random variables. In this case the random variables are the languages of the world, and the values they can take are the numbers of mother tongue speakers of each. A Gaussian distribution, also called 'bell curve' (Figure 1.2), is symmetric about its mean and is more than zero over its entire real line (here: all languages). The variation of languages by number of speakers follows this pattern. The graph tells us that the median of 50 per cent is a bit less than 10,000, that is, the number of languages with up to 10,000 speakers account for slightly more than 50 per cent of all languages. Beyond that size the number of languages diminishes, the real titans with more than 100 million speakers being just 8 or 0.1 per cent of all languages.

Another interesting characteristic of the distribution of the world's languages is about continents. It again bears witness to population movements in the distant past and the nature of the habitats where migrants settled. As we have seen in Figure 1.1, the languages are dis-

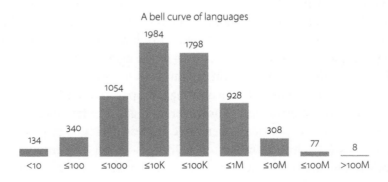

Figure 1.2 Gaussian distribution of languages by number of native speakers.

persed very unevenly across continents. The disparities are even bigger when we compare continents by percentage of world population and percentage of languages. A simple division of the latter by the former gives us a linguistic diversity index (Table 1.3).

The linguistic diversity index (LDI) of a given territory, in the event continents, is the quotient, a/b, of its share of the world's languages (a) and its share of the world population (b). On the basis of this calculation, Oceania is the most linguistically diverse continent by a large measure, since it is home to 18 per cent of all languages, but of only half a per cent of the world population. Considering the natural environment, this is not surprising. While in the period of earliest human migration the other continents were connected to each other by land bridges, Oceania has been completely separated. Many thousands of islands were first inhabited by small groups of seafaring migrants who then lived there for many generations with little or no contact with the outside world. Archaeological evidence suggests that the earliest inhabitants of Australia and New Guinea similarly lived a secluded life in small groups (O'Connell and Allen 2003). Inhabitation of Australia and New Guinea is thought to go back to the oldest migration out of Africa, maybe some 50,000 years ago. The great time depth of some 1600 generations and the fractured landscape, provided the environment for a high number of languages to develop, many hundreds in Australia and as many as 1,000 in New Guinea.

The natural environment was not the only force that favoured linguistic fragmentation—you can also call it language richness—but it did play an important role. As Daniel Nettle (1998: 357) quoting Breton (1991) and Nichols (1992) has noted, language diversity is greatest in

Table 1.3 Linguistic diversity index calculated by dividing percentage of languages by percentage of world population per continent.

Continent	Percentage of world population	Percentage of languages	Linguistic diversity index	Rank
Asia	60	32	0.53	4
Africa	15.5	30	1.94	2
Americas	14.2	15	1.1	3
Europe	10.4	5	0.5	5
Oceania	0.5	18	36	1

Source: following Wunderlich 2015: 39, with adjustments.

tropical regions near the equator where the diversity of natural species is also the greatest. Language diversity is often thought of as being analogous to natural species richness. The idea that this might not be fortuitous goes back to Charles Darwin.

1.2 Family affairs

The languages of the world differ in many ways exhibiting an astounding range of variance; but they also resemble each other in non-arbitrary ways. English resembles Dutch more than both resemble Cantonese, and Tamil has more in common with Yerukala than with Polish. English and Dutch, and Tamil and Yerukala are genetically related to each other and are therefore customarily said to belong to the same language family, the former two to the Indo-European family and the latter two to the Dravidian family. This metaphor carries a long way. It allows us to bring some order into the confusing array of languages and their inexhaustible variety.

The idea that a family of languages may be more than just a plausible analogy was first put forth by Charles Darwin in his famous treatise *On the Origin of Species* which exerted a huge influence on many sciences in the nineteenth century. As its subtitle explains, it is about 'the preservation of favoured races in the struggle for life'. Darwin proposed a classification of the natural system in which different groups are ranked 'under different so-called genera, sub-families, families, sections, orders, and classes'. And he went on to illustrate this view of classification 'by taking the case of languages' which he saw as directly linked to 'the genealogical arrangement of the races of man'. He explained that 'the various degrees of difference between the languages of the same stock, would have to be expressed by groups subordinate to groups; but the proper or even the only possible arrangement would still be genealogical' (Darwin 1859: 406).

That different languages share certain features of phonology, syntax, and lexicon is apparent to anyone who has studied a foreign language. The degree of similarity depends on the amount of shared features. For instance, Mandarin, Cantonese, Vietnamese, Thai, and many other languages spoken in China and in Southeast Asia use pitch to distinguish lexical meaning. These languages are therefore known as tone (or tonal) languages. However, tone languages are also found in Africa and in North and South America. Pitch is one of many features that humans

8

can use to make distinctions in their speech. Similarly, noun class systems, a grammatical organization principle to categorize nouns, is a characteristic feature of Niger-Congo languages. However, Japanese and Korean also have elaborate noun class systems. Or take vowel harmony, an assimilatory process of vowels which is a distinctive feature of Turkic languages, but also of Igbo, a language spoken in south-eastern Nigeria, and Telugu of South India, among others. The occurrence of a single feature is thus not enough to establish any genealogical relationship between languages, but a clustering of features in combination with shared vocabulary does.

In the nineteenth century, Darwin's suggestion of a substantial relationship between 'human races' and languages fell on fertile ground in linguistics where the historical-comparative method made great progress putting 'the various degrees of difference' on a solid empirical footing that measures the degree of variance and distance between different members of a group of languages. Lexicostatistical methods determine the distance between languages on the basis of shared vocabulary, while linguistic typology classifies languages according to structural features, such as the use of tone, word order, morphology, etc. The set of the features that distinguish languages has been likened to a gene pool in population genetics. Progress in and standardization of language description worldwide have made reasoned classifications of languages possible. They are now commonly presented as family trees in the manner of the simplified tree of Sino-Tibetan languages in Figure 1.3. The whole family is much larger, comprising some 450 languages.

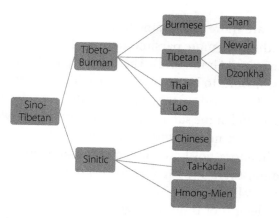

Figure 1.3 Family tree of Sino-Tibetan languages, greatly simplified.

Physical anthropologists, archaeologists, and linguists have joined forces to put Darwin's idea into practice quite beyond the metaphorical level, demonstrating that the genetic structure of population groups is significantly correlated with linguistic affiliations (e.g. for Europe: Sokal et al. 1989; for Africa: Scheinfeldt et al. 2010). There is still much controversy about particular aspects of language classification, and research about the connection between linguistic and genetic classifications continues. However, in the light of findings so far, language families must be seen as a reality that incorporates much information about the dispersal of modern humans in prehistoric times. It also invites conclusions, or at least hypotheses, about social patterns because it suggests that groups carry their languages with them and tend to stick to them. The time depth of early population movement is not definitely known, and from the number of extant languages we cannot conclude that there always were that many groups, or when and where they formed.

The following list is how *Omniglot*, an online encyclopaedia of languages, sorts languages into 45 families:

Afroasiatic, Algonqian, Altaic, Arawakan, Austroasiatic, Australian, Austronesian, Aymaran, Barbacoan, Cariban, Cahuapanan, Caucasian, Chibchan, Dravidian, Eskimo-Aleut, Guaicuruan, Hmong, Indo-European, Iroquoian, Japonic, Jivaroan, Khoisan, Mayan, Mirndi, Misumalpan, Muskogean, Na-Dené, Niger-Congo, Pama-Nyungan, Panoan, Peba-Yaguan, Oto-Manguean, Nilo-Saharan, Quechuan, Salishan, Sino-Tibetan, Siouan, Tai-Kaidai, Tucanoan, Tupi-Guaraní, Uralic, Uto-Aztecan, Yenisei, Zaparoan.

Other indexes are more fine-grained, recognizing up to 300 language families. Yet others are more parsimonious making do with just 22 families (Wichmann and Grant 2012). These discrepancies suggest not only that there is still work to be done. Classifications are systems that help us to organize the world. If they are good they are derived from the world of objects and at the same time add something to what is directly perceptible. They are never quite independent of the researcher's point of view and therefore not hewn in stone. Disagreements about detail notwithstanding, there is virtually no dispute that languages can be classified genetically and that degrees of similarity and distance bear witness to the length of time since groups split up—however difficult it may be to draw a realistic timeline into the ancient past—and that conclusions about migration flows can be drawn from the geographical distribution of languages.

Language classification systems often contain the caveat that the transplantation of European languages to other continents during the past 500 years is left out of consideration, and for good reasons, because this half millennium has seen more drastic population shifts than ever before. Yet, this self-imposed limitation is a bit ironic, for the first major discovery of genealogical relationships between languages was a by-product of the European expansion. In 1786, William Jones, a British judge stationed in Calcutta who took a serious interest in Indian languages, observed that Sanskrit had more commonalities with Greek and Latin than could reasonably be thought to be coincidental. Greece and Bengal are separated by a distance of 6,000 kilometres and a sea lane half way round the world, how could this be? The most convincing explanation: migration. Darwin's point was to relate linguistic diversity to what he called the 'arrangement of the races of man', and that is all about migration.

1.3 Richness of languages and the wealth of nations

The first migrants out of Africa went east along the coast to India, reaching Southeast Asia and Australia. They moved in small groups staying in moderate climate zones. Nomads ventured to northern latitudes of Asia and Europe only later, eventually crossing the land bridge that connected Asia with the Americas. After all continents had been colonized, the human journey continued, and it still does, changing the linguistic face of the planet; but the geographic distribution of languages still testifies to early migration flows. Today, the ten countries with the most languages are without exception in the tropics: Papua New Guinea, Indonesia, Nigeria, India, Mexico, Cameroon, Democratic Republic of the Congo, Brazil, Chad, and Myanmar, listed in Table 1.4 in descending order of number of languages.

Since countries differ widely in size and population, the number of languages per country is not a meaningful measure of linguistic diversity. The linguistic diversity index (LDI) in column F of Table 1.4, which matches percentage of world population with percentage of languages, offers a more expressive assessment. It reveals at a glance that Papua New Guinea is the real outlier, housing just 0.11 per cent of the world population but 11.81 per cent of all languages. It also shows that despite

Table 1.4 Diversity index of the ten countries with the most languages, C/E.

A	B	C	D	E	F
Country	Number of languages	% languages	Population (millions)	% of world population	C/E
PNG	802	11.81	8	0.11	107
Indonesia	742	9.95	258	3.54	2.8
Nigeria	427	7.41	186	2.56	2.8
India	405	6.39	1284	17.6	0.36
Mexico	243	4.07	122	1.67	2.4
Cameroon	275	3.96	23	0.33	12
Dem. Congo	219	0.92	85	0.65	1.4
Brazil	209	3.22	205	2.82	1.14
Chad	126	1.84	14	0.2	9.2
Myanmar	105	1.65	54	74	3.01

its many languages, the degree of India's linguistic diversity is not very high, because of its huge population.

The ten countries in Table 1.4 are clustered around the equator, and except Brazil they are poor as measured in per capita income. Taking this observation a little further, we can try to find out whether this is coincidental or indicates an interesting correlation. In a seminal contribution to charting the languages of the world, American linguist Joseph Greenberg proposed, quite in the spirit of Darwin, that by comparing disparate geographic areas, it will be possible 'to correlate varying degrees of linguistic diversity with political, economic, geographic, historic, and other non-linguistic factors' (Greenberg 1956: 109). As quoted in section 1.2, Darwin was concerned with 'the preservation of favoured races in the struggle for life'. Again, at the risk of sounding rather anthropomorphic, this notion can be applied to languages. There is a great disproportion between the number of languages of language families and their demographic strength. The six biggest families, Indo-European, Sino-Tibetan, Niger-Congo, Austronesian, Afro-Asiatic (formerly called Hamito-Semitic), and Dravidian, account for close to 90 per cent of the world population, but comprise only 65 per cent of all languages. With roughly 21 per cent or 1,524 languages the Niger-Congo family is the largest, followed by 1,221 Austronesian languages (17 per cent). The Indo-European family comprises about 5.5 per cent of all languages, but almost twice that share of the world population. Evidently, some of these languages were 'favoured in the struggle for life'. So have Austronesian languages been, for now. They have been passed on through the generations, although their speech communities were invariably very small.

This was possible because for a long time, the region was left alone, bypassed by history, as it were. Like other peoples in remote areas, Pacific islanders were left behind in the tropics which the arrival of the white man turned into the *Tristes Tropiques*. This phrase was coined by French anthropologist Claude Lévi-Strauss in his famous melancholic memoire of his encounter with a people he studied in the rain forest of Brazil in the 1930s, and whose way of life he knew had no future. That tropical countries are rich in languages and poor in material wealth may be two sides of the same coin. For longer periods than other parts of the world they were deprived of, or protected against, the development that comes with the upheavals of war, colonization, and the ever faster rolling wheels of progress. In Oceania this is perhaps most obvious, but the general tendency can be observed in many other areas too.

Ferdinand de Saussure ([1916] 1985: 281), pioneer of structural linguistics, recognized two influences in the history of the world's languages, provincialism [*esprit de clocher*] and intercourse [*force d'intercourse*], which he thought counteract each other, but in modern times were skewed towards the side of intercourse. Isolation fosters idiosyncrasy and continuation of heredity, while intercourse propels adaptation and change. Adaptation and heredity are the key ingredients of Darwin's concept of natural selection. Evolution theory explains (predicts) that those individuals survive who are best equipped to adapt to their environment. Genetic alterations (mutations) may help organisms to adapt more quickly to their environments or, by contrast, lead to extinction. The merits of applying evolution theory to the world of languages are anything but clear, however, although languages are not living organisms but tools used by living organisms (humans), it is customary in present-day discourse to speak of the extinction of languages (Romaine and Nettle 2000). Many linguistic traditions are discontinued, as parents no longer hand down their language to their children or children refuse to use them. No mono-causal explanation can do justice to this complex social process, but on a very general level it can be said that relatively sudden exposure to modern life left the communities concerned with not enough time to adapt their languages to a drastically changed environment and they were therefore abandoned in

13

favour of others better adapted to and more useful for the functions of modern-day life.

This is another way of saying that every language is a system of signs governed by interrelated rules that follow their own principles, but are not invulnerable to non-linguistic factors and deliberate intervention. To every generation of speakers, their language is both a ready-made structure they acquire in early childhood, and what they make of it by adding to, transgressing, and bending the rules they were offered by their elders. Is one's mother tongue destiny? Yes, in the sense that we cannot choose the first words we hear; no, in the sense that we can decide to affiliate ourselves with a different language later in life. To answer this question more theoretically, we can apply the conceptual framework of 'structure and agency' used in the social sciences to explain social reproduction. From this point of view, human behaviour is the result of a complex interplay of objective factors—structure—and subjective factors—agency. Languages cannot evolve but as a mode of human behaviour. In many ways, they reflect the social existence of their speakers—for example kinship terminology—and their interaction with the ecosystem in which they live. Speakers can change their language, for instance by introducing generic *she* or singular *they*; they can change functional domain allocations of languages, for instance by opening the school to immigrant languages; and they can opt out of a language in favour of another. Whether they do one or the other is strongly influenced by the socioeconomic conditions in which they live.

For languages adjusted to the communication needs of hunter-gatherers, the conditions to be handed down to future generations are nowadays very unfavourable. The small size of many speech communities is an important factor, because the marketization of ever more spheres of life does not stop before languages. To linguists, the size of a language's community of speakers does not matter, to economists it does. Linguists are fascinated by the inventiveness of the human mind and the endless variation of structural options the many languages embody. Economists, by contrast, think in terms of efficiency and possibilities of reducing transaction costs. Economies of scale have produced the big companies that now dominate many markets, and similar forces favour big over small languages, and few languages over many languages. As large-scale global surveys have found, 'bilateral merchandise trade flows are higher between pairs of countries that share a common language' (Helliwell 1999: 5; see also Ginsburgh and Weber 2011: 60).

There is mounting evidence that not just trade but the world economic system as a whole works against linguistic diversity. On the basis of large-scale international comparative surveys, Fishman observed as early as the 1960s, that 'linguistically homogeneous polities are usually economically more developed, educationally more advanced, and politically more modernized' (Fishman 1968: 41). In another early study, Jonathan Pool (1972) correlated countries' per capita gross domestic product with linguistic homogeneity and arrived at the conclusion that homogeneous countries could be poor, but very heterogeneous countries could never be rich. No one would assert that the degree of linguistic homogeneity is the only determiner of a polity's per capita income, but looking at the association between richness of languages and the material wealth of nations half a century later, there is no reason to revise the general account Fishman and Pool presented. If anything, the tendency they uncovered has become stronger, lending support to the hypothesis that global linguistic diversity will continue to diminish.

Table 1.5 confronts the ten poorest countries with the ten richest countries in terms of per capita GNP and linguistic diversity. The general picture that emerges from this table reconfirms the correlation of wealth and homogeneity observed by Fishman (1968): The linguistic

Table 1.5 The ten poorest countries, A, and the ten richest countries, D.

A	B	C	D	E	F
Country	LDI	GNP p.c. US$ 2013/14	Country	LDI	GNP p.c. US$ 2013/14
C. African Rep.	17	600	Norway	3	103,050
Somalia	1.3	600	Switzerland	3	90,670
Dem. Congo	1.4	700	Qatar	5	90,420
Malawi	1.4	800	Luxembourg	10	69,880
Burundi	0.4	900	Sweden	2.4	61,400
Liberia	7	900	Denmark	3.7	61,310
Niger	1.1	1000	Kuwait	1.6	55,470
Mozambique	1.9	1100	Austria	2.5	50,390
Eritrea	13.7	1200	Finland	3.7	48,910
Guinea	26	1300	Germany	0.8	47,640
Mean	7	910		3.57	67,874

Data source: World Bank.

diversity of the rich countries is half that of the poor countries. At the same time, Pool's (1972) claim that rather homogeneous countries can be poor is also borne out by a few countries, notably Burundi and the Democratic Republic of the Congo, with a low LDI. Luxembourg seems to be an exception to the observed correlation, but its high LDI is of a special nature, having to do with being the seat of many international (European) institutions and cross-border labour migration from neighbouring countries. If we take Luxembourg out, the LDI of the richest countries is 2.8, which is more representative of the general picture.

1.4 A complex system

The available evidence suggests that economic development favours linguistic homogenization and standardization and it is, therefore, not farfetched to assume that economic progress in developing countries will bring in its wake reductions of linguistic diversity/fragmentation. Since the economically motivated snowball effect of languages being abandoned for fear of desertion can be observed in many countries, language endangerment has become a research field in its own right.[2] It is nevertheless difficult to make numerically precise and testable predictions about the future linguistic stock of humanity. For, although no one would deny that nowadays economic thought holds more sway than linguistic ideas, economic valuation is not all that counts when it comes to language, and market forces are not the only factors working on the distribution of the world's languages.

The languages of the world constitute a highly complex system (De Swaan 2001) precisely because language plays an important role in several different spheres of human life. The conditions that make some languages thrive and other perish cannot be reduced to economic parameters alone. The political, legal, social, medial, ideological, cultural, and religious dimensions of languages must also be taken into account, as well as a language's state of development, and, last but not least, the ill-defined but important issue of multiple layers of identity

---

[2] See, for example, the UNESCO Atlas of the World's Languages in Danger at http://www.unesco.org/languages-atlas/; the Documentation of Endangered Languages at http://dobes.mpi.nl/, and the Endangered Language Project at http://www.endangeredlanguages.com/.

(individual, social, ethnic, national) that may feed the desire against all odds to maintain a language that seems at the brink of extinction.

The most noticeable feature of the world language system is the inequality of its elements, the languages. This is worth mentioning because linguists prefer to emphasize the equality of all human languages in the sense that theoretically they can all express whatever human beings need to express. In practice, however, languages are not just diverse, but in many ways unequal, as might be expected on the basis of the numerical differences between their speech communities discussed above.

The first dimension of inequity is status. The United Nations recognizes six official languages, Arabic, Chinese, English, French, Russian, Spanish, as do other international organizations, such as the World Health Organization and the International Criminal Court. Rather than economic conditions, this selection reflects political conditions at the time when these organizations were founded after the Second World War (notice the absence of German and Japanese!). On national and subnational levels, just 211 languages enjoy some kind of formal status as official, co-official, or national language, less than 3 per cent of all languages. Notice that while 211 is not the exact same number, it is the same order of magnitude as the number of sovereign states that constitute the world system.[3] Status recognition is directly related to the political world order. There is no state without official language, and only very few languages are used in this capacity. In many instances when languages are conferred official status or that of 'national language' they are subject to elaborate ideological support structures, such as linguistic nationalism that are also part of the world system of languages. Again, this holds for few languages only, as there are only a small number of states and an even smaller number of would-be states, such as Kurdistan, a vast territory spread across four countries which has a national language, but is not a nation state.

All of the languages listed in Table 1.6 enjoy official status somewhere, but there are great disparities between them. The dominance of European languages as a lasting remnant of the age of discovery and colonization is very conspicuous. English, French, Portuguese, Spanish, Dutch, and Italian were carried overseas to become indigenized on continents far afield, whereas the other languages with official status in multiple polities were spread in contiguous areas.

---

[3] The United Nations lists 206 states which are divided into three categories: 193 member states, two observer states, and eleven other states.

Table 1.6 Languages with official status in several countries (2017).

Language	Official status in number of countries
English	64
French	34
Arabic	26
Spanish	23
Portuguese	10
Russian	8
German	7
Fula	7
Dutch	6
Chinese	5
Italian	5
Malay	4
Swahili	4
Persian	3
Turkish	3
Swedish	3
Tamil	3
Tswana	3

Languages further differ in whether or not they are used in formal education and at what level. Higher education is the exclusive domain of a small number of languages. An overwhelming number of all languages have never been used in this function and never will be, as they lack standardization and orthography. No textbooks or any other literature are available in these languages, making them unsuitable for the representation and acquisition of knowledge outside face-to-face contexts. A related dimension of inequality is foreign language education. Only very few languages are taught systematically as foreign languages, and fewer still are those found worthy by interested governments to be promoted abroad. Foreign language education is a huge market generating tens of billions of dollars annually as well as a field of fierce diplomatic competition which, however, is dominated by very few players. The size of a language's native speaker community, its official status in the world, and the relative wealth of the countries where it is spoken work together to produce network effects that favour 'big' languages, particularly English (Wiese 2015). Languages spoken by many speakers are attractive for learners and literary producers (authors as well as publishers), and the reverse is also true. All attempts at solving the world communication problem by establishing a neutral artificial language were frustrated by the impossibility of attracting a sufficiently large number of learners to overcome the initial hurdle of the absence of a community of interlocutors (Pool 1991). Choices of foreign languages to study are not entirely determined by economic considerations, but to a very large extent. Traditional curricula, cultural attractiveness, and emotional motives play subsidiary roles which, however, can also be assessed as values that have a bearing on language competition. Foreign language learning is thus the component of the world language system that is most susceptible to market forces and, therefore, most amenable to economic modelling of supply and demand and agents making choices.

A final differentiation inherent in the world system concerns minority status. A speech form may or may not be granted minority language status for political reasons, but the process of recognition is also often tied to difficult questions of language differentiation having to do with the well-known problem of language vs. dialect. In some cases, such as Picard, both kinds of considerations overlap. In France, this variety is a French dialect, in Belgium a minority language.

The picture that this brief overview of the world system of languages reveals is one of a hierarchical order comprising a large set of disparate components that are subject to several interacting forces. The dynamics of the system are clearest at its extremes, which is also where the inherent inequities are most pronounced. At the top, one superpower language, English, has everything going for it: a large community of native speakers, international standing, official status in a large number of countries, worldwide demand as a foreign language, and a rich literature of every genre in print and online. At the bottom, thousands of minor languages have none of these properties. They are local, confined to a small community, enjoy no official status, are not used in formal education and are not in demand as foreign languages, have no literature, and for the most part no ideological backing. In the middle range of the system, conditions are more diffuse, but the dimensions along which languages are set to compete with each other are the same:

demographic strength;
international standing;
official status;
market as foreign language;
standardization and literary development;
ideological support structure.

*Portuguese, German, Hindi, Persian, Swahili, Malay, Fula

Figure 1.4   The world language system.

The languages that differ along these dimensions can be thought to exist in a five-tier system as shown in Figure 1.4.

Figure 1.4 is a scheme that offers some orientation, no more than that. There are many open questions, especially concerning the middle-range languages, but not only those. All of the problems of separating and counting languages have not been solved. By way of concluding this chapter, a brief look at some of them will be useful, as they will be relevant in subsequent chapters.

1.5 Counting

Suppose you have a stamp collection and you want to know how many stamps you have collected over the years. You start counting, a tedious business. Looking at the various designs, shapes, and colours your mind is wandering. There are interesting stories behind the stamps. Some are extremely rare, others run-of-the-mill. Do they have any value? You lost track. Have you counted that one? You start over again only to realize that two stamps are stuck together. And then there is the question of what counts as a duplicate. There are problems, but with some patience you will come to a definite result, the correct number of the stamps of your collection, a result that can be checked and replicated by a bookkeeper.

Instead of stamps you may want to count languages or just verify the counting of others, such as the latest edition of *Ethnologue*, 7,102, for example. There are problems, too, but diligence, attentiveness, and patience will not clear things up for good. Stamps are discrete objects, languages are not. The multiplicity of languages, therefore, is different in kind from a pile of stamps. Japanese and Italian are two languages; that is a clear case. The grammars are completely different; there is no common lexical stock, except for a few loanwords—such as *opera*, *mezzo*, and *tempo* in Japanese and *tofu*, *otaku*, and *tsunami* in Italian, for example—and speakers of Japanese and Italian do not understand each other. That is a good start, but things do not stay that simple. There is no need to draw a line between Japanese and Italian, they are just different for everyone to see.

Grammatical typology, shared lexical stock, and mutual intelligibility are the three most common criteria used for language classification and hence for counting. They are not fool proof, however. Are Venetian and Italian two languages or one? Opinions are divided. Is what people in the Okinawan islands speak a language, or perhaps several languages, or dialects of Japanese? Opinions are passionately divided. The Shaaxi (陝西) and Gansu (甘肃) Mandarin dialects are understood by the Dungans of Central Asia who, however, cannot really understand Beijing Mandarin. Should Dungan be regarded as a Mandarin dialect? Opinions are divided, again. Are Korean and North Korean two different languages? You will find 'North Korean' in some statistics.

If we incorporate the time axis in our quest to count languages, things get messier still. Should what was considered one language yesterday be counted as one today? Serbo-Croatian also known as Croato-Serbian was the dominant language of Yugoslavia, but when Croatia broke away from Yugoslavia and established an independent state, it declared Croatian its national language which, upon Croatia's accession to the European Union in 2013, also became an official language of the EU (Busch 2016). Its grammatical similarity, shared vocabulary and inter-communicability with Serbian has hardly changed. In the wake of the dissolution of Yugoslavia, language status was claimed for two other varieties, Bosnian and Macedonian, which were not recognized previously in international contexts. Further along the time axis into the past, consider Latin and Sanskrit! In the event, there is no question about their status as languages, but should they be included in an inventory of living languages? Opinions are divided.

The above examples are striking, but in no way exceptional. Rather they illustrate the general problem of naming, categorizing, and counting languages. Measuring the size of a language community by assigning speakers to languages is no less problematic. Some people cannot honestly answer the question what their mother tongue is in the singular, but for various reasons may do so.

These problems are compounded by relatively simple matters such as multiple names of languages. Take Memi, for example, a language spoken by some 20,000 people in Nagaland, India. 'Memi' is what they call it, but to other people in Nagaland it is known as 'Mao' or 'Sopvoma'. Or Yi and Mizo, two Sino-Tibetan languages spoken in Yunnan. In the bulk of English-language literature they are known as 'Lolo' and 'Lushai', but these names have pejorative connotations and are therefore avoided by speakers of Yi and Mizo.

And finally, there is the issue of the 'Bible translation-based overcounting of languages imposed from outside' which Kamusella (2012: 76) identified as a principal flaw of the language recognition work done by Ethnologue, an organization initiated by evangelical societies which has become something of a global authority that imposes its own methods and purposes on speakers of other tongues without taking their point of view into account. For the 'mission-(pre)ordained making of a dialect into a language was not to meet any needs of a concerned speech community, but a missionary organization's self-adopted chiliastic and proselytizing belief in the Christian God-inspired imperative to make the Bible available in all the world's languages' (Kamusella 2012: 74).

These concerns bring us back to the predicament of the 'point of view' problem discussed at the beginning of the chapter. They are valid, and the difficulties of delimiting, recognizing, naming, and counting languages are real and must be borne in mind when dealing with the multiplicity of languages in a given geographical area or a defined population. However, they do not reduce the polyphony of human voices or make the world's linguistic diversity less fascinating. Whether this multiplicity is a curse or blessing is a question about which positions have been divided since antiquity.[4] To settle the issue is not our task. For present purposes it must suffice to note that, since antiquity, it has been a part of the human condition and as such is deserving of our attention.

1.6 Conclusions

Humanity speaks in many tongues. For as long as can be ascertained (which is not very long) this has always been so. As this chapter has shown, the multiplicity of languages constitutes a complex system that is an outflow of and reflects other aspects of the multiformity of human life, genetic, economic, political, and cultural. Populations can be distinguished by their genes, and it has been established that genetic differences correlate with linguistic differences. These correlations bear witness to a common history of diffusion and inheritance, but they cannot explain any differences between languages with regards to the demographic strength of speech communities, their economic importance, and political status—the principal dimensions of the inequalities that characterize the world language system. However, because the geographic distribution of languages is in various ways associated with these inequalities, the study of the polyphonic world in all its facets is above all about inequality.

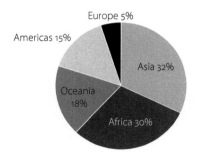

Figure 1.5   The distribution of languages across continents.

[4] The voices that have bemoaned the diversity of language as a great calamity have been somewhat louder, it must be admitted, than those celebrating it as proof of human ingenuity. Just think of the proverbial 'Babylonian confusion of tongues' described in the Book of Genesis 11:1–9; or Confucius' plea for linguistic standardization, based on his reasoning that if names are not correct, language (in the singular!) is not in accordance with the truth of things.

Problems and questions for discussion

1. What is the linguistic diversity index (LDI) of your class? Make a research design to determine your university's LDI!
2. What are the principal differences between counting stamps and counting languages?
3. What if any is the relationship between language diversity and national wealth?
4. In what sense are languages equal, and in what sense disparate?

Further reading

De Swaan, Abram. 2001. *Words of the World*. Cambridge: Polity Press.

Grin, François. 2003. On the costs of cultural diversity. In: Philippe van Parijs (ed.), *Cultural Diversity versus Economic Solidarity*. Brussels: De Boeck Université, 193–206.

Nettle, Daniel. 1999. *Linguistic Diversity*. Oxford: Oxford University Press.

Ruhlen, Merritt. 1994. *On the Origin of Language: Studies in Linguistic Taxonomy*. Stanford, CA: Stanford University Press.

2

Multilingualism is...

Twenty definitions and more

The previous chapter has set the scene. There are a great many languages in the world, and we have to deal with them somehow. In the first overview, we have avoided the term 'multilingualism' because in scholarly writing it is not advisable to use important terms without proper definition, and if any term is important in this book, it is 'multilingualism'. Intuitively, it is clear what it means. *Multi-* is a common prefix meaning 'many' occurring in almost 1,000 English words. *Lingual* is an unremarkable adjective that means 'relating to language', and *-ism* is an extremely productive suffix. Anything can be an *-ism*: ibsedixitism, doomsdayism, fallibilism (the doctrine that knowledge is always provisional, never definitive), Hamletism; closer to home: linguicism (discrimination based on language) or, why not: not-on-my-smartphoneism. Most -isms fall into one of the following categories: a system of thought (e.g. Darwinism, Postcolonialism), a political or religious ideology (e.g. communism, creationism), a special practice (exorcism, cronyism), an artistic vogue (Dadaism, constructivism), a linguistic phenomenon (e.g. archaism, Latinism). Thus we may conclude that *multilingualism* refers to a multiplicity of languages and their coexistence.

2.1 Dictionary definitions

Assuming that this is the core meaning—multilingualism refers to a multiplicity of languages and their coexistence—the question that then arises is which category does multilingualism belongs to, if that can be decided. To some people it may be a practice, to others an ideology, and to yet others a fad. Another question which, perhaps, brings us closer to a reasoned decision is why we need a term for it at all. The 1971 edition of the *Oxford English Dictionary*, the only one I ever bought, lists nothing between 'multilineal' and 'multiloquacious'. The latter comes pretty close to the target, but isn't quite it. Even if the *OED* dispensed with the '-ism', 'multilingual' would have to be there, between these two entries. The present online edition has an entry for it. Why is it worth including in the dictionary now, but was not then?

Actually, upon enquiry, the Oxford Dictionaries team courteously supplied the following information:

Multilingualism was first published in A Supplement to the OED, volume II (1976) as a subentry of 'multilingual, adj. and n.'

Pronunciation: Brit. multilingualism#_gb_3.mp3 /ˌmʌltɪˈlɪŋgwəlɪz(ə)m/ , multilingualism#_gb_2.mp3 /ˌmʌltɪˈlɪŋgwlɪz(ə)m/, U.S. multilingualism#_us_1.mp3 /ˌməltiˈlɪŋgwəˌlɪz(ə)m/ ; see also multi- comb. form.

Etymology: Formed within English, by derivation. **Etymons:** multilingual adj., -ism suffix. Compare earlier bilingualism n.

The state or condition of being multilingual, or the policy of promoting this; the ability to speak many languages; the use of many languages.

Further, according to the publication history of *multilingualism*, which is documented on a separate page of the current *OED* online edition,[1] the term first appeared in print on 26 June 1916 in the *Manitoba Free Press*, a fact of some significance to which we will return below. Seven years later, in 1923, the *OED* began to approach the subject, including as a new entry 'multilinguist, n. *A person who is able to speak several or many languages; a student of or expert in many languages.*' The definition is cogent and in keeping with the etymology, but it leads us down the wrong alley exemplifying the general

---

[1] See online companion page to this chapter.

principle that etymology is not a reliable predictor of current meaning. What the *multilinguist* indicates is that, when he or she caught the *OED*'s attention, multilingua*lism* was not an issue. Half a century later it was.

Many things of historical dimension happened in the meantime, most notably the Second World War, but it was the drawn-out process of decolonization as one of its lasting consequences that produced the phenomenon we now call 'multilingualism'. As territories formerly dominated by European imperial powers (and to a lesser extent the USA) became independent states, population flows from Africa, Asia, Oceania, and the Caribbean to Europe brought about significant social change. Between 1945 and 1960, three dozen new states in Asia and Africa achieved independent statehood and forty-five states acceded to the United Nations Organisation. In the 1970s another twenty-six followed. While independence was desired by many, its achievement was accompanied by much hardship, turmoil, and often bloodshed that drove many inhabitants out of their newly independent countries to seek refuge in their former motherlands.

South Asians began arriving in the UK shortly after their countries gained independence and in the wake of the partition of India in 1947. They were followed by tens of thousands of Asians who were driven out of Uganda in the early 1970s. In the 1960s, France received an influx of North African migrants along with the exodus of some 900,000 Pied-Noirs, as French residents of their former colony were known. The Netherlands became home to almost one third of the population of Suriname when this small South American colony gained independence in 1975. Without going further into the details of post-colonial migration, these three examples may suffice to illustrate the general point. Whereas the colonial regime had Europeans migrate to various places around the world invariably carrying with them their mother tongue as the language of rule (Calvet 1974), the process of decolonization instigated a reverse population flow that changed the demographic composition of Western European countries (and continues to do so), as the former colonial subjects also carried their languages with them.

It was in this context that multilingualism became a matter of general interest, as opposed to an individual capacity or pursuit. When new words break out of the confines of nonce occurrences and eccentricities becoming more widely used in society, they qualify for entry in the dictionary. By the mid-1970s, *multilingualism* had made the grade for the

OED. Major dictionaries of other European languages followed. For instance, in the very same year, 1976, the tenth edition of *Grote Van Dale*, the most comprehensive Dutch dictionary, included for the first time the entry *meertalig* 'multilingual', although it does not list *meertaligheid* 'multilingualism', an omission on which the project leader of the dictionary comments as follows: 'Although it often happens that, for reasons of limited space, dictionaries do not include derivations such as this one, I do find it strange because in the event it is a common word.'[2] It is a common Dutch word because following the independence of the Dutch East Indies and Suriname, the Netherlands absorbed a large population of non-Dutch mother tongue speakers.

At about the same time, the French word *multilinguisme* became a dictionary entry in the 1975 edition of *Le Grand Larousse de la langue française*. The word had first appeared in print two decades earlier in Marcel Cohen's book *Pour une sociologie du langage* in which he also used the term *plurilinguisme*. Both terms are commonly used in French today. Cohen was sensitive to the coexistence of various speech forms early on, beginning his scientific career with a thesis about the Arabic dialect of Jews in Algiers, published in 1912. When his book 'For a sociology of language' appeared in 1956, some 400,000 French troops were fighting in Algeria, engaged in one of the bloodiest decolonization wars of the epoch and which ended in Algeria's gaining independence from France.

The lexicalization of multilingualism in German offers a conspicuous contrast. *Mehrsprachigkeit*, was first included in the authoritative *Duden* dictionary only a decade later than English *multilingualism*, Dutch *meertalig*, and French *multilingualisme*, in its nineteenth edition of 1986. No exodus of people from former colonies settled in Germany. Since the 1960s, West Germany had recruited foreign labour, without, however, adjusting any policies to recognize the coexistence of culturally and linguistically diverse populations. Accordingly, public discourse about multiculturalism, and derived from it, multilingualism, began later in Germany than in other Western countries. Notice also that *Mehrsprachigkeit*, like Dutch *meertaligheid* means 'multilinguality', referring to a state of affairs rather than an attitude or policy as implied in the '-*ism*'.

---

[2] Rob Tempelaars, Projectleider Algemeen Nederlands Woordenboek (ANW) http://anw.inl.nl, personal communication.

The lexicalization of 'multilinguism' in Spanish also lags behind other European languages. The first appearance of the word *multilingüismo* in a Spanish dictionary was in *Diccionario de la Lengua Española* (2014, paper edition) (2015, online edition), edited by Real Academia de la Lengua Española. Other dictionaries, such as, *Diccionario histórico de la lengua española* (1933–1936) and *Diccionario Histórico* (1960–1996) do not list *multilingüismo*. The *Diccionario del Español Actual—Manuel SECO* (1999) contains the word *plurilingual* but not *multilingüismo*. There is no tangible evidence that this apparent omission is a reflection of the fact that linguistic diversity has long been perceived in Spain as a threat to national unity, but it is perhaps an idea worth investigating.

The general propensity of comprehensive dictionaries to reflect social realities with a certain delay[3] is borne out in lexical traditions outside the Western world as well, Chinese, for example. According to a dictionary of technical terms in linguistics published in 2011, *duōyǔxiànxiàng* (多语现象) means 'multilingualism', literally 'multilinguality'. The term *duōyǔzhǔyì* (多语主义) is also used in this meaning, the former referring to the phenomenon of multiple languages being used, the latter to the policy of dealing with language difference.[4] Semantically quite transparent, both terms are readily understood, but they are not listed in any general Chinese dictionary. That various other languages in addition to Mandarin are spoken in China is nothing new, and many of them have been studied by Chinese scholars in depth. However, no need has ever been felt to conceptualize the condition of language difference and coin a term for it.

The situation is similar in Japanese, though not quite the same. *Tagengoshugi* (多言語主義), a direct calque of 'multilingualism', is widely used among specialists and even in the press. (Japanese *shugi* corresponds to Chinese *zhǔyì* '-ism'.) Additional evidence for the currency of the Japanese term are 144 books and magazines listed in the 2016 catalogue of the National Diet Library, with *tagengoshugi* in the title. Yet, there is no such entry in any of the seven biggest Japanese dictionaries. Two major dictionaries, *Sanseidou kokugo jiten* (三省堂

---

[3] The technological shift from print to online publication has greatly reduced the delay. The first edition of the *OED* was published in fascicles, 1884–1928. Supplements published as of 1933 were integrated to produce the second edition in 1986, followed in 1992 by the first CD-ROM edition. Nowadays, the *OED* is published online with four updates a year.
[4] Yǔyánxué míngcí (语言学名词) Chinese Terms in Linguistics. Beijing: Commercial Press, 2011, p. 192.

国語辞典) and *Daijisen* (大辞泉) have an entry of the English loan-word *bairingaru* (バイリンガル) 'bilingual', and the second edition of the largest and most influential *Nihonkokugo daijiten* (日本国語大辞典第二版) of 2000, also includes the entry *marutiringarizumu* (マルチリンガリズム) 'multilingualism', likewise an English loanword, using *tagengoshiyou* (多言語使用) 'use of multiple languages' in its explanation. In Japanese, loanwords, especially English loanwords, suggest that the phenomena designated by them are modern and of foreign origin. By contrast, Sino-Japanese and Japanese terminology indicate that the phenomenon is an authentic part of the cultural heritage.

Inspecting the situation of another major non-Western language, Arabic, we see a comparable picture. There are two competing terms, *alta'dud al-lughawi* (التعدد اللغوي) 'multitude of language' and *ta'dud al-lughaat* (اللغات تعدد) 'plurality of languages', but there is no fixed dictionary lemma or an agreed-upon term for an attitude or policy concerning linguistic diversity. Once again, it is not a new insight that, in addition to Arabic, many other languages are spoken in the wider Arabic-speaking world, but their presence has not prompted the coining of a term that warrants inclusion in a dictionary.

Our short review of the lexicalization of linguistic diversity in several European and non-Western languages indicates that, as a social phenomenon and as an object of scholarly attention, multilingualism originates in Western countries. It is not so much about a multiplicity of languages which, as we have seen in the first chapter, is ubiquitous throughout the world and nothing out of the ordinary, but about attitudes, policies, and ideologies. As we learnt form the *OED*, the English term *multilingualism* first appeared in 1916 in the Manitoba Free Press. Perhaps it was coincidental that it was this particular newspaper that first used it; however, in hindsight it is easy to see that the local and temporal context of a classical immigrant country at the beginning of the twentieth century were germane to the term's appearance.

Manitoba is today one of Canada's most ethnically diverse provinces. As early as 1871, the Province signed treaties with the leaders of the Aboriginal population. At the time, some 50 per cent of its inhabitants spoke French, but because of immigration from neighbouring Ontario, this was down to less than 8 per cent twenty years later. In the early years of the twentieth century, renewed shifts occurred, as immigrants from Eastern Europe poured into the province. During the thirty-year period from 1881 to 1911, the population of the province grew rapidly from 66,000 to 450,000.[5] No wonder that national origin, ethnic mix, and linguistic diversity became topics of public discourse there and then. On 26 June 1916, still using a hyphen, the Manitoba Free Press discussed abolishing multi-lingualism and establishing English as the medium of instruction in Manitoba's public schools.

In sum, there were two key occurrences in the twentieth century that turned the multiplicity of languages in certain contexts into a social issue deserving of a label, the lexical term *multilingualism*, which at the time of writing this book, is a hundred years old. The scientific study of multi-lingualism is not quite that old but came about in the wake of decolonization. In the meantime, as sometimes happens when an issue is first addressed by scholars, rather than having been made clearer, the more attention it received, the more involved it seems to have become, as ever more aspects of the phenomenon were discovered which cannot be covered in a dictionary definition. In order to determine the crucial characteristics of multilingualism, it is better to rely on experts in the field.

2.2 Expert assessments

Thus, a number of well-known scholars were requested to supply a one-sentence definition by completing the simple phrase: 'Multilingualism is...'. Their responses can be grouped into four clusters according to whether they focus on multilingualism as a capacity, a practice, an attitude or ideology, or an object of theorizing. While they overlap and concur in some ways, they bring a remarkable variety of features to the fore.

2.2.1 Capacity

Hartmut Haberland is Professor of German Language and the Socio-linguistics of Globalization at Roskilde University, Denmark. One of his many interests is in language choice in higher education (Haberland 2013). A native speaker of German and naturalized Dane, he welcomes you on his personal homepage in four languages, English, German, Danish, and Japanese. Multilingualism, according to him, means

---

[5] Manitoba, DigitalResources on Manitoba History: http://manitobia.ca/content/en/themes/ias.

(1) to be able to function in some type of contexts in more than one language,

a definition that is almost identical with that offered by Reem Bassiouney (ريم بسيوني) who is an Egyptian author and professor of sociolinguistics with a special interest in the sociolinguistics of Arabic dialects (Bassiouney 2009), affiliated to the American University in Cairo, Egypt:

(2) Multilingualism is the ability to communicate in more than one language.
(3) Multilingualism is having a linguistic repertoire of more than one (two if you want to keep bilingualism separate) language; this can be applied to groups of people (e.g. families, communities, societies, nations, or individuals).

The third definition is the one supplied by Marilyn Merritt, a specialist in literacy and professor in the Department of Anthropology, The Catholic University of America, Washington, DC. She has lived and worked in India and several African countries where she supported literacy and education programmes in multilingual settings (Merritt 1992). Being concerned, as she is, with literacy, the repertoire of languages at the disposal of various agents that any literacy curriculum has to take into account is of paramount importance to her.

Kutlay Yagmur is a native speaker of Turkish and professor of language, identity, and education at the Tilburg School of Humanities, Tilburg, Netherlands. A keen observer of evolving new speech patterns in urban settings (Yagmur 2016), he likewise puts aptitude at the centre of his definition:

(4) Multilingualism is **the ability** of individuals and communities **to communicate** in multiple languages.

His definition is in accord with the preceding one in that it specifies that both individuals and communities can have the ability in question. In this regard, Rita Franceschini, professor at the Faculty of Education, 'trilingual and intercultural', Free University of Bolzano, Italy, goes a step further explaining that

(5) The concept of multilingualism is to be understood as the capacity of societies, institutions, groups and individuals to engage on a regular basis in space and time with more than one language in everyday life.

That the agents which have the ability to communicate in multiple languages are of various kinds has implications for the analysis, for an individual's capacity to function in a certain way clearly differs from that of institutions or groups where a division of labour may be relied upon.

Franceschini moreover adds that 'multilingualism is a product of the fundamental human ability to communicate in a number of languages', highlighting her view that what is at issue is an ability that characterizes the human species (Franceschini 2016). This explanatory elaboration not only adds weight to the importance of this trait, but must also be understood as a theoretical position opposed to those who would portray multilinguality as an unusual, if not abnormal condition. A similar stance underlies Maher's account, which speaks of 'a global norm'. John C. Maher is a pioneer of metrolinguistics and teaches sociolinguistics in the Department of Society, Culture and Media, International Christian University, Tokyo (Maher 2010). His definition is:

(6) Multilingualism is a complex social phenomenon and a global norm, a situation of language contact, a multidimensional distribution of languages—spoken, written or signed—where groups or communities or an individual in society, communicate, with varying proficiency, in a number of languages, in addition to a national or official language.

Maher draws our attention to mediatization, that is, the technological aspects of language as expressed in speech, writing or signing. In later chapters, especially Chapter 10, we will have occasion to discuss the implications of multilingualism for the language system, however multilingual communication can be realized only in one of the said media, and what is more, it can be studied only where situated communication happens, that is, in practice.

2.2.2 Practice

Being actively involved in research, several of our experts characterize multilingualism as a practice or assign language use a notable position in their definitions. Accordingly, Li Wei (李嵬), professor of Applied Linguistics at the Institute of Education, University College London, defines multilingualism as

(7) the co-use of multiple languages by individuals and societies,

and elaborates that

co-existence is not enough. Unless there is co-use, we do not get genuine multilingualism.

A native of Beijing where he was trained as a teacher of English, Li Wei speaks Mandarin as his first language. He came to Britain early in his career, studied diasporic Chinese in England and became a specialist of bilingualism in education (Li Wei 2014). His definition accords with Shana Poplack's which likewise stresses actual language use. She declares:

(8) Multilingualism is *regular interaction* amongst community members in more than one language.

Poplack, born in Detroit, Michigan, and raised in New York City, is professor of linguistics in the University of Ottawa with a long-standing interest and research record in bilingual speech patterns, much of her work focusing on Romance languages—French, Spanish, Portuguese—in New World environments (Poplack 2009).

Xu Daming (徐大明) and Li Chor Shing David (李楚成) also concentrate on language use. The former is professor of linguistics in the Department of Chinese Language and Literature, Universidade de Macau, studying the effects of urbanization on language (Xu 2015). He defines multilingualism as

(9) the use of more than one language in a community of a territory (politically or otherwise defined).

Xu directs our attention to the equally obvious and important fact that for the purpose of meaningful discussion language diversity must be indexed to a territory. In the event, what he adds in parentheses may be interpreted as reflecting the environment in which he works, Macau. It is in another postcolonial territory, 'politically or otherwise defined', that Li Chor Shing David works. He is professor in the Department of Linguistics and Modern Language Studies, The Hong Kong Institute of Education, where he uses three languages regularly, his native Cantonese, Mandarin, and English. In addition to these three, he commands several other languages, having written his doctoral thesis in German. Language use in multilingual settings is his principal field of research (Li, David C.S. 2013). His definition is:

(10) Multilingualism is a characteristic of a community in which two or more languages are used by its members in their everyday lives; a multilingual community is typically made up of plurilingual speakers who find it necessary to use two or more languages depending on the contexts and/or people they interact with, including monolingual speakers.

David Li, as he also calls himself in English (The three characters 李楚成 are read Li Chor Shing in Cantonese and Lǐ chǔ chéng in Mandarin.), reserves the terminological distinction between *multi-* and *pluri-* for groups and individuals, respectively. This allows him to give *mono*lingual speakers a place in his definition which furthermore makes it clear that multilingualism is not a pastime, but a necessity. The *multi–pluri*-differentiation is in keeping with official terminology used, for example, by European institutions, which Elizabeth Lanza brings to bear in her definition:

(11) Multilingualism is understood as the ability of societies, institutions, groups and individuals to engage on a regular basis, with more than one language in their day-to-day lives. This broad definition embraces the distinction made by the Council of Europe between 'multilingualism' and 'plurilingualism' where multilingualism refers more to social organization, and plurilingualism to an individual repertoire of linguistic competence. However, the terms 'bilingualism', 'plurilingualism', and 'multilingualism' are often interchanged. Traditionally, 'bilingualism' was used to refer to more than one language, while the default term today has become 'multilingualism'.

Elizabeth Lanza is Professor of Linguistics at the University of Oslo and Director of the Center for Multilingualism in Society across the Lifespan. She has worked in various environments from Norway to Ethiopia; her most recent work focuses on issues of language, culture, and identity in multilinguals (Lanza 2004).

Among the variables that determine the proportion of multilinguals in a population and to what extent multilingualism is practised, the size of the speech community plays a critical role. Hence Matthias Brenzinger's definition:

(12) Multilingualism is inversely correlated with the size of (L1) language communities, communal language repertoires shrink with increasing numbers of speakers.

Brenzinger is an Africanist and champion of language diversity affiliated to the University of Cape Town where he is Director of the Centre for African Language Diversity, and Curator of The African Language Archive (Brenzinger 2008). He is professionally concerned with the territorial distribution and dispersion of language groups, especially with small language communities whose plentiful presence in Africa informs his definition. As his field research has shown time and again, the likelihood of people's control and use of multiple languages has something to do with the size of their mother tongue group: the smaller the group, the less likely it is that its members speak only one language. This is his thesis, which brings the dimension of power into play, and with it ideas and ideologies.

2.2.3 Attitude and ideology

In definition (6) above, John Maher characterizes multilingualism as 'a complex social phenomenon and a *global norm*'. The latter can hardly count as a factual description, but when it comes to definitions there is not always a sharp dividing line between what is and what should be. In fact, a definition can be understood as a stipulation, as in 'defining their rights and obligations'. Riikka J. Länsisalmi puts forth a definition that expresses an awareness of this ambiguity:

(13) Multilingualism is often associated with a kind of parallel monolingualism (in major World/European Languages), be it in the (educated) individual or in society at large, inspired by prescriptive, educational, societal and political ideologies, and ignoring the creativity, versatility and real-life unboundedness of ordinary human interaction.

Riikka J. Länsisalmi received her education mainly in Finland, which has two official languages, Finnish and Swedish plus a number of smaller indigenous and immigrant languages. After living and working in Japan for many years, she returned to Finland where she teaches Japanese at the University of Helsinki (Länsisalmi 2012). By juxtaposing multilingualism and monolingualism, her definition introduces a theme that permeates the discourse on multilingualism implicitly or explicitly: without (prescribed or professed) uniformity, no diversity (worth noting). In other words, if the coexistence and communal use of multiple languages were considered the normal state of affairs, no one would talk about it or need a term for it. Since, notwithstanding the avowed 'global norm', this is not the case in certain places, multilingualism *is* an issue. Knowing where and what kind of places these are, is indispensable for understanding the phenomenon.

A resident of one such place, Monica Heller supplied the following definition, terse and to the point:

(14) 'Multilingualism' is an idea produced by the nation-state construct of unified languages, cultures, populations and territories.

Heller is professor in the department Social Justice Education, University of Toronto and Ontario Institute for Studies in Education (OISE). Her research focuses on the interaction of language and social difference and inequality in the globalizing economy, paying particular attention to francophone Canada (Heller 2011). Multilingualism, it follows from her definition, is not a state of affairs, but an idea produced by, and predicated on the existence of, the nation state as a political unit. Heller thus fills a gap by pointing at the important fact that, whatever it may be, multilingualism is historically contingent. Others, however, prefer to release multilingualism from its historical boundedness, calling it

(15) a basic condition of human society.

This definition was proposed by Goro Christoph Kimura (木村護郎クリストフ), a Japanese-German bilingual professor of sociolinguistics and Germanic studies at Sophia University, Tokyo, with a strong interest in language management (Kimura 2014). Among the languages he has mastered and which he studies, Esperanto plays a special role, being an artificial language created to overcome the hostile feelings often associated with linguistic fragmentation.

As an ideational as opposed to a natural occurrence, multilingualism can be an object of affection or dislike. In some of the definitions this aspect is foregrounded, as in C. J. Daswani's definition:

(16) Multilingualism is a positive attitude towards languages other than your mother tongue, and willingness to communicate with speakers of other languages spoken in your community.

Chander Daswani (चंदर दासवानी) is Professor Emeritus of Linguistics at Pune University and Jawaharlal Nehru University in New Delhi. He dedicated most of his professional life to the advancement of literacy in India, serving for many years as head of Non-Formal Education at the National Council on Educational Research and Training, New Delhi (Daswani 2001). A native speaker of Sindhi and prominent representative of the Hindu Sindhi diaspora[6] in India, he is sensitive to the importance of cultivating positive feelings towards minority languages not used in formal education. The willingness to understand the other is part of successful communication under any circumstances, but particularly so where language difference is involved. In India, the presence of linguistic diversity in a community is normal, frictionless communication across the divide of language, ethnicity, or caste not always so.

According to Daswani's definition, positive feelings are localized on the giver's side, directed from you to others in the best interest of mutual understanding. With a shift in perspective, we can also think of the emotional benefits of being able to interact in diverse environments

---

[6] For Daswani's account of Indian Sindhi, see https://hindusofsindh.wordpress.com/tag/daswani/.

making use of different languages. The following definitions by Federica Guerini and Penelope Gardner-Chloros bear witness to such a point of view.

(17) Multilingualism is feeling at home in different countries.
(18) Multilingualism is living in a large house in which each of the rooms has a completely different beautiful view; if you live there, you do not envy the neighbour with a small house and a single window.

Guerini's definition (17) refers to countries, suggesting immigration as a sub-theme of multilingualism. She is professor of linguistics in the Dipartimento di Lettere, Filosofia, Comunicazione, Università di Studi di Bergamo, Bergamo, Italy. She is a specialist of Akan, a West African Niger-Congo language, and studies sociolinguistic outcomes of language contact, for example by Ghanese immigrants in Italy (Guerini 2006). Language contact is also Gardner-Chloros's main field of research. On the basis of her long-standing interest in code-switching, she is working on a comparison of multicultural London English and multicultural Paris French where she studies varieties spoken by major communities of immigrant origin, including Afro-Caribbeans in the UK and French Caribbeans and Maghrebans in France (Gardner-Chloros 2009). She is professor of sociolinguistics and language contact in the Department of Applied Linguistics, Birkbeck, University of London. Her poetic definition (18) reveals an attitude likely to provoke adverse reactions on the part of those who feel comfortable in 'a small house with a single window'.

2.2.4 Object of theorizing

Scientific inquiry, many think, should be guided by disinterested objectivity, rather than passion, but this is easier said than done. This may be one of the reasons for Frans Gregersen to define multilingualism as

(19) the most obvious theoretical and practical challenge of post-modern super-diverse information societies.

Gregersen is professor in the Department of Nordic Studies and Linguistics, Københavns Universitet, specializing in variation and historical language change. For several years, he headed the Danish National Research Foundation Centre on Language Change in Real Time.[7] Working

---

[7] For documentation of LANCHART, see http://lanchart.hum.ku.dk/.

in an environment where cross-language communication is common and the separation of languages in the course of time is a matter of public discussion, Gregersen (2011) is keenly aware of the theoretical problems generated by language contact. No matter how you look at it, the mixing, alternate use, and mutual infiltration of languages that exist in close proximity, albeit in cyberspace only, as Gregersen's definition implies, pose enormous theoretical problems for a linguistics that is predicated on the assumption of clearly distinct, non-overlapping linguistic systems. For linguists, in contradistinction to, for instance, political scientists with an interest in language, the dynamics and effects of exogenous change are at the centre of interest. Hence Paulin G. Djité's definition:

(20) Multilingualism is on-going language contact in the same territorial space.

Djité is professor of linguistics in the Laboratoire des Théories et Modèles Linguistiques, Université Felix Houphouet Boigny, Abidjan, the metropolitan centre of Côte d'Ivoire, where in addition to official French and local varieties of French an estimated sixty vernacular languages from all over the country are spoken. His research is focused on the nexus of modernization, development, and the place of language in education, health, the economy and governance, mainly, but not exclusively in the African context where the co-use and intermingling of multiple languages is more prevalent than in many other parts of the world (Djité 2008).

Very few areas get as complex as in Abidjan, although they are complex enough in many places to make scholars throw up their hands, at a loss as to how to set a practical research agenda. Yet, some do not allow themselves to be discouraged, such as Massimiliano Spotti, a native speaker of Italian and Assistant Professor in the Department of Culture Studies Tilburg University, who is affiliated to the Centre for the Study of Superdiversity. In the light of his research in multilingual classrooms (Spotti 2011), he offered the following definition: 'Multilingualism is 'an almost obsolete absolute mess but because of that still so much fun!'

Rather than a definition, this is an expression of enthusiasm for his job and, therefore, gets no number in the list; but because it highlights the difficulties that, after decades of research, scholars still confront when trying to develop a reasoned approach to the study of multilingualism, it is a valuable contribution to the present discussion. Few scholars in the field have a clearer understanding of these difficulties than Albert

Bastardas Boada. He is professor of sociolinguistics, language ecology, and language policy at the Facultat de Filologia, Universitat de Barcelona and has explored every corner of it. Of all the experts I asked to provide a definition of multilingualism, Bastardas Boada was the only one who refused, but not without telling me why. His explanation was as follows.

I don't feel comfortable trying now to improvise a definition of 'multilingualism'. It is not a simple matter. Besides I think that **it is better not to approach the concepts starting with the word, but do it from the opposite way, from the facts to the word.** To such and such we call it 'multilingualism'. (I take it from Popper: non essentialist definitions[8]).

It is not a simple matter; indeed, it isn't. On this point, all of our experts undoubtedly agree with Bastardas Boada, as do I. And their travails proved him right. The definitions of multilingualism they volunteered not only range from the flamboyant to the profound, but are so multifaceted that it seems hard to identify an essential nucleus of meaning, which a dictionary is compelled to provide. These definitions are, moreover, informed by different concerns and points of view. It is hard to think it coincidental that

- a definition that stresses 'a positive attitude towards languages' (16) comes out of a country with a history of community conflict;
- multilingualism is defined as a construct by a citizen of the country with the most elaborate language laws (14);
- multilingualism is characterized as 'a basic condition of human society' (15) by a scholar from a country used to playing down heterogeneity;
- a definition focused on 'on-going language contact' (20) comes out of a city that saw its population mushroom a hundredfold during the past half-century.

Twenty is an arbitrary number. More definitions could easily be added that would draw attention to yet other aspects of language diversity in society. But the above collection is quite sufficient to make the point that *multilingualism* is deserving of a plural. It is kinds of multilingualism we have to come to terms with. Chapter 3 will discuss the relevant

---

[8] Bastardas Boada refers to philosopher Karl Popper who criticized the view, common in Western thought since antiquity, that it is possible to categorize all things and concepts of the universe because they are instances, though often imperfect ones, of ideal types that are characterized by essential, i.e., indispensable properties.

distinctions, address terminology, and introduce a typology of language diversity.

2.3 Conclusions

After reviewing a number of dictionary entries and the lexicographic history of *multilingualism*, this chapter has presented twenty definitions of the term by experts in the field. From these definitions several conclusions can be drawn. (1) One multilingualism is not like all others. The term is variously applied to many different situations that have in common the presence of multiple languages, but for the purposes of analysis and theorizing should be differentiated. We need a typology of multilingualism, and several of the terms and concepts so far used quite innocently need theoretical grounding. (2) Multilingualism is a paradigm case of the messiness of social reality where clear-cut categories are in short supply. Since it occurs in different political settings, interacts with other social characteristics, poses challenges to schooling and is economically relevant, while having to do with languages, it does not concern only linguistics, but other disciplines as well, including political science, sociology, education, and economics, among others. As will be discussed in greater detail in Chapter 3, it is no easy task to analytically separate the social from the linguistic aspects of language. (3) Researchers not only observe, but also experience multilingualism, and, as witnessed by many of the twenty definitions, they do so on the basis of their experience and from their specific point of view. This makes it more difficult than in the natural sciences to reduce the object of investigation to objective facts, retaining a disinterested attitude. While objectivity in the sense of unbiased investigation and reproducible tests and measurements is an aim common to all scientific research, complete freedom from personal perspective and value commitments is hard to attain in research concerning a complex phenomenon to which the researcher's experience can contribute.

Problems and questions for discussion

1. In the light of the definitions discussed in this chapter, can multilingualism be described as a natural state of affairs?
2. Take the definition of multilingualism that appeals to you most and explain why!

3. Do any of the definitions contradict each other or are in other ways incompatible? If so, try to resolve the contradiction.
4. Why was *multilingualism* not an entry in the 1971 edition of the *Oxford English Dictionary*, but is one now? Explain when and why the term became lexicalized.
5. If English is not your first language, is there a generally agreed-upon term for multilingualism? Is it in the dictionary? If so, since when? Answer these questions and compare the situation with that of English!

Further reading

Fuchs, Stephan. 2001. *Against Essentialism: A Theory of Culture and Society.* Cambridge, MA: Harvard University Press.

3

Descriptive and theoretical concepts

Murder

Subject to three exceptions (see Voluntary Manslaughter below) the crime of murder is committed, where a person:

- of sound mind and discretion (i.e. sane);
- unlawfully kills (i.e. not self-defence or other justified killing);
- any reasonable creature (human being);
- in being (born alive and breathing through its own lungs—*Rance v Mid-Downs Health Authority* (1991) 1 All ER 801 and *AG Ref No 3 of 1994* (1997) 3 All ER 936);
- under the Queen's Peace;
- with intent to kill or cause grievous bodily harm (GBH).

The Crown Prosecution Service[1]

We all know what murder is, but then we don't. Lawyers know what murder is and students of law, magistrates, and prosecutors. You can say, 'that

[1] http://www.cps.gov.uk/legal/h_to_k/homicide_murder_and_manslaughter/#b3.

was plain murder', but that's just your opinion (or C. S. Forester's[2]); if you want to prevail in the courtroom, you have to know the legal definition of 'murder'. Even though we use the same word, the meaning of the common-sense term and the legal term may not coincide. The same holds for scientific knowledge expressed in plain words. In everyday language, every concept cannot be easily transferred to a scientific concept. The former we know on the basis of use, for the latter we need a definition.

This chapter discusses and defines a number of concepts that are important for the study of multilingualism, some of which have been used without definition in the foregoing chapters. Others will be introduced anew.

3.1 Concepts and definitions

Concepts can be defined from two different points of view, known as extensional and intensional. The extension of a concept is the set of all instances to which the concept applies, while the intension of the same concept consists of the attributes an object must have to qualify as an instant. Clearly, intensional and extensional definitions are related, but they are not the same. For example, if a ballpoint pen is shaped like a race car or a syringe or incorporates a radio, that will not play any role in the intension of 'ballpoint pen', but all ballpoint pens so shaped will be part of the extension. Extension means we are concerned with objects that can be counted. Intension means they can be identified on the basis of some indispensable properties. (If something does not have a ball-point, it is not a ballpoint pen.)

In the social world, both intensional and extensional definitions are often difficult to get. Take race, for example. We all know what race is. In some countries, race categories are listed on immigration forms and contained in census questionnaires. However, among the categories listed there is usually one that gives us cause to sit up and take notice: 'other'. Not a race like, presumably, the rest, 'other' tells us that the racial categories at hand are not completely selective and exhaustive. Biologists have known this for some time and no longer use the concept of race without qualification. It is a concept hard to pin down on scientific grounds, yet in certain administrative contexts it continues to be used

---

[2] C. S. Forester, *Plain Murder*. Penguin Classics, first published 1930.

and in social relations it plays an important role. In short, race is a bio-logical fiction, but a social fact. In recognition of the increase in recent decades in our knowledge of human genetics, public administrations have supplemented racial with ethnic categories and at the same time shifted from allegedly objective definitions to self-identification: Your race is that which you most identify with. Data on race, their geneticist limitations notwithstanding, are still used to study economic, social, educational, and health variables across population groups, although the differences that have occurred within data sets over time are well known. For example, in decennial US census data, Indians from India were counted as 'Hindus' from 1920 to 1940, as 'White' from 1950 to 1970, and as 'Asians or Pacific Islanders' in 1980 and 1990. If these re-classifications are curious, more curious still it is that people hailing from anywhere between the Himalayas to the southern tip of the Indian Subcontinent were in all of the censuses counted as one 'race'.

From this example, three lessons can be learnt:

1. Categories and definitions change over time.
2. That categories lack a scientific foundation does not necessarily render them socially meaningless.
3. Taken together, (1) and (2) lead to the conclusion that in the social world the object of investigation is not given but must be constructed.

For the purposes of multilingualism research, this has important impli-cations. Where there are many, there must be one. Multilingualism does not exist and cannot be studied without more than one language; better: more than two, for two hardly count as 'multi'. Hence, it is necessary to tally languages, or at least to distinguish one from the other. To this end, we need to specify the concept of language, which we can do in two ways: one, human language as distinct from other kinds of communica-tion (an intensional definition); two, one language as distinct from another (an extensional definition). Both are difficult questions, but in the given context the second is more important than the first, for we are not concerned with Dolphin chatter, flag signals, or Python (a program-ming language). We can be satisfied, therefore, with a rather circular definition to the effect that human languages are languages used by 'any reasonable creature (human being)'. How many there are, is a trickier question, as we saw in the first chapter.

Like genetics, linguistics has made much progress in recent decades, increasing our knowledge of human languages significantly. One of the most important insights is that variation across the whole spectrum of languages is both more fine-grained and multifaceted than formerly thought and that, therefore, the number of languages has increased. Whether it has increased because the lens through which we look at them has become sharper or they have actually multiplied is an issue that is hard to decide, if only because our knowledge about the human population on earth increased simultaneously with the population itself. In the eighteenth century, the number of the world's languages was commonly thought to range in the hundreds, nowadays it is seen to be in the thousands. In 1800, the world population was just about to reach its first billion. Since then, within two short centuries, it has increased more than sevenfold. Do these two increases have anything to do with each other? Not many scientists would flatly deny it, but conclusive evidence in support of a positive answer is also all but absent. Many a scientist would say, 'it depends', and it does. It depends on how you define a language more specifically than the general definition given above, which in turn depends on your point of view, for instance, whether you conceive of language as a natural growth or a tool shaped by its users.

Concepts of language have always at some level contained mixtures of classification based on genetic relatedness (e.g. Romance languages, Dravidian languages, etc., see Chapter 1) and culture (e.g. orality vs. literacy). The changeability of the concept of language is particularly obvious when we examine what language means to different scientific disciplines, for while linguistics is properly the science of language, it is by no means the only discipline that takes a legitimate interest in its investigation. There is a conspicuous lack of correspondence between linguistic conceptions of language and those of other disciplines.

As an illustration consider some of the properties of language most salient in a number of disciplines that are relevant to the study of multilingualism. Language can be seen in any of the following ways:

Linguistics I: an innate capacity consisting of cognitive categories that distinguish humans from other primates (Chomsky 2012);
Linguistics II: a set of distinct but systematically related speech forms (Schilling-Estes 2006);
Political Science I: a means of persuasion (Martin 2013);

Political Science II: a source of conflict (Mabry 2011);

Sociology: social capital which affords its holders symbolic power (Bourdieu 1982);

Social History: a historical construct of social homogenization (Marfany 2010);

Economics: the product of a 'fictitious optimizer' who operates behind a 'veil of ignorance' (Rubinstein 2000: 5);

Neuroscience: a mental occurrence whose diversity affects the density of grey matter in the brain (Mechelli et al. 2004);

Education: a norm that can be taught, learnt, and transgressed (García 2009).

Other conceptions could be added, but the above suffice to demonstrate the great diversity of perspectives on language. Language is all that and more. Although the cited views are not necessarily incompatible, they are only marginally relevant to each other, if at all. Linguists do not study whether a language has any economic value or is subject to optimization, while to the political scientist who wants to know whether and under what circumstances language triggers community unrest, it is immaterial how it is acquired, taught, or organized in the human brain.

What counts as a language is historically contingent and discipline-dependent. Because of the indeterminate character of the concept of language, the object of investigation is not given, ready to be examined in the same way as we might, for instance, examine layers of rock or the number of legs a centipede has, but it must be constructed by the scientist. A technical terminology is an important part of this exercise. Supplementing everyday vocabulary, it lets us see that an occurrence is, or has perhaps recently become, an object of systematic research. The term 'multilingualism' itself is an example. The remainder of the chapter discusses a number of technical terms needed to account for various aspects of linguistic diversity and to overcome the limitations of an understanding of languages as clearly separated bounded systems.

3.2 Technical terms

Language. In the light of the above considerations about the impossibility of defining the concept of language in isolation, it is not surprising that this term is often used with some qualification indicating an aspect of language of particular significance to a theoretical context or scientific discipline. Thus, in political science and sociological contexts, languages are characterized as 'official', 'national', 'standard', and 'minority' language, often with further specifications, such as, 'indigenous' and/or 'immigrant' minority language. The extension of these terms is more restricted than 'language'. They all point to the issue of status, something a language has as a result of being used under certain circumstances rather than by virtue of some inherent properties. Whether or not a language is a national or official language can be decided, precisely because such a status is not a natural attribute of any language but a position accorded it by law or quasi-legal authority. Such a position is only rendered to what are now commonly called 'named languages', a term which implies that there are also unnamed languages, that is, speech forms for which no one has claimed or successfully tried to claim language status. There is, in other words a grey zone of speech forms that defy or have escaped clear-cut classification (not unlike the 'other' among the racial categories).

These unnamed speech forms are not typically used in writing and have no codified standard. Speakers are able to judge whether or not a certain expression is an expression of their language, but no one ever laid down the rules of correct usage to define a standard. The term 'standard language' is ambiguous. In one meaning it refers to standardized languages, such as French, German, Dutch, etc. In this sense, we can say, for example: 'The European standard language is the product of five centuries of cultural development.' In the other meaning it refers more narrowly to the standard form of a particular language, standard Mandarin, for example. The second usage implies that in addition to the standard there are other forms of a given language, such as dialects, sub-standard jargon, etc. Standard languages are clearly distinct, by definition. Dutch linguist Joop van der Horst (2009) described them as having a fence built around them. Languages that lack a standard and non-standard speech forms are not so easily demarcated, which is yet another analytic and terminological challenge.

Variety. Whether what a group of people speak is a language or a dialect is not so easily determined, as mentioned above (Chapter 1, section 1.4). Like racial distinctions, linguistic ones are fluid, which was one of the reasons for linguists to introduce the term 'variety' which, moreover, is less prone to be used in a derogatory way, as 'dialect' in everyday speech often is. As a technical term, 'dialect' is coterminous with 'regional or local variety'. A variety is always a variety of X, where X is a genetically related superposed standard variety or language in the common sense of the word. Another technical term with a similar meaning is 'lect'. A local or regional variety is a *dia*lect, for example Viennese German (Russ 1990). A variety that is specific to an ethnic group in an immigration setting, is called '*ethno*lect', for example Dutch as spoken by Turkish immigrants in the Netherlands (Doğruöz and Backus 2010). (Notice in passing that English as spoken by the American community in Singapore is highly unlikely to be called an ethnolect.) Next, a variety indexed to a social class is a *socio*lect, for example, Public School English (Hitchings 2011). Further differentiations lead to the notion of *idio*lect, an individual speaker's speech form which may combine features of regional, ethnic, and social variation.

Distinctions between varieties of all sorts are more or less pronounced, ranging from minute differences in pronunciation noticeable only to insiders to marked alterations in syntax, morphology, and vocabulary also perceptible to outsiders. Historically, sub-standard or local varieties can be promoted to language status, if their speakers so desire. The emergence of the Southern African dialect of Dutch as a language in its own right, now known as Afrikaans, and its codification early in the twentieth century is an example (Den Besten 2012). When Dutch as the written standard was officially replaced in South Africa by an Afrikaans standard in 1925, a new fence had been built and the number of named languages had grown by one (cf. Chapter 10). Boundaries can shift, for the varieties of a language constitute a multidimensional continuum which for descriptive and analytic purposes is dissected into meaningful parts.

Diglossia and heteroglossia. Because different varieties are associated with different people and different communicative functions, the sociology of language takes an interest in the perception of and relationship between varieties. A regular pattern of alternations of varieties between functional domains, such as, formal education and government administration, on one hand, and communication with family and friends, on the other, is called 'diglossia'. French Orientalist William Marçais (1930) used this term to describe an aspect of the language situation in North Africa. He observed that the distance between formal Arabic and the colloquial Maghrebi vernacular was extraordinarily wide, to the extent that these varieties were not mutually intelligible for all speakers, but were nonetheless considered varieties of one and the same language. The notion of diglossia later became topical in sociolinguistics when Ferguson (1959) argued that similar socially motivated patterns of usage also obtained in other cases, such as the alternating use of Standard German (which the Swiss call *Schriftdeutsch* 'written German') and Swiss German in Switzerland. Following that, Fishman (1967) argued that functional domain allocations in a speech community of genetically unrelated varieties, such as Yiddish and Hebrew, should also be subsumed under this concept. The ensuing debate about it demonstrated once again the theoretical difficulties of clearly and uncontroversially defining technical terms for social phenomena.

Suffice it to note that diglossia is closely associated with writing. Once applied to a language, writing tends to embody a standard of correctness and arrest change, while colloquial speech continues to evolve. Hence, for example, in Arabic the gap between the 'high' (H) written variety and the 'low' (L) vernacular variety grew very wide over the centuries (Albirini 2011). Yet, held together by a community, motivated not least by their religious texts to consider H their language and the only proper written language, the Arabic diglossia has survived, while the above-mentioned tension between the Southern African dialect of Dutch and standard Dutch, which in the nineteenth century was a kind of diglossia in the Fergusonian sense, eventually broke up when Afrikaans acquired a written standard. In oral societies—almost none survive today—no diglossia obtains. Although variation is present even in the smallest language group, the split between H and L that characterizes diglossia is a by-product of literary culture. No matter how defined, diglossia is a pattern of linguistic alternation observed in various settings and is as such indicative of the human capacity to control more than one variety.

Ferguson (1959) described diglossia as a stable arrangement of a society that uses two distinct but genetically related varieties, H and L, in functionally complementary domains where both H and L were also conceived as relatively stable entities. A more dynamic concept to deal with the diversity of speech forms within a single language was proposed by Russian philosopher and semiotician Michail Bakhtin (1935). His term 'heteroglossia' refers to the stratified multiplicity of 'dialects' of social groups, professions, generations, etc. which interact and are in constant flux. Heteroglossia articulates a counterpoint to the literary language (Ferguson's H), while exercising an influence on it.

Patois. In literate societies all varieties are not deemed suitable for written communication, as exemplified by the L-variety in diglossia situations. 'Patois' is another term that gives expression to this notion. It is commonly defined as a variety other than the standard or literary variety, but eschewed by linguists who consider it a derogatory term. Take Occitan, for example, a Romance language like French and Spanish, according to some linguists, but a patois according to many who speak it. Linguists tend to downplay the role of writing, whereas for historians and laypeople it is a decisive criterion of languagehood. To French linguist Louis-Jean Calvet (1987) the fact that people in southern France think they speak patois is proof of the low status of Occitan and the speakers' lack of self-esteem. Catalan historian Joan-Lluis Marfany criticizes this view from a sociohistorical perspective: 'What the old lady [a field work informant, FC] knows and Calvet apparently does not, is that, when she speaks patois, she speaks patois, not a language; when she wants to do that, she speaks French' (Marfany 2010: 5). Calvet relies on instruments of descriptive linguistics, Marfany on how common people categorize their own speech.

Patois or language? Can this issue be resolved amicably and objectively? The answer is no, because linguists and historians do not speak the same language. The former find it hard to provide valid linguistic criteria to distinguish patois from languages, while to the latter and, it must be admitted, the majority of women and men in the street, a patois is simply a social fact, distinguished from proper languages by the lack of a written standard. This casts doubt on Juliette's optimistic belief that 'a rose by any other name would smell as sweet'—at least when it comes to trying to gain the upper hand in a scholarly debate. As we will see in Chapter 4, it is not so easy to put the issue aside as a semantic squabble; for in this case labels have social, political, and, perhaps, legal consequences. A language by any other name just would not smell as sweet.

Pidgin. Take pidgin, for example! Linguists' fascination with the phenomenon notwithstanding, most speakers of English would object when told that they speak pidgin; for like 'dialect' and 'patois', in common parlance 'pidgin', while lacking a clear definition, has pejorative connotations signifying broken or corrupt speech, an incompletely acquired or mixed language. Technically speaking, a pidgin is defined by a number of specific features. A pidgin:

- is an auxiliary language created by speakers of different languages who have no common language;
- limited to fulfil restricted communication needs;
- has no native speakers (and is hence, in the public mind, not a language at all);
- draws its lexicon largely from one language, often called 'superstrate language', and its grammar from another, called 'substrate language'.

Since a pidgin is not acquired as a native language it follows that its speakers have other linguistic resources to make use of, their first language and maybe other languages, as the case may be. Pidgin speakers are, therefore, not constrained in their communicative potential by the expressive limitations of the pidgin. Because pidgins emerged in colonial settings when local people made an effort to learn without instruction the language of the colonialists (mainly English, Portuguese, Dutch, and French), they were indeed restricted in expressive power, and their speakers were accordingly, if unjustly, often denigrated in Western accounts for not being able to speak properly.

What makes these reduced varieties so interesting to linguists is that they dispense with all unnecessary frills, of which there are many in all languages, concentrating on essentials. Pidgins are, by definition, spoken in multilingual settings, and when they enter private households where a new generation is exposed to them as their first language, pidgins are developed by their new speakers into full-blown languages, known as 'creoles'—which brings us back to English, a language that feeds on Germanic and Romance sources. After the Norman Conquest (1066 CE), English became subject to heavy French and Latin influence, as a new pattern of linguistic divide came to hold sway. For some three hundred years the language of ordinary people was Middle English, but the official language and that of the social elite was (Anglo-Norman) French. Whether this arrangement led to pidginization or creolization or produced a mixed language, a hybrid language, a syncretic language, or a converted language is an academic question about which libraries could be written (cf. Matras 2009 for an overview). No answer is attempted here other than that diverse inputs into the formation of a language are a matter of degree and a matter of how far you look back.

The analogy, even parallel, with miscegenation or genetic admixture is quite apparent. It is encapsulated in the term 'creole'—Spanish 'criollo',

Portuguese 'crioulo', French 'créole', Dutch 'Creool'—which refers both to people of mixed descent and to languages formed in European colonies from European and local languages. Precise meanings vary across languages testifying to different colonial histories, as do the connotations of these and related terms. The fictitious ideal of pureness is reflected in many derogatory terms for persons of mixed parentage, such as 'mulatto', 'mongrel', 'sambo', 'half-blood', 'metis', and 'mestizo', just as 'pidgin', 'patois', 'lingo', 'argot', and other terms for unlettered or otherwise substandard speech forms of the socially weak which, if used by outsiders, are nowadays considered offensive. The idea of racial or ethnic homogeneity and the attachment to it is not the same in all countries, and therefore connotations cannot be transferred from one language to another, even if they include similar or identical terms. For instance, while in some English-dominant countries 'mulatto' is considered a racial slur, Spanish 'mulato' is a socially acceptable term in Latin America. Like any other social aspect of language diversity, connotations are an interesting object of study, but for research and theory building they can be distracting. Neutral technical terms are preferred.

Code. One such term that helps to circumvent the thorny language-or-dialect-or-what issue is 'code'. It became current in the literature when, in the 1960s, British sociologist of education Basil Bernstein recognized linguistic discrepancies between working-class and middle-class pupils as a major cause of differences in scholastic achievement. Pupils of all social backgrounds were, supposedly, speaking the same language, English; but the school, Bernstein (1971) argued and demonstrated, favoured the 'elaborated code' associated with middle-class speech to the detriment of the 'restricted code' more common in working-class speech. Because of profound differences between the two codes, what theoretically counts as the same language does not guarantee equal access to educational contents taught at school. Influential though it was for some time, the theory of codes and its terminology has been largely superseded by variationist sociolinguistics and 'sociolect' as a general term for varieties indexical of social stratification.

Code-switching. However, 'code' is an important term in another subfield of multilingualism research, 'code-switching' (also 'codeswitching'). It is indifferent to whether what are being switched are languages or dialects or other varieties. Code-switching, understood as alternating use of more than one variety by individual speakers in the same conversation, but variously defined more narrowly by different scholars

53

(Gardner-Chloros 2009), has grown into a huge field of investigation, upsetting many naïve assumptions about linguistic communication.

As is the case for other terms discussed in this chapter, 'code-switching' is not a term that refers to an entity in the world of objective facts waiting to be studied, but a label that helps researchers to organize heterogeneous speech data. Attempts have been made to refine the terminology by distinguishing, for example, between 'borrowing', 'nonce-borrowing', 'interference', 'intersentential (i.e. within one sentence) code-switching', 'intrasentential (i.e. between sentences) code-switching', and 'code-mixing', but a congruent usage of these term was never accomplished. Different researchers drew the lines between these concepts differently, and the growing research literature about various forms of speech that deviate in one way or another from the fictitious ideal of a monolingual conversation brought with it a proliferation of arcane terminology of limited usefulness.

The linguistic behaviour whereby an individual uses different *codes* in one conversation attracted scholarly attention for three main reasons. First, it is not random, but exhibits a certain systematicity in that regularities in switches can be discovered. Code-switching thus differs from deviant speech caused by incomplete acquisition, although this is not always appreciated by laypeople educated in strongly monolingual settings. Second, code-switching is a matter of choice, constituting a separate component of bilingual speakers' linguistic capabilities which they utilize in order to fulfil communicative and social functions. Thus, code-switching is socially meaningful. Third, the codes in question are not just named languages, but may be dialects or other varieties as well.

Wherever different codes are used regularly in a community they assume different tasks, be it in terms of communicative or social functions. A conspicuous dividing line first noted and described for instances of code-switching in such diverse places as Norway and India by John Gumperz (1982) is that between 'we-code' and 'they-code', the former being preferred for in-group communication, the latter more commonly used in out-group relations. Language is used in many ways as a social tool to form groups, mould social relationships, and establish dominance. In multilingual settings of increasing ethnolinguistic diversity, 'we-codes' and 'they-codes' have been employed in new, more complex ways, including the alternation between the two as a marker of group identity. For example, features of immigrants' 'we-codes' have been observed to be integrated into the repertoire of local speakers.

Rampton (1995) observed the adoption of Punjabi and Creole features by Anglo adolescents in urban Britain who, according to his interpretation, in this way created a trans-racial common ground. By way of distinguishing this very particular and socially significant kind of code-switching which occurs not on the basis of anything resembling bilingualism, but as an act of accommodation or association, he introduced the telling term 'crossing', which has been widely adopted in the field (see Chapter 10).

Bilingual. Switching languages requires a command of at least two languages, in other words, to be bilingual. A bilingual is defined as a person fluent in two languages; however, by now we know that this is probably not the end of the story. And indeed, once we leave the domain of common sense, things become more involved. If we want to understand the particulars of this kind of language behaviour we cannot colour all bilingual speakers with the same brush, for they differ in various respects. There are several ways of classifying bilingual speakers, each of which has its utility. Most typologies that have been proposed are organized along two dimensions, skill and age of acquisition, which reveals the interesting fact that age of acquisition does not strictly determine degree of proficiency. 'Early bilinguals' acquire two languages at a young age and, depending on whether they were exposed to both languages from birth or one after the other in early childhood, are categorized as 'simultaneous' or 'sequential' bilinguals (see Chapter 5). Both are distinguished from 'late bilinguals' who acquire the second language (L2) significantly later than the first (L1) (Hoffmann 1991).

Along the skill dimension bilinguals are classified as 'equilingual', 'balanced bilingual', 'dominant bilingual', and 'passive bilingual', where the first has perfect and indistinguishable competence in both languages; the second is highly proficient in both languages, but may on occasion prefer one over the other for specific purposes; the third, dominant bilingual, has a clear dominance usually in L1, although it is not unheard of for speakers to change their dominant language in the course of their lifetime. The fourth type is a bilingual speaker who has more or less fluent comprehension but only limited speaking proficiency of his or her L2. Developmental psychology and language acquisition are the research domains where these distinctions are relevant. Many studies have been carried out over the past decades designed to answer the question of how bilingual competency is acquired, whether bilingual children develop their L1 and L2 separately from one another, and whether there are any useful strategies to help parents raise them (Grosjean 2010).

'Native-like fluency' is the presumed benchmark against which proficiency is measured, although native exposure does not in all cases guarantee fluency. In this connection yet another type of bilingual must be mentioned whom we come across in a different field of research, semi-speakers (Dorian 1980). In the case of semi-speakers or semi-linguism, the issue is not setting standards of acquisition and progressing proficiency, but the reverse: decay and fading proficiency, that is, loss of a minority or immigrant language forgotten or used with ever decreasing frequency by their bilingual speakers who by necessity or choice use the majority language. The semi-speaker is the central figure in endangered languages research, although language attrition, degeneration, and abandonment are also of interest to psycholinguistics and migration studies. Imperfect proficiency and maybe only passive knowledge of a language are features the semi-speaker shares with other types of bilinguals, but because of the different gestation of limited competence in both cases the concepts are distinct.

Native speaker. While semi-speakers retain only partial competence and fluency, they are, like pidgin speakers and bilinguals, not limited to one language, but likely have full competence in another language, even native competence. 'Native competence' and 'native-like competence' are often treated as primitive terms not in need of further explanation. For example, the balanced bilingual speaker has been defined as one who 'can be recognized as a native speaker in either one of the languages' (Hamers and Blanc 1989: 132). This looks as if a balanced bilingual were two native speakers packed into one. Yet, such a definition bags the most interesting question of what happens when two languages are simultaneously put into one brain: whether the native competence of a bilingual differs from that of a monolingual speaker, and if so, how.

The native speaker is a creature of modern linguistics, the witness of the 'homogeneous speech community', who 'has been exposed to one and only one language during his entire life' (Paikeday 1985: 48). Within the assumed monolingual context of grammatical studies of one language the native speaker is a convenient reference figure, but in the field of bilingualism research his or her role must be different. Is the native speaking bilingual possible? Or does it 'make sense to speak of a native speaker of more than one language?' asks, for example, Davies (1991: 75). Upon reflection, the native speaker reveals itself as a rather shady figure with many faces (Coulmas 1981; Dasgupta 1998). Once taken out of the monolingual ghetto, his or her role as a reliable arbiter of deciding what does and does not constitute part of a language can no longer be taken for granted (Mufwene 1998).

Native speaker, native language, and native-like competence are abstractions properly put into the same box with the fenced-in 'standard language'. These are highly ideologized notions that can be useful when clear cases are at issue, for instance, differences in proficiency between a speaker's L1 and foreign languages learnt at school. They are premised on the idea that languages are clearly distinct systems and that the relevant distinctions are acquired from birth. In families whose everyday speech is close to the standard language this may be a justifiable abstraction, but in many environments where new-borns are exposed to more than one language or variety, the concept is problematic and should be used with circumspection.

Mother tongue. The same holds for 'mother tongue'. The term itself speaks of sentimental attachment which lends itself to metaphorical conflation with kinship and by extension race. Conceptually the mother tongue speaker is a close cognate with the native speaker. Since typically people have but one mother, one's mother tongue, too, is supposedly just one. To persons whose mother's L1 is not their own L1, who grow up with more than one language, or whose primary linguistic model in early life is their father or another relative rather than their mother, this concept is not easily applicable without qualification. Tracing the history of 'mother tongue' and 'native speaker' in philology, Bonfiglio (2010) has shown that these concepts entered both common and scholarly discourse on language in connection with emergent ethnolinguistic nationalism in the early European nation states where the national language became the focal point of an ideology of congenital communities and claims to political independence.

Notwithstanding its ideological loading and conceptual vagueness, the term 'mother tongue' is widely used in various settings, such as, for example, mother tongue education programmes and census surveys.[3] In scientific contexts it has been largely superseded by more descriptive terms referring to both immigrant and indigenous languages, such as 'home language', 'language of origin', 'heritage language', and 'community language' (e.g. Clyne 1991; Van Deusen-Scholl 2003). 'Heritage language'

---

[3] See the companion page for some examples.

has not escaped criticism, suggesting, as it does something like DNA, a trait gained through birth, which is just what opponents to the native language ideology want to avoid; for, from studies on language maintenance and shift, it is well known that L1-affiliation is fluid and ambivalent among children born to parents speaking such languages.

At the present time, 'home language' and 'community language' seem to be the least problematic terms; however, no matter what you call it, the language in question is one that is in an inferior position relative to the dominant language of the wider environment, while it may or may not be the speakers' L1. It constitutes in any event a component of bi-/multilingual speakers' repertoire which makes itself felt in their language behaviour. In the wake of increasing numbers of bilinguals entering the educational system in Western societies, researchers have studied how these speakers strategically draw on different linguistic resources, repeatedly traversing between languages, in order to carry out complex cognitive and social tasks (García and Li Wei 2014). Defying any categorization in terms of native speaker or mother tongue and resembling in many ways other modes of code-switching, this particular kind of language behaviour has been called 'translanguaging', a recent term first used in educational contexts where code-switching has often been viewed as undermining the effectiveness of language teaching. Translanguaging, by contrast, has been promoted as a positive strategy of language learning that exploits the learner's linguistic resources to maximize communicative potential. The concept has also been taken out of the classroom to account for the strategic employment by bi-/multilinguals of two or more languages.

3.3 Conclusions

In this chapter we have examined a number of concepts that are in various ways related to the study of multilingualism. By identifying patterns of behaviour and aspects of language ignored or abstracted away by a system-centred science of language, they are designed to deal with the vagueness, fluidity, inconsistency, and dynamics of linguistic diversity situated in the social world. Most of them have grown out of the insight that the complexities of multilingualism are impossible to grasp if the two or more languages that coexist in countries, homes, classrooms, and in the street are treated as bounded autonomous systems. Rather, languages and varieties in multilingual settings are related in manifold ways which, although fluid and dynamic, have identifiable commonalities that warrant investigation. On the basis of the concepts reviewed in this chapter, we can record that theories of multilingualism are about the dynamics of socially situated languages in contact.

As a way to summarize the discussion, the following matrix sorts key concepts along a static vs. dynamic dividing line and thus highlights a core characteristic of multilingualism, its fluidity.

Static	Dynamic
Standard language	Multiple varieties, Patois
National language	Pidgin, Creole
Mother tongue	Home language
Heritage language	Community language
Diglossia	Heteroglossia
Monolingual speech	Code-switching, crossing, translanguaging
Native speaker	Bi-/multilingual speaker; Semi-speaker
Uniformity	Diversity

The fluidity of the object of investigation and the general multifacetedness of the social world forces students of multilingualism, as pointed out repeatedly, to delineate meaningful phenomena for research, rather than just look carefully at the given facts. The terms discussed in this chapter bear witness to this necessity. They are themselves subject to constant review and modification. None of them is made forever, and in the hope of laying a screen on an ever-changing picture-puzzle that reveals hitherto hidden features, new terms keep getting introduced together with new theories.

Problems and questions for discussion

1. Take any language of your choosing and find out what conventionally used terms it has for racially mixed people, if any, and whether these terms are neutral or value-loaded! How do such terms as you can find relate to terms for broken or mixed language?

2. Can you in your everyday communication distinguish a 'we-code' from a 'they-code'? If so, describe a situation in which you would switch from one to the other.

3. Explain the difference between the terms 'diglossia' and 'heteroglossia'.

4. What is a fenced-in language? Explain the meaning of the concept and discuss its implications for an extensional definition of 'language'.

Further reading

Goertz, Gary. 2005. *Social Science Concepts: A User's Guide.* Princeton, NJ: Princeton University Press.

Woolard, Kathryn A. 1985. Language variation and cultural hegemony: Toward an integration of sociolinguistics and social theory. *American Ethnologist* 12: 738–48.

4

Power, inequality, and language

4.1 Restricting choice

In 1978, the Indonesian government banned the use of Chinese characters on public signage, a measure designed to deny the ethnic Chinese minority a legitimate presence in the linguistic landscape of Indonesia.

After having been banned from schools and the public sphere under General Francisco Franco's dictatorship (1936–1975), the Catalan language re-emerged in public when Catalonia regained a degree of autonomy within the Spanish state in 1979.

In February 2014, the parliament in Kiev rescinded the Ukrainian 2012 language law that allowed the country's regions to grant other languages official status in addition to Ukrainian provided they were spoken by more than 10 per cent of the population, notably Russian. As a result of this action, relations between Ukrainians and Russians deteriorated, contributing to the tensions that led to the secession/annexation of Crimea by Russia in 2014.

Power is the ability to restrict choice. In the extreme case, the choice is about life itself—capital punishment. In less dramatic ways it is about regulating many aspects of social life: on which side of the road to drive, when to go to school, whom to marry, what names to confer on one's offspring, among many others. The three cases just mentioned, although different in nature and for a proper understanding in need of more detailed information, are all about restricting language choices in multi-lingual settings. Relations with ethnic Chinese in Indonesia, never free from tension even in colonial times, worsened after independence was achieved from the Netherlands and the People's Republic of China was proclaimed in Beijing. Chinese Indonesians were summarily suspected of sympathizing with communism and subject to discrimination. Since the 1950s, various regulations have gradually reduced the visibility of Chinese outside the private sphere. The importation of printed material from China was banned, Chinese newspapers and magazines were shut down, and the number of Chinese-language schools was drastically reduced (Willmott 1961: 96–7). Banning the display of Chinese characters in public was the ultimate expression by the Indonesian government which let the Chinese know that they were not wanted in Indonesian society (Tan 2005). In the event, the Chinese minority bore the brunt of tense relations between Indonesia and China, Chinese characters serving as the obvious symbol for those determined to stamp out the Chinese presence as well as those who wanted to display it.

The disputed status of Catalan, too, extends further into the past than its ban under Franco. Ever since the Catalan Rebellion against the Spanish Habsburgs in the seventeenth century many Catalans imagined Catalonia as a third sovereign state on the Iberian Peninsula alongside Spain and Portugal. The Catalan language always played a central role in their claim to statehood which, however, the Castilians continued to deny them. In the interest of a strong Spanish state, for centuries Castilian government policy imposed the Castilian language onto the Catalans, as stated by José Rodrigo Villaplando, senior officer of the Council of Castile, in 1716: 'The importance of making the language uniform has always been recognized as great, and it is a sign of dominion or superiority by princes or nations' (quoted from Major 2013: 86). Franco's ban on the use of Catalan in public was just an echo and continuation of long-established policies designed to promote Castilian.

Frictions between Ukrainophones and Russophones are likewise not a recent occurrence. In the Tsarist Empire the Ukraine was commonly referred to as 'little Russia' (малоросский). The Ukrainian language, called a 'Russian dialect contaminated by Polish' (Hosking 1997: 379), was forbidden between 1876 and 1905. Prior to and during the Russian Revolution, Lenin advocated a more conciliatory policy towards the many national minorities of the Soviet Union (Coulmas 2016: 189–92), but under Stalin discriminatory attitudes re-emerged, and while there was not much open repression, Ukrainians and other non-Russians came to realize that insistence on speaking their language, especially among Russophones, was understood as hostility towards the Soviet state (Kuzio and D'Anieri 2002). What is more, many Ukrainians had ambivalent attitudes to Ukrainian which, like the Russians, they perceived as provincial, preferring to use cosmopolitan Russian for literary and non-intimate forms of communication. The revocation of official status for Russian in independent Ukraine must be seen in the context of a young country still in the throes of nation building.

In all three cases, as in numerous others, restricting language choice is a long-standing historical issue. If we want to understand to what end power over language use is exercised, it is necessary to be aware of the historicity of our present circumstances. Political scientists and sociologists often treat language as a background reality, a necessary condition for the constitution of society and for power to unfold. This view, though true, is too narrow as it ignores the fact that language choices, even unmarked choices that pass unnoticed as normal procedure, always reflect power relations. Where such relations seem to put one of the involved parties at a disadvantage or appear in other ways to be unjust, they are particularly conspicuous; however, in itself the exercise of power is not illegitimate or to be equated with coercion. It may be based on or result in consent; in any event it is the product of historical processes and as such subject to deliberate or accidental change. Existing restrictions may be lifted, new ones established, more often than not for other than linguistic reasons.

The complexity of analysing power relations with a linguistic dimension is compounded by the fact that, as our three examples illustrate, linguistic divisions are inextricably linked with an array of social, political, and economic cleavages. Language often serves as the stage on which power relations involving inequalities of various kinds are acted out. Our three model cases do exemplify inequality of languages: Indigenous Bahasa Indonesia (and other Indonesian languages) vs. immigrant Chinese; hegemonic Spanish vs. minority Catalan; minority Russian vs. national Ukrainian. In all three cases it is the majority that restricts the minority's language choices. However, we must beware of simple generalizations, for these inequalities are very different. Chinese is an immigrant language in Indonesia, but one representing a high culture and prestigious literary tradition that affords its speakers self-confidence and connections to a powerful state. Bahasa Indonesia, by contrast, is the national language which was promoted to serve the functions of high culture only in conjunction with Indonesian independence from colonial rule. Catalan has always been limited in geographic extension to a small region along the southern coast of the Iberian Peninsula and the Balearic Islands, a provincial rival to Castilian which is the national language of Spain and also one of the most widely spoken languages in the world. Russian used to be the dominant language of Ukraine when it was part of the Tsarist Empire and when it was one of the Soviet republics. As the language of many Ukrainian writers it also forms part of the common cultural heritage of Ukraine and Russia. However, most Ukrainians speak Ukrainian and Russian fluently and would find it hard to say which one is their 'mother tongue', unless as a vow of commitment. What is more, while Russian is now a minority language in Ukraine, it is also the language of its powerful neighbour and as such still extensively used in business, in the media, and in education.

Classifying the three groups in question only as linguistic minorities obscures the picture, for linguistic minority status intersects in multiple ways with other social divides. A small group of some 1.2 per cent of the total population, the Indonesian Chinese are economically strong; their religious affiliation is mostly Confucianism and Taoism (lumped together with Buddhism in Indonesian statistics) with a small number of Christians; and they are racially distinct from the majority which is of ethnic Malay extraction. This group are therefore defined as a minority on multiple dimensions: economic, religious, racial, and linguistic. If multiple reasons for the majority to see one group as a minority increases the risk of intergroup conflict, as political scientists have suggested (McRae 1989), then the ethnic Chinese in Indonesia are a case in point, having been targeted repeatedly by anti-Chinese riots. However, similarities according to structural traits and genetic closeness are no safeguard against violent conflict, as the Ukrainian case attests. The Russians and Catalans are neither racially nor religiously distinct from the respective majorities. In Spain, Catalonia is one of the economically wealthier provinces, and many Catalans are resentful of a state-wide redistribution system over which they feel they have too little control and receive too little benefit. For Catalan activists today, this is a weighty reason to oppose the Spanish government which for three hundred years has worked to construct a unified centralized nation state with no regional differences, but has not been able to eradicate a Catalan self-image centred upon the Catalan language (Bel 2013). In contrast, the minority language status of Russian in Ukraine is of very recent origin, having been brought about by the 1996 Constitution of Ukraine. Many of its speakers alive today remember a time when they were part of the majority speaking the majority language. In terms of religion, race, and culture little separates them from the majority in newly independent Ukraine, which, to the chagrin of Ukrainian nationalists, is economically still strongly involved with and dependent upon Russia (D'Anieri 1999).

In sum, the three linguistic minorities discussed in this chapter are as diverse as the reasons why their language choices are curtailed. They represent three types of minorities which we might call 'indigenous', 'immigrant', and 'postcolonial'; but there are many other types and sub-types. The subject of language, power, and inequality is a large and multidimensional one that is hard to subsume under a unified theoretical framework. The following questions may provide some orientation for a reasoned conceptualization of power in multilingual settings.

1. Whose language choices are restricted?
2. Who decides on restricting language choice?
3. How are restrictions on language choice justified?
4. Who enforces such restrictions and how?
5. Are restrictions on language choice contested, and if so, by whom?

Examination of these five questions about restrictions on language choice should disprove the common belief that language is but a background condition of social and political life.

4.1.1 Whose language choices are restricted?

The principal language users are individuals and it is their choice on which restrictions apply, but institutions are also subject to limitations in the languages they may use. Government agencies are not free to make legally binding announcements in any language they see fit. Without official approval they cannot even issue tax return forms or driving licences in any but the officially sanctioned language(s). The language(s) of public broadcasting is commonly regulated by law or institutional statute. National reserve banks are limited in the number of languages they may use on the banknotes they issue. For instance,

Swiss banknotes feature Switzerland's four national languages, German, French, Italian, and Romansh; the Chinese Yuan has inscriptions in five languages, Chinese (Mandarin pinyin), Mongolian, Tibetan, Uyghur, and Zhuang; on the Indian Rupee fifteen languages appear; and on the South African Rand, 'South African Reserve Bank' is translated into two different languages each for each denomination, ten languages in all. The British Pound and the US Dollar are monolingual.

Another example of a restriction on institutional language choice is the oath of office administered when officials are sworn in. Typically, the wording allows for no choice, nor is the oath taker free to choose the language. For instance, the oath of allegiance in British courts is prescribed as follows:

I, _____ , do swear by Almighty God that I will be faithful and bear true allegiance to Her Majesty Queen Elizabeth the Second, her heirs and successors, according to law.

Since, however, 'Almighty God' may not be relevant for all those qualified and willing to practise law, provisions are made for followers of other religions. Thus, members of the Hindu faith and the Muslim faith can swear 'by Gita' and 'by Allah', respectively;[1] but they are not allowed to do so in Hindi, Bengali, Arabic, or any other language. An interesting difference between religious and linguistic affiliations comes to the fore here. In many modern constitutional states, freedom of religion is guaranteed, and it is accordingly considered inappropriate to force anyone to recognize the authority of the majority god, while in many institutions the sole authority of the majority language is taken for granted.

Many other examples could be cited to show that restrictions on the languages that individuals and institutions may use are pervasive; and in many cases these restrictions are accepted as a matter of course. A trickier question is whether groups can be restricted in their language choice. On the face of it this seems obvious; however, an affirmative answer implies that a group can carry out actions, hold rights, be held liable for transgressions, and be subject to limitations, which is not so clear. Repression, racism, and pogrom are directed at collectivities, but opinions are divided as to whether groups can suffer, or only individuals. Does a group have a being or an identity separate from the individuals

---

[1] Cf. Courts and Tribunals Judiciary: https://www.judiciary.gov.uk/about-the-judiciary/the-judiciary-the-government-and-the-constitution/oaths/.

who make it up, standing between the individual and the state's citizenry? Does it change with each member who joins or departs from it? In the philosophy of law these are hotly debated questions which cannot be discussed here.[2] There is, however, wide agreement that groups exist; that the subjective sense of the members to be part of a group is essential for a group to exist; that groups differ in the significance such a sense of belonging has for their members; and that since the dissolution of the multilingual Habsburg, Ottoman, and Tsarist Empires and in the wake of decolonization ethnolinguistic groups aspiring for nation status proliferated. Language, like religion, appears to be an evident criterion of group formation, except that, as discussed in the previous chapter, boundaries are fluid. Am I a member of a group by virtue of the fact that I speak Japanese? What kind of group would that be? Not all speakers of Japanese may want to associate with that group. Do they belong to it anyway?

These are not just moot questions. They pertain to the problem of diversity within the modern state which puts the individual human being at the centre of the legal system. Liberty of abode, protection against discrimination and unlawful detention (*habeas corpus*), and freedom of expression, among others, are rights granted to individuals. The individual is the principal holder of rights which is in keeping with the fundamental idea of human rights. Yet, collective interests are brought to bear as legitimate grounds to restrict individual rights. For example, a naturalized deputy of country X may be prohibited from addressing the national assembly in his or her first language Y in the interest of the collective, the assembly, most of whose members would not understand a speech delivered in Y. In the event, the individual's language choice is restricted. Suppose there were several naturalized deputies who are denied their wish to address the assembly in their L1. Does this amount to restricting a group's language choice, or is it only the choice of each one of the deputies that is restricted?

In the abstract the question whether a set of individuals constitutes a group whose language choices can be restricted or accommodated does not lead to a satisfactory solution and the status of group rights and limitations thereof remains a theoretically controversial issue (for an

---

[2] For instance, Kymlicka (1995) makes the case for group rights, in particular with respect to culture and language. On the other hand, Ellis (2005) argues against the notion of group rights on the grounds that all rights are possessed by individuals who belong to groups.

overview cf. Jones 2016). An obvious and convincing argument for the possibility of groups' language choice restrictions is that languages are collective products and collective goods[3] designed to enable people to communicate with each other. Bar some eccentrics, speakers speak in order to be understood by those who speak the same language, a group. But whenever a language is not admitted for use in a certain domain, this is a restriction on the language choices of individual speakers of that language. In other words, group choices are reducible to individual choices.

However, when the language choices of a large number of individuals are restricted, their individual claims to have such restrictions lifted may carry more weight. It is not theoretically satisfying that, if individuals' choices are restricted, numbers should make a difference, but in practice this is exactly what happens. Individuals have a better chance to suffer fewer restrictions if they are many, where 'many' is a rather elastic and context dependent measure—or another attestation to the 'messiness' of social life.

4.1.2 Who decides on restricting language choice?

Most states have official or national languages which explicitly or tacitly imply restrictions on language choice.[4] Our three examples illustrate government actions effectuating restrictions on the use of languages in certain domains. Such restrictions may be legitimized by constitutions or individual laws, forming an integral part of the state's power structure. Non-sovereign states, such as the states of the USA, may formulate restrictions in statutes or constitutions. For instance, the Constitution of the US State of Idaho stipulates in article 2-209 that a 'prospective juror is not qualified to serve on a jury because he or she is unable to read, speak, and understand the English language'. The Constitution of the State of Florida, Article 2, 9 declares: 'English is the official language of Florida.' Given that Hispanics account for 23 per cent of Florida's population, this looks like a strong restriction on language choice in the public sphere. However, general provisions of this sort are often

---

[3] Collective goods, also called 'public goods', are a class of goods characterized by two very special criteria: (1) they cannot be withheld from an individual without withholding them from all (non-excludability), and (2) they do not diminish by additional users (non-rivalrous).

[4] Gauthier et al. (1993), if somewhat dated, is still a useful overview of language clauses in national constitutions worldwide.

qualified by more specific regulations, implementation statutes, and institutional rules of procedure, including exceptions (see Chapter 6).

In the absence of and in addition to formal regulations, effective restrictions are brought about by habit, common practice, and social pressure. For, contrary to what linguists assert, languages are not equal but are subject to attitudes and valuations on the basis of which speakers of lesser-used, peripheral, immigrant, and otherwise marginal languages are often shamed into silence, a mechanism to which children are particularly susceptible. But it is not only children who avoid using their L1 in environments where it is stigmatized, using the dominant language of their environment instead. Such indirect means of control also form part of the power relations in society and as such influence the interpretation of existing legal provisions.

A third force that works against the equality of languages and brings about covert but very effective restrictions on language choice are market forces. The commodification of language in the knowledge society has produced language industries which, according to Duchêne and Heller (2012: 13) are 'among the hallmarks of late capitalism'. These industries interact with technological developments in complex ways. Thus computer-mediated communication facilitates the expansion of minor vernaculars into domains hitherto restricted to standard languages, while at the same time strengthening further the big languages that can generate a profit, for example, in publishing and providing translation services. According to current neoliberal ideology, markets are moved by quasi-natural forces, but reflecting as they do political and social power differentials, the world market of languages and national language markets are not in any way free markets. Like other markets they are subject to power and political opportunities.

In sum, to answer our second question, it can be said that statutory law, sub-state level institutional regulations, social attitudes, and market forces interact to restrict language choices. This very general statement only identifies the forces at work in a language regime and serves to call attention to the fact that the power of restricting language choice resides in various quarters. How governments intervene in the linguistic behaviours of their citizens; where beliefs about and valuations of languages come from and how they take hold in a society; how market forces influence inter-language relationships; and how these forces are balanced and integrated, to uphold or change a language regime are questions to investigate empirically for specific contexts and languages.

4.1.3 How are restrictions on language choice justified?

In premodern times a multitude of languages in a single polity was nothing out of the ordinary. There was not much communication between ruler and ruled, and at the same time it was a matter of course that if subjects wanted to speak with their ruler, they had to speak the ruler's language or rely on an intermediary. For this arrangement not much formal justification was needed, although religious organizations tended to justify their language regimes with otherworldly authority. In modern societies, in contrast, ideas of sovereignty by culturally defined population units, participation, equality, and justice play a prominent role. They underlie linguistic nationalism, the dominant language ideology in post-French Revolution Europe and still very potent today: If everyone speaks the same language, so the rationale goes, the problem of exclusion and discrimination can be eliminated.

From our contemporary point of view and under conditions of ever stronger claims of equal rights in liberal democracies, linguistic nationalism appears as an instrument of repression that disadvantages weaker language groups. However, when this ideology took shape and began to influence political developments, it was seen more positively as a strategy of empowerment. Notably in France the idea was to turn left-behind backwoodsmen into citizens by liberating them from the narrow confines of their patois. The diffusion of standard French throughout the republic was an important revolutionary aim. Abbé Grégoire (1750–1831), the chief architect of the new government's language spread policy, was a progressive Catholic priest who championed many of the revolutionary causes of his day, such as the emancipation of slaves, the right of Jews to full French citizenship, and the establishment of compulsory public education (Grillo 1989: 24). He and many of his contemporaries thought that the universal promotion of standard French was a precondition of bringing the truth of liberty and progress to the provinces and for every French citizen to have equal opportunities.

Linguistic nationalism always had the two objectives of claiming power over a territory where a language is spoken, if only in an educated elite's imagination, and unifying a populace across regional and social divides to enable all citizens to understand the laws passed by an elected government and to communicate directly with each other. The convergence of nation, language, and territory favoured by French revolutionaries and German romanticists alike brought about what Clyne (2008) called a 'monolingual mind-set'. The idea that multilingualism is a liability for democratic government and that, accordingly, restrictions on language choice are legitimate in the name of democracy is still current among some political scientists (e.g. van Parijs 2007), although in recent decades there has been an ideological shift towards a positive evaluation of diversity extending the equality imperative to languages. The important point to note here is that regimes of restricting language choice are justified by ideologies that make such restrictions look reasonable, appropriate, and even inevitable. These ideologies are historically grown components of power structures that make people see languages, dialects, and other elements of their linguistic resources in certain ways, and make them act in certain ways. It is only when particular interests that are at variance with the extant regime are articulated strongly enough that the legitimacy of a language ideology is called into question. It should also be borne in mind that ideologies are more easily recognized in retrospect for what they are and what functions they fulfil. For most contemporaries they are an integral part of the normal order of things not requiring any reflection.

Language choice restricting ideologies may accord with widely supported political designs or be accepted as practical necessities, as, for example, in the context of nation building or establishing an effective system of education. What is more, one's own positions and attitudes are always less ideological and more reasonable than those of former times. With regards to restrictions on language use, there is no simple solution. The actual state of affairs is the result of power struggles, which may have lain dormant for a long time, but become obvious when the dominant ideology is contested by those who have a just case to make or are at least convinced of having one. The paradigm case, linguistic nationalism, was seen as a liberating philosophy when it appeared on the European scene in the eighteenth century and was later taken for granted. In modern industrial society, it played a central role, mediated through the school system, in establishing an effective common culture (Laitin 1998). Nowadays it is regarded as an obsolete ideology by many intellectuals in the Western world, but not so by minorities (e.g. Catalans) or recently independent nations (e.g. Ukraine). Whether this change of perspective is to be welcomed or condemned is a political question. Of scientific interest is why such changes occur and what causes them.

4.1.4 Who enforces restrictions on language use and how?

French sociologist Pierre Bourdieu (1982) used the notion of the 'legitimate language' to refer to the officially sanctioned standard language as distinct from dialects, patois, and other sub-standard varieties. According to his theory, the legitimate language is associated with the variety spoken by the educated socially dominant classes, and its promotion in the national school system is a crucial mechanism of reproducing social inequality. While Bourdieu is concerned first and foremost with the suppression of local and social varieties of the standard language, other unrelated languages are treated similarly as non-legitimate languages.

The legitimate language is the dominant language within a polity and often but not necessarily (a variety of) the majority language. Colonial and post-colonial situations are characterized by a mismatch between demographic strengths and power which finds expression in the colonialists' language obtaining the position of legitimate language of rule and maintaining it even in many post-colonial states. There is a wide range of variation in the extent to which legitimate language status implies a denial of human differences in terms of other social cleavages, but in any event power and politics rather than communication are at the heart of the language regime.

The most drastic restriction of language choice is categorical language proscription. It can emanate from government agencies invested by law with the power to determine the linguistic norms to be observed in various domains of the public sphere. Private organizations and religious institutions can exercise similar power. Restrictions can also take the form of language recognition or positive prescription of one or some languages which implies the exclusion of others. To cite an early well-known example of marginalizing an indigenous language by establishing another as sole legitimate language, the Act of Union of England and Wales of 1536 places restrictions on the language choice in courts of law and other government agencies.

Also be it enacted by auctoritie aforesaid that all Justices Commissioners Shireves Coroners Eschetours Stewardes and their Lieuten'ntes, and all other Officers and Ministers of the Lawe, shall proclayme and kepe the Sessions Courtes hundretes letes Shireves and all other courtes in the Englisshe Tongue and all others of officers iuries enquestes and all other affidavithes verdicted and Wagers of lawe to be geven ond done in the Englisshe tongue (quoted from Davies 2014: 34).

If there was no coordinate policy of eradicating Welsh and other Celtic languages from the British Isles, establishing the use of English as the only legitimate language in the courts and other branches of the administration in Wales was a measure that functioned as an exclusion of Welsh and could only foreshadow its decline, as the educated Welsh elite were thus faced with the uncomfortable choice between insisting on using their language or partaking in power.

Official status allocation is an effective means of enforcing language choice restrictions because it implies exclusion. A dramatic case occurred shortly after the partition of British India along religious lines when, on the occasion of his visit to what was then East Pakistan in 1948, Muhammad Ali Jinnah, the leader of Pakistan, declared:

> Let me make it very clear to you that the state language of Pakistan is going to be Urdu and no other language. Anyone who tries to mislead you is really the enemy of Pakistan. Without one state language, no nation can remain tied up solidly together and function (quoted in Islam 1978: 144).[5]

Jinnah, who spoke in English, had come to the eastern province to celebrate liberation from the colonial yoke and the formation of an independent Muslim state, but his insistence on imposing Urdu and 'no other language' as the official language on a population that did not speak Urdu provoked protests among the Bengali-speaking majority of East Bengal, giving rise to the Bengali Language Movement which became a key element of the undoing of Pakistan and the establishment of Bangladesh as a separate state in 1971, after a bloody civil war.

For a more recent and less violent example of exclusion by status allocation consider Italy. Its Law no. 482 of 1999, art. 2, subsection 1 lists twelve languages deserving protection: Albanian, Catalan, German, Greek, Slovenian, Croatian, French, Franco-Provençal, Friulian, Ladino, Occitan, and Sardinian.[6] Not included in the schedule are Sicilian, Venetian, and Ligurian. The implicit conclusion that can and must be drawn from this schedule is that the latter three are not languages enjoying state protection or are not languages at all but Italian dialects and,

---

[5] A recording of Jinnah's speech can be found at http://www.londoni.co/index.php/history-of-bangladesh?id=118.

[6] Legge 15 Dicembre 1999, n. 482, 'Norme in materia di tutela delle minoranze linguistiche storiche', http://hubmiur.pubblica.istruzione.it/alfresco/d/d/workspace/SpacesStore/a838f175-f878-4b2d-b249-bbbfbd7d6of9/legge-482.pdf.

therefore, not worthy or in need of protection, a view that may or may not be shared by these varieties' speakers.

Lists of this sort enforce, however tacitly, language choice restrictions by offering simple selection criteria for job applications, the allocation of funds, drafting syllabi, and for the allowance of a language as the medium of instruction in schools. Because for most people it is the first institution outside the family in which they consciously experience regulated language use, the school is the most important agent enforcing language choice restrictions. Power relations within this institution are clearly defined, and those at the receiving end, the pupils, are not in a position to call its modus operandi or the content that is being transmitted into question. They cannot but accept the restrictions on which languages are used inside and outside of the classroom, just as they have to accept which words are to be written and how they must be spelt. Modern flexible educational practices notwithstanding, the school is not a place where anything goes, but a place of right and wrong where the right resides with the authority. In the modern state, formal education is a load-bearing pillar of social reproduction which, as we have seen, is intimately bound up with linguistic divisions and language choice restrictions. Since schools are disposed to stick to established practices and education reform is inevitably subject to rival political interests, change, though possible, tends to be slow.

4.1.5 Are restrictions on language choice contested and, if so, by whom?

Evidence in support of an affirmative answer to the first part of this question is not hard to find, for the majority of language related conflicts are about restrictions and privileges. Another postcolonial situation can illustrate this. In Sri Lanka a majority of Sinhalese Buddhists live together with a minority of Tamil Hindus. In the British Crown Colony (1817–1948), English was the language of rule, while Sinhalese and Tamil were used in everyday life by their respective speech communities. In the deterioration of community relations after independence, language played a critical role. When in 1956 the government passed the Sinhala Only Act—which replaced English by Sinhala as the only official language of the country—the Tamils felt excluded from the highly coveted government jobs and rebelled against Sinhalese hegemony

(DeVotta 2004). The Sinhalese, on the other hand, felt they had to defend themselves against the well-educated Tamils who were a minority in Sri Lanka, but whose language—which is also spoken by tens of millions of Tamils in India—had a much larger speech community than Sinhala. The Sri Lanka Tamils were systematically discriminated against by various policies, for instance by regulating access to university on the basis of language group size rather than academic merit. After more than two decades of tension and repeated riots, a new constitution was adopted that made some concessions to the Tamils by assigning Tamil National Language status along with Sinhala (Art. 19), while, however, retaining Official Language status for Sinhala only. By that time, many Tamils had been radicalized and were ready to fight for a separate state. The burning by a Sinhalese mob in 1981 of the Tamil library in Jaffna made it clear for everyone to see that language was at the heart of the conflict. Outright civil war erupted in 1983 and lasted for the next twenty-five years.

The Sri Lanka language conflict was driven by linguistic nationalism, which for decades undercut all attempts to create an atmosphere of mutual toleration towards managing the inequalities in terms of language, religion, demographic strength, and education that divide the major ethnolinguistic groups in the country. Language related conflicts are rarely accompanied by so much bloodshed, but this particular case serves as a warning that language choice restrictions are prone to being contested by disadvantaged groups and of how explosive their grievances can be.

Language regimes are part of the overall social system and as such are likely to be affected by developments in other parts of the system. Therefore, the fact that multilingualism is not just about language is in evidence wherever one looks. Demographic shifts following decolonization resulted in growing tensions between entrenched monolingualism in Western nation states, including traditional immigrant countries such as the United States and Australia, and an increasingly multilingual social reality. Over the past half-century, the privileged status of national languages as the sole medium of instruction in national school systems has been contested by ever greater numbers of pressure groups led by intellectuals pitting the theme of ethnolinguistic identity against the dominant ideology of national unity. The supposedly homogeneous cultures of Western nation states are undergoing a process of re-heterogenization, as the battle cries of language maintenance and linguistic rights[7] challenge the professed advantages of linguistic uniformity. The quest for identity tagged to language is voiced by immigrant communities, on one hand, and indigenous minorities, on the other.

In Australia, insistence on the maintenance of immigrant languages other than English has effectively undermined long-standing English monolingualism and led to the creation of a multicultural and multilingual environment with several hundred languages being spoken (Australian Bureau of Statistics 2009). In the United States the awakening of Black consciousness in the 1960s was a catalyst for the 'ethnic revival' (Fishman 1983) which did not obliterate Anglo-dominance, but has brought into existence 'an active pressure group demanding that society assist pluralistic goals through legislation and public funding' (Weinstein 1983: 154). By making the identity assertion of ethnolinguistic groups increasingly acceptable, such pressure has also contributed to exposing the melting pot ideology for what it always was: a myth (Lichter et al. 2015). Western European countries were and continue to be confronted with a ceaseless influx of immigrants with their own language needs that have proven rigid assimilation policies impractical. In many countries, multiculturalism became an issue of public debate, echoing many of the themes that were topical in the USA (Modood 2013). On both sides of the Atlantic the chorus of immigrant voices has been supplemented by indigenous minorities challenging their disadvantaged position and demanding equal rights and more tolerance of cultural and linguistic diversity.

It should be noted that the great ideological shift from the glorification of uniformity in the name of linguistic nationalism, in industrial society, to the appreciation of diversity, in the knowledge society, emanated from the West. Scholars, media, activists, religious units, and educators have called for 'mother tongue education', a policy repeatedly advocated by UNESCO for the past six decades (UNESCO 1953). Given the commitment against discrimination on the grounds of race, gender, religion, and language enshrined in the 1948 Universal Declaration of Human Rights and many subsequent documents, this is an honourable goal, but in light of the fact that only a fraction of the languages of the world have ever been used in writing and even fewer provide access to

---

[7] See the 1996 Universal Declaration of Linguistic Rights which 'takes language communities and not states as its point of departure [...] and aims to encourage the creation of a political framework for linguistic diversity based upon respect, harmonious coexistence and mutual benefit', http://www.linguistic-declaration.org/versions/angles.pdf.

any body of literature to speak of, it is quite unrealistic. It is hardly surprising, therefore, that the enthusiasm for minor languages and their use in education by Western intellectuals is not unconditionally shared in other parts of the world.

Nigerian linguist Ayọ Bamgboṣe (1998) has shown that established restrictions on language use in the educational system of many African countries are not necessarily challenged by excluded language groups, but that, on the contrary, Western-educated African intellectuals have difficulties convincing their compatriots of the merits of vernacular education because 'with years of indoctrination, many people have come to accept that "real" education can only be obtained in a world language such as English' (Bamgboṣe 1998: 88). The power of a language ideology and the difficulties of replacing it with another are in evidence here. In keeping with current Western discourse on linguistic diversity Bamgboṣe supports the notion of language rights, in particular the right of children to receive education in their own language which, he maintains, cannot be denied without violating their cultural identity and heritage. Considering the practical consequences of such a stance, he adds the caveat that 'the sociolinguistic situation may make absolute insistence on language rights impossible' (Bamgboṣe 1998: 85), but he does not question the validity of the general idea of cultural identity and heritage affixed to a language, however small.

The romantic idea of one's proper language and its essential links with cultural identity and heritage has gained many followers; however, that its claim to universal validity is as debatable as linguistic nationalism appears from a critical appraisal by Indian linguist E. Annamalai. Against the background of dynamic multilingual practices in South Asia he notes:

The social construct of native language is to sustain an asymmetrical power relation through the ideology of otherness. It ensures that some speakers of a language are defined by shared grammar as others in contrast with the self. This ideology operates at the level of the individual, the community and the State (Annamalai 1998: 149–50).

What we can learn from Bamgboṣe's and Annamalai's observations is that ideas about language regimes in a society are never neutral or detached from experience and context, but modulated according to traditions, practical expediency, and philosophical persuasions. While this is not a plea for unconditional relativism, it may serve as a reminder of the historical contingency of current Western ideas about contestations of restrictions on language choice. Nowadays identity and heritage are big topics in Western discourse about just rule, equal opportunity, and the 'inalienable right of people to preserve their way of life'. We must not forget that these ideas arose against the background of the colonial experience, which many see as an injustice, but which cannot be undone by promoting these ideas in other parts of the world. It is also worth considering to what extent acceptance and promotion of diversity depend on national wealth or, more generally, on the level of economic development. However that may be, challenges to established restrictions on language choice can only be understood if these restrictions are seen as part of a political strategy, cultural repression, economic necessity, or, most likely, a combination of all three. Where language choice restrictions have no or almost no social and economic correlates, as in Switzerland (see Chapter 8) they often stay uncontested. However, to answer the fifth question, wherever they are contested this may occur at the institutional, community, or national levels.

4.2 Conclusions

Restrictions of choice reflect power differentials and are an expression of inequality. As such they are an integral element of the language regime in most societies. With regard to political entities that designate a national or official language and make use of, command, or tolerate more than one language, it is particularly obvious that complete equality of the languages involved, nominal or factual, is the rare exception.

While the power differential between languages is most relevant in the national political arena, it is also present in smaller communities, families, as well as with respect to the proficiency of individual speakers. The notion of 'dominant language' which implies a hierarchical order is applicable on all of these levels. Restrictions on language choice can be more or less severe, installed by explicit regulation or habit, generally accepted or contested. The coexistence of several languages in one community without any restriction is, however, conceivable at best as an ideal, if only because societies are constantly evolving and their linguistic resources are evolving with them. There is, therefore, a need to justify restrictions on language choice, a function fulfilled by language ideologies that connect individual languages with states, territories, membership, heritage, historical myths, authenticity, and culture.

Ideologies furthermore legitimize evaluations of monolingualism or multilingualism that inform legislation and public discourse and in this way enable individual and institutional agents to enforce restrictions. Whenever language choice restrictions are coupled with privileges and the rationalizing ideology loses credibility, language divisions tend to become politically more salient, bearing the risk of conflict. Even where a system of restrictions is firmly established, language can always be politically charged and therefore never be discounted as a factor in intercommunity relations.

Problems and questions for discussion

1. Do you have to write a term paper or sit for an exam? In what language? Do you have a choice?
2. Who has the power to decide in your country in which language(s) banknotes are issued?
3. Do persons elected to the national or regional assemblies in your country have to take an oath of office? If so, do they have any options about the language in which they take it?
4. How can positive status allocation of languages cause intercommunity frictions? Are there any examples discussed in this chapter?
5. Is an official restriction of language choice a limitation of freedom of speech?

Further reading

Bauman, Richard. 2003. *Voices of Modernity: Language Ideologies and the Politics of Inequality.* Cambridge: Cambridge University Press.

Bourdieu, Pierre. 1982. *Ce que parler veut dire. L'économie des échanges linguistiques.* Paris: Fayard [English translation: *Language and Symbolic Power.* Oxford: Polity Press, 1991].

5

The polyglot individual

> Rare linguist, whose worth speaks itself, whose praise,
> Though not his own, all tongues besides do raise:
> Than whom great Alexander may seem less:
> Who conquered men, but not their languages.
> In his mouth nations spake; his tongue might be
> Interpreter to Greece, France, Italy.
> His native soil was the four parts o' the earth;
> All Europe was too narrow for his birth.
> A young apostle; and, with reverence may
> I speak't, inspired with the gift of tongues, as they.
>
> John Dryden, 1649[1]

5.1 Preparing the ground

That children grow up with more than one language is not uncommon.
Strict monolinguals, in the sense that they learn and use only a single

---

[1] From the first published poem by John Dryden, 'Upon the Death of the Lord Hastings', mourning his friend Henry Lord Hastings who died prematurely of smallpox at the age of 19. *The Poems of John Dryden.* 1913. London: Oxford University Press, p. 175.

language, are likely a minority in the world as a whole. There are, therefore, good reasons to study linguistic issues from the point of view of people who use several languages in their daily lives, be it in multilingual countries such as South Africa and Singapore or in allegedly monolingual countries such as France and Germany.

The central figure in this chapter is the polyglot, the individual who has command, to various degrees, of two or more languages. It begins with a number of autobiographical reports by writers who have commented on their life with multiple languages. While their accounts lack immediacy and may not always draw a clear line between fact and fiction, they are the result of conscious reflections of greater depth than can usually be elicited from the millions who are leading a multilingual life. On the basis of their accounts we will take a closer look at some of the more mundane issues of individual multilingualism. In particular, we will address the following questions. When is a multilingual? Is there enough room for several languages in one brain and if so, for how many? How important is the order of acquisition? Do multilinguals always have a dominant language? Is growing up multilingual a burden? For children? For their parents?

But first consider what some extraordinary people had to say about their multilingualism, for much in science comes from descriptions of the peculiar and exceptional.

(1)   William Gerhardie.
Of the four languages taught me in childhood my knowledge of English was least and, until I was eighteen or so, inadequate. With our parents, as a matter of duty, we spoke English. But it was the language we children knew least—a language mostly confined to our parents in conversation with each other. Among ourselves we spoke Russian, and now that we have passed into the habit of speaking and corresponding in English, in a fit of sincerity we mechanically lapse into Russian. With our French governesses (of which there were a succession) we conversed, very unwillingly in their tongue. With 'Fräulein', who remained with the family seventeen years, we talked fluent German of the Reval variety. When in danger, as in a rocking boat or in an overturning vehicle, we, by association of ideas, exclaim in German. We expostulate, as indeed you must, in French. But English, peppered with Russian, is now our more or less natural mode of expression.

These lines are from the autobiography of William Gerhardie (1895–1977) who grew up in pre-Revolution St Petersburg and upon settling in England became a celebrated novelist of the 1920s and 1930s. Perhaps his best-known novel, *The Polyglots*, first published in 1925, is about a young man of Anglo-Russian upbringing who tries to make sense of the world which, in a sense, he finds in a group of multilingual expats stranded during the Great War in the Far East. That Gerhardie's multi-linguality was a defining element of his life appears from the title of his autobiography: *Memoires of a Polyglot*.[2]

(2) Vladimir Nabokov
I think like a genius, I write like a distinguished author, I speak like a child. Throughout my academic ascent in America, from lecturer to Full Professor, I have never delivered to my audience one scrap of information not prepared in typescript.... My hemmings and hawings over the telephone cause long-distance callers to switch from their native English to pathetic French.

I don't think in any language. I think in images. I don't believe that people think in languages. They don't move their lips when they think. It is only a certain type of illiterate person who moves his lips as he reads or ruminates. No, I think in images, and now and then a Russian phrase or an English phrase will form with the foam of the brainwave, but that's about all.

Vladimir Nabokov (1899–1977), son of an old aristocratic Russian family and perhaps the best-known post-1917 émigré author, made a career in American academia and wrote in Russian and English. The first paragraph is from the foreword of a collection of interviews, appropriately entitled *Strong Opinions*, the second from one of the interviews.[3]

(3) Arthur Koestler
Interviewer: Was German your first language?
Koestler: I was bilingual—Hungarian and German. I believe I'm the only writer who twice changed the language in which he writes, from Hungarian to German at seventeen years old, and from German to English at thirty-five. Since 1940 I have written only in

---

[2] First published 1931; quoted from reprint 2008, London: Faber and Faber, pp. 47, 48.
[3] Vladimir Nabokov. 1973. *Strong Opinions*. New York: McGraw-Hill, xii. Vladimir Nabokov, 1962, from a BBC Interview by Peter Duval-Smith and Christopher Burstall, http://lib.ru/NABOKOW/Intero2.txt.

English. But in any language it is a struggle to make a sentence say exactly what you mean.

Interviewer: Is English better suited to your purposes than German?

Koestler: Oh yes, much. English has a muscularity with the fat massaged away. German is a very woolly language. French has a so-called Cartesian lucidity, but it's deceptive because it misses so much, a pseudolucidity because...no, cross that out, it's getting too complicated.[4]

This interview with Arthur Koestler (1905–1983) was carried out near the end of his life. Born and raised in Budapest, he became famous as an author and journalist in the English language, although he also wrote in German and French. After decades of moving about Europe between Vienna, Berlin, and Paris and repeated stints in Palestine, he made his home in Britain in the 1950s.

(4) Elias Canetti

The first language I spoke was the old Spanish, Spaniolo, then I learnt English as second language, and then, because my parents who thought highly of themselves took in a French governess, I learnt French as my third language. After my father died at young age, my mother who loved Vienna where she had gone to school, moved with us, we were three boys, to Vienna.

Interviewer: And you learnt German only then?

Canetti: No, it was before that. On the way to Vienna, in the summer, my mother stopped in Lausanne to teach me German in three months, by almost terrorist means, to make sure I could enter school in Vienna in the right grade. Thus German was only my fourth language. When I learnt it I was eight years old.[5]

Elias Canetti (1905–1994) who recounts his linguistic childhood in this quote was born in Ruse, Bulgaria, where he lived the first six years of his life. After that he grew up in Manchester, Vienna, Zürich, and Frankfurt. He moved to London in 1938 and obtained British citizenship in 1952. Throughout his career as a writer, he wrote in the German language, crowned in 1981 with the Nobel Prize in Literature.

[4] Arthur Koestler 1984. In an interview by Duncan Fallowell in the *Paris Review* http://www.theparisreview.org/interviews/2976/the-art-of-fiction-no-80-arthur-koestler.

[5] Elias Canetti, 1971, in an interview by *André Müller*, published in *Über die Fragen hinaus*, dtv, 1998, available at: http://www.a-e-m-gmbh.com/andremuller/elias%20canetti.html (translation from the German original F.C.).

These four renowned writers led eventful and vibrant lives. They have been selected here because of their testimonies about their various languages, representing many others who share similar experiences: Józef Teodor Konrad Korzeniowski (1857–1924), better known as Joseph Conrad was conversant in Polish, Russian, and French before he learnt English, in his twenties. Léopold Sédar Senghor (1906–2001) spoke Serere and Wolof before he learnt French, the language of his illustrious writing, recognized by the highest authority of that language when he was made a member of the Académie française. Samuel Beckett (1906–1989) switched from English to French and sometimes back. Beat-Generation cult author Jack Kerouac (1922–1969) grew up speaking Québécois French and later wrote in English and French. Alain Mabanckou (1966–), today a prominent French writer, grew up in the Republic of the Congo where he spoke Bembé, Laari, and Munukutuba before he went to a French-medium school. Wole Soyinka (1934–) was raised in Nigeria with Yoruba and English to become the first African winner of the Nobel Prize in Literature. Francesca Marciano (1955–), an Italian dramatist, writes in Italian and English. In *The Other Language* she explains that languages, identities, and races will continue to intertwine, and that she shares her linguistic duality with many others. Ying Chen (1961–), born in Shanghai and living in Canada, writes mostly in French and self translates into Chinese.[6]

These vagabonds of language belie all those inclined to use the concept of native language in a reductionist way as an inescapable and irreplaceable element of 'individual identity', in this day and age the dominant index word for sorting people into closed categories. The idea of mother tongue as destiny is quite common.[7] Ginsburgh and Weber (2011), for example, in a essay about linguistic diversity entitled, *How many Languages do we Need?* do not allow for individuals equally conversant in more than one language. The native language, they insist, is distinct. Similarly, Akerlof and Kranton who like Ginsburgh and Weber are economists have proposed an 'Identity Economics', because

---

[6] For more contemporary examples, see Yildiz (2012) who speaks of 'the postmonolingual condition'.

[7] Twentieth-century linguists have contributed their share to the promotion of the idea that a second language can be acquired only at the expense of the first. So says, for example, Otto Jespersen in his influential book *Language* that whatever advantages there were for children to be familiar with two languages, they were 'purchased too dear'. With immediate relevance to our present context, he continues with the rhetorical question, 'Has any bilingual child ever developed into a great artist in speech, a poet or orator?' (Jespersen 1964: 148).

identity [boundaries of race, ethnicity, and class] 'may be the most important determinant of economic position and well-being' (Akerlof and Kranton 2010: 16). In their view, one's native language is a fatality, especially for immigrants: 'They may try to "pass", or to integrate with the dominant group, but they cannot be fully accepted. They are unable to fit the ideal to which they aspire, and instead, in their language, culture, and background, they are made to feel inadequate' (Akerlof and Kranton 2010: 101). Although, in my view, these two authors see society too much as working like the military, that is, in terms of norms, loyalties, and strict adherence to a code of conduct, discrimination on the grounds of language is indeed a common occurrence. However, for all we can infer from their accounts, our four polyglots did not suffer from it. All of them wrote in their 'adopted mother tongue', to use Gavrousky's (1982) felicitous term, considering language a matter of choice rather than destiny. What unites them with other bi- and multilinguals is that they can contemplate questions about language choice and language use that do not and cannot occur to monolinguals. Allowing for the possibility of difference comes easily to them. It should be noted, though, that their multilingualism is of the kind that has often been called 'elite bilingualism' as opposed to 'folk bilingualism' (e.g. De Mejía 2002). This distinction draws attention to the importance of social characteristics of multilingualism, even when individuals are at issue.

5.2 Language skills and critical age: when is a multilingual?

Our four polyglots are thought remarkable for their command of languages other than their L1 to an extent that goes far beyond facility of use for everyday purposes. They achieved mastery of a style that distinguishes great writers. Language proficiency, we can conclude, is an acquired ability. Suggestive as the terms 'mother tongue' and 'native language' are, they should not obscure this fact, or be taken to mean that language proficiency is an inborn aptitude. Tests have been developed to assess language aptitude (Meara et al. 2001), and it is uncontentious that some people are better than others at handling language, just as some people have an ability with numbers; but our examples suggest that this does not necessarily depend on whether or not one has acquired a language as L1.

While it cannot be denied that the said individuals were or are highly competent in their respective languages, sociolinguists and psycholinguists are likely to point out that in the cases at hand the focus is on competence in the written language, which should not be confused with language skills in general because—discounting Tarzan who learned language from text[8]—children typically acquire speech before writing. This is true, but it is equally true that literacy is indispensable for modern life and considered a deficit where it is lacking. Let us note, then, that command of the written language is a part of the language skills that can be measured and compared. There are other parts. In the context of language learning and teaching, four skills are usually distinguished along two dimensions, active and passive, and oral and literate: writing and reading, speaking and listening comprehension. Productive and receptive control of sign languages must be added, and among the many kinds of multilinguals, bimodal bilinguals who are proficient in both sign language and oral language occupy a position of their own. Language skills can be mastered to different degrees. The written mode facilitates, even requires, conscious reflection on language in ways and to an extent not practical in oral speech.

Our four polyglots had several languages at their disposal about which they entertained different feelings and ideas. To Gerhardie German came most spontaneously when in danger, and Russian was the language of intimacy with his siblings. Koestler, when asked about the suitability of different languages for his writing, started to expound some ideas about English, German, and French, but then interrupted himself, apparently to sidestep any untenable generalizations. Nabokov, aware of both his genius and his limitations, spoke 'like a child', by which he meant that, in English, he lacked fluency and an unmarked accent. Technically speaking the metaphor was not fitting because 'hemmings and hawings' and a strange accent are not what characterize children's speech; on the contrary, they, unlike Nabokov, acquire a native accent effortlessly, as, if we believe his testimony, Gerhardie did with German 'of the Reval variety' offered him as primary input by his nanny.

Nabokov had been taught English by a private tutor, but emigrated from Russia to England when he was twenty, too late, defenders of the

---

[8] *Tarzan and the Apes*, a novel by Edgar Rice Burroughs, first published in 1912. In it, Tarzan, who was orphaned at the age of one and grew up in the jungle, performed the well-nigh impossible feat of teaching himself English from books, including some primers he found in his parents' deserted cabin.

'critical period hypothesis' would argue, to acquire a native-like accent in English. This hypothesis (also: 'critical age' or 'sensitive period') has played a significant role in language acquisition research in an attempt to explain learning differences between children and adults (Birdsong 1999). It assumes that the apparent ease with which young children master a language or more than one is attributable to the greater cerebral plasticity at a young age. And if language acquisition is delayed and does not occur by puberty, full mastery of language is unlikely ever to be achieved. While the hypothesis has given rise to much controversy (Harley and Wang 1997) and many questions remain to be answered, a consistent finding based on anecdotal evidence as well as systematic research is that adult second-language learners are more likely than children to retain an identifiable accent, but there is no unequivocal explanation why this is so. Nabokov seems to be a case in point. Yet, because of the many circumstantial, individual, psychological, and social variables that may impact the language acquisition process, conclusive evidence is hard to establish. Birdsong (2005) has shown that native-like proficiency can be attained by adult learners and argued that no sensitive period can be delimited. Furthermore, the question has been raised whether accent—the tonal accent of the language and the speaker's regional accent—may not actually be a misleading attribute for age effects in second language acquisition (Cook 2001: 495).

Perhaps Nabokov, to return once again to his individual case, had better things to do than fine-tune his accent, while children are more affected by peer pressure, and sounding like 'the others' is for them a high priority. Clearly he did not suffer from lack of self-esteem (he thought 'like a genius'). Could such a personality trait have an effect on the felt need to blend in with the environment? If so, its influence is likely to increase with age. However, the critical period hypothesis does not take into account personality traits or social variables but posits that synaptic patterns established in early childhood in the brain to hold the L1 will be relied on when learning another language later in life and therefore affect the learner's mastery of that language. Where the phonology is very different from L1, the result is a foreign accent (Flege 1999). This is a plausible theory supported by many adult L2-learners' initial difficulties in pronunciation of sounds not present in their L1, but it cannot explain why some adult learners are able to acquire a native-like accent, while others never lose the accent of their L1. And it does not enable us to draw a sharp line between age effects and structural interference.

Another unresolved question is what distinguishes a foreign accent from a native one. Upon reflection this is not so clear. If your English betrays your Scottish, Australian, Singaporean, or Californian origin it is native; but sounding as if you come from France or Russia is qualified as a foreign accent? Of an elderly friend of mine who was born in London and had never lived anywhere else, I thought that I could detect not just a German but a Frankfurt accent in his English. He laughed at me, but then he told me that his father grew up in Frankfurt, Germany. Can accents cross languages and generations? Most people are more aware of the accents of others—national, regional, social, and individual— than of their own. Nabokov, a professional wordsmith, was very much aware of his own accent in English. Was he too old, too lazy, untalented (unmusical), or ill-suited as a personality to get rid of it? This has to remain an open question; however, the individual case is indicative of the variables that may be involved and may in any event prove hard to isolate.

Children learn both first and second languages faster than adults. There is plenty of evidence for this, yet identifying unequivocally the reasons why this is so has not been so easy. As mentioned above, the greater flexibility of children's brains has often been cited as the main reason, but proof is elusive (partly because of the general difficulty of empirical research with very young children). If we conceive of an infant's brain as an empty shelf, it is perhaps easier to fill it up than an adult's shelf which is already crammed with all sorts of materials. Or perhaps children just have more time to do the job; or they suffer from fewer psychological and social inhibitions. All of these factors come into play, among others. This demonstrates, once again, that we are not dealing with categorical distinctions, but gradual processes of acquiring skills to variable degrees. Any typology of multilingual speakers should be seen in this light.

Various such typologies have been proposed in the literature in which the temporal dimension figures prominently. Basic distinctions are between 'early'—that is, from birth—and 'late'—that is, after adolescence— and between 'simultaneous'—learning two languages at the same time— and 'sequential'—learning one after another. Cutting across this dimension are differences in proficiencies in the languages involved (L_1, L_2, L_n), major types being balanced vs. dominant and productive vs. receptive. The recessive bi-/multilingual is sometimes included as an additional type to describe speakers whose competence in one language is fading.

In this manner, multilingual speakers can be classified by age, according to degree of fluency and by the context of acquisition, that is, 'natural' (by which no one thinks of Tarzan alone in the jungle, but rather of a family setting in the civilized world) vs. 'formal', in a classroom setting.

Since these dimensions are interrelated, our question, 'When is a multilingual?' is best answered in a minimalist way. Rather than getting lost in a maze of blind alleys, we settle on a simple definition proposed by Mackey (1962: 52) when this field of research was still young, for a half a century of research has not produced a more cogent unified definition. Accordingly, a bi-/multilingual is a person who has 'the ability to use more than one language'. On the basis of this definition, subgroups may then be defined in terms of varying degrees of competence in the four skills mentioned above. Our four polyglots would qualify for the highest ranking in the language of their writing, but might score differently in the other skills for that and their other languages.

5.3 Is there enough room for several languages in one brain and, if so, for how many?

The obvious answer to the first part of this question is an unqualified 'yes'. Hundreds of millions of bilinguals testify to that. The second part is trickier. Is there a limit? Unless you believe in immortality, there must be, for learning a language, no matter how good you are at it, takes time. The brains of our four polyglots held at least four languages each allowing them to speak, write, read, and understand them. Russian philologist Roman Jakobson was fluent in six languages, and Hungarian-born Australian linguist Stephen Wurm spoke nine. If you want more, consult the Guinness Book of Records! Hudson (2008) refers to persons who speak twelve or more languages as 'hyper-polyglot'. Learning languages, many polyglots have reported, gets easier with each subsequent language. Anything gets easier when you do it more often. It is particularly true for learning closely related languages, such as the European languages, which share a huge part of their vocabulary. That should help but could also be confusing. How do polyglots keep track and make sure they do not get mixed up? They must not say *buono* when *gut* is expected or talk about an 'ancient lady' when she is just old. It distinguishes proficient polyglots that they are able to keep their languages apart and not be misled by false friends. Function and person specific language choice is characteristic of their language behaviour. Their linguistic skills thus include not only separate lexica, grammars, phonologies, and, as the case many be, orthographies, but also the capacity to manage these resources and make the right choice.

This capacity has been the focus of a great deal of research on the bilingual brain; for choose they must, given that their languages are stored in their brains. At what point in the process of cognition and verbalization this happens and to what extent volition and deliberate search are involved are questions which have interested neuroscientists for some time, in a search for evidence by means of experiments and diagnostic tests. For example, picture naming and translation tasks were designed to determine differences in the processing speed of the two languages and for monolingual controls (e.g. Bialystok 2001). Dementia research (Bialystok et al. 2007) and clinical studies of brain injury induced aphasia (Paradis 2014) are other approaches to shed light on the mysteries of bilingual cerebration. Brain injuries resulting in 'pathological language switching' (defined as the uncontrolled alternation between languages for no apparent reason) suggest that there is in the healthy bilingual's brain a special language control system. From the fact that it can malfunction, Green (1998) has concluded that this mechanism is normally employed to select the intended target.

What Nabokov, on the basis of introspection, described as a phrase of one language or the other suggesting itself when thinking can be equated with what in scholarly terms has been called the *language activation threshold*. The Activation Threshold Theory posits that in the bi- or multilingual brain languages compete with each other, and that for using one rather than another, the activation level of that language is higher than that of the competing language(s), which are at the same time deactivated or blocked from contributing to the speech output (Paradis 2004). Frequent use, according to this theory, lowers the activation threshold of a language, while conversely prolonged disuse raises the activation threshold which may find overt expression, for example, in temporary word-finding difficulties or, when disuse continues over a long period of time, in language attrition (Schmid 2011).

New brain imaging implements and methods have greatly enhanced neurologists' ability to localize functions and processes in healthy brains and compare them with diseased brains, but it remains difficult to investigate very specific questions, such as whether bilinguals have a localizable language control system that governs language separation and choice. Comprehensive meta-studies (e.g. Hull and Vaid 2005; Mouthon, Annoni, and Khateb 2013) conclude that in spite of a wealth of interesting findings, no conclusive evidence for a language control centre in the bilingual brain is yet available. More generally, almost every review of research on language localization in bilinguals includes repeated caveats of the kind, 'but see XYZ, for counterevidence'.

In sum, much more is known today about the bi-/multilingual brain than a vague intuition that in the process of verbalizing thoughts one language or the other comes to the fore, but the entire field is in a state where every answer generates a multiplicity of new questions. Mouthon et al. (2013) offer a brief and accessible synopsis of research about how the bilingual's brain organizes, differentiates, and uses the different languages (for more comprehensive overviews, see De Groot 2011; Hernandez 2013; Pavlenko 2014). What we do know is that people can pick up new languages as the need arises and, while learning new skills tends to get more difficult with advancing age, no one has yet reached a hard-wired limit of the number of languages he or she can pack into their brain, this side of the grave. The more languages a speaker has, the less likely it is that they are all on par. What this means for the hierarchization of multilinguals' languages is one of the questions that continues to puzzle researchers. In at least one respect, if in no other, the languages of hyper-polyglots and indeed of all non-simultaneous multilinguals differ. They were acquired at different points in their speakers' lifetime—which brings us to the next question.

5.4 Simultaneous or sequential: how important is the order of acquisition?

Three of our protagonists came to literary acclaim in a language that was not their L1 and the fourth, Gerhardie, did not feel comfortable in the language in which he would become a writer until he was eighteen years old. These examples tell us that the question of whether the order of acquisition has any significance must be made more precise. 'Important with regards to what?' we must ask. The above discussion about accent suggests that phonological patterns established with L1 acquisition are more likely to affect subsequent languages than the other way round. Notice, however, that both immigrants developing a 'foreign' accent in their L1 and L2 speakers acquiring a native(-like) accent are not unheard of. For instance, investigating with empirical tests constraints on second language pronunciation Hopp and Schmid (2013: 361) come to the conclusion that 'acquiring a language from birth is not sufficient to guarantee nativelike pronunciation, and late acquisition does not necessarily prevent it'.

If we order language skills on a scale ranging between most spontaneous and most consciously controlled, pronunciation is at one extreme and (creative) writing at the other. From studies such as Hopp and Schmid (2013) it follows that it is impossible to establish a categorical effect of order of acquisition on proficiency in bilinguals' languages. The best we can hope for is discovering general tendencies. L2 speakers are much more likely than L1 speakers to have a perceptible foreign accent in their speech, for example. Notice that we are talking about probabilities rather than constant causalities.

In the same vein, some empirical studies based on functional brain imaging techniques suggest that exposure to L2 is more important than order of acquisition (Abutalebi, Cappa, and Perani 2001). Again, amount of exposure and frequency of use are graded rather than categorical variables. For those seeking definitive rather than probabilistic answers this is a disappointment, but the latter certainly give us a clearer view of reality. After decades of research about the impact of order and age of acquisition on proficiency, we are forced to realize that the search for clear-cut distinctions and categories is destined to be frustrated, and that its pursuit is a distraction. We have to accept messiness, vagueness, and a wide range of individual variation as inherent to multilingualism, not as something we should strive to eliminate by sharpening our research tools. For many people who live in an environment where they are exposed to and speak their first-learnt language the most, order of acquisition is de facto decisive, but this may be so as a matter of probability rather than causality. For others who move from their L1 environment to one where they use their L2 (L3) more, the order of acquisition may prove to be of lesser importance. Yet, a distinction is commonly made between *simultaneous*, that is, those who acquire two or more languages from earliest childhood, and *sequential* or *late* bilinguals, that is, those who add one or more languages after adolescence or as adults.

As we have seen in the above discussion about the critical age/sensitive period hypothesis, age and order of acquisition interact with several other factors that influence L2 proficiency. We must confine ourselves to rather general statements about the effect of order of acquisition. Bar any external factors such as, for example, immigration, a temporal hiatus between L1 and L2 acquisition typically results in L1 dominance, and, everything else being equal, the longer the time the more this is so. This is not to say that order of acquisition determines the hierarchy and relations between a multilingual speaker's languages for life. It may be overruled by other factors that bring about changes in language behaviour, preference, and dominance.

5.5 The foam of the brainwave: do bilinguals always have a dominant language?

'And what language do you think in?' is a question bilinguals are frequently asked by monolinguals who have learnt a foreign language, but cannot imagine handling two languages with equal ease. The language in which one thinks, they believe, can only be one. The question, however, already includes the important presupposition that thinking is done in a language. Coupled with vulgar conceptions of linguistic relativism, it results in simplistic and misleading ideas about the intricate links between cognition, language, and culture.

Nabokov commented on this question in no uncertain terms: He did not think in any language and did not believe that people think in languages. His answer marks one of two extreme positions that characterize a longstanding debate about the relationship between thought and language. The other extreme position known as linguistic determinism holds that the language we speak makes us think in certain ways and thus limits our knowledge. Linguistic determinism or, in its weaker form, linguistic relativism goes back to the nineteenth century and is closely associated with the name of Wilhelm von Humboldt (1767–1835) who linked cultural to linguistic differences arguing that lexical and grammatical structures coincide with the cognitive classification of experience. In the twentieth century, the idea was popularized as the Sapir–Whorf hypothesis (so named for their principal proponents Edward Sapir and Benjamin Lee Whorf), whose names were, however, abused for a deterministic view on the influence of linguistic categories on cognition that they never held. Vulgar Sapir–Whorfianism, became quite influential, not least because of the fundamental difficulty of conceiving of thinking without language and because it is so fascinating to contemplate a world in which people who do not speak our language cannot understand what we think. Obviously, we need language to talk about thinking, but that does not mean that thinking and articulating thoughts are the same, or that, once acquired, language becomes a prison house that contains us, rather than an adaptable instrument we control.

Yet the ideas that our thoughts are channelled by our language and that in the case of bilinguals it can only be the dominant language that is fit for the task are firmly rooted in the public imagination. However, Nabokov recognized in himself different stages of the thought process, images and phrases of his two principal languages, Russian and English, 'formed with the brainwaves'. Koestler's above-quoted terse remark is also worth repeating in this connection: 'In any language it is a struggle to make a sentence say exactly what you mean.' Habit and routine aside, if you have something to say that others have not said before, it is not easy to find the right words—regardless of the language. The task is to achieve congruence between the meaning you intend and the meaning expressed by a sentence. That is a struggle, Koestler says. So who is doing the struggling? And who is there to judge whether the result is or is not satisfactory? There are two distinct activities or phases that together constitute the process of verbalizing a thought; and one precedes the other, first forming a thought and then putting it into words. Some psycholinguists posit a third phase in between the two, called 'inner speech', a kind of silent soliloquy which involves the manipulation of linguistic resources for sorting out 'how to put it'. In any event, there is a non-linguistic part of the cognitive process, of which both Nabokov and Koestler were clearly aware.

This, however, is not the end of the story about cognition and language, a field of inquiry in which psycholinguists, cognitive scientists, and anthropologists are equally interested. Because the links between the two are largely hidden from view and hard to reduce to empirical investigation, they are susceptible to fashionable expectations and biased views. Pavlenko (2014: 18) makes the connection that needs to be made about linguistic relativity and its significance for the study of bilingualism by pointing out that the fascination with Humboldtian and Sapir–Whorfian ideas arose in a period of history and in societies where monolingualism was strongly favoured. This is in keeping with the fencing off of languages discussed in Chapter 3 above. Language standardization and linguistic nationalism informed politics, education, and also scholarship, to the effect that the normalcy of the monolingual native speaker gained universal acceptance, referring the multilingual speaker to a marked position whose deviation from the norm calls for explanation. Koestler's and Nabokov's observations open up a different view, pointing to the general difficulty of achieving concord between intended and expressed meaning which involves, among other things, groping in a black box we call mental lexicon.

Whether and to what extent multilingual speakers search in different places in the black box and whether separate brain networks are engaged when they perform various tasks involving one or two languages are questions pursued in ongoing research, which may be a more promising approach to resolving the question of dominance in a piecemeal fashion than starting out from the preconceived superiority of the mother tongue (alias standard or national language). For present purposes, suffice it to note that many multilinguals have a dominant language; that this is not necessarily their L1; that dominance may shift over their lifetime; and that even if one language is dominant overall, they may prefer another for certain communicative functions such as counting and calculating, professional discourse, talking about emotional subjects, or singing.

The factors that may have an influence on language dominance are many, both learner internal and learner external. Here is just a selection: individual characteristics, such as personality, age, age at onset of L2 acquisition; family characteristics, such as birth order, that is, learner's position among siblings, first-born child or child with older siblings, parents' level of education and socioeconomic status, and parents' attitude towards language maintenance; characteristics of milieu and location, such as ethnolinguistic homogeneity or diversity, educational provisions for the languages concerned, frequency and quality of language exposure; language characteristics, such as minority/majority, closely related or distant, literary or oral. With so many variables coming into play, language dominance itself is bound to be a highly volatile trait which, moreover, is subject to social modulation.

5.6 The social setting: is growing up multilingual a burden?

Yes, but. The 'but' is about conditions that determine how heavy a burden it is and whether shouldering it is worth being celebrated as a hero superior to Alexander the Great who conquered just peoples but not their languages, as in the case of Henry Lord Hastings in the quote at the outset of this chapter. The deservedness of such an accolade is, perhaps, debatable, but it is beyond doubt that becoming bilingual requires more brain work and is, therefore, a burden. Canetti's after-thought about his mother's teaching him German, 'by almost terrorist means', suggests that even in retrospect coping with several languages as a child is experienced as an onus rather than a privilege or pastime.

Just looking at the mental lexicon as one part of language acquisition, a simple calculation will illustrate this point. If five-year-olds have an expressive vocabulary of 2,500 words—a rough and ready number, but the right order of magnitude—they have learnt on average some 1.4 words every day since birth, with no day off. Can some of them fairly be expected to learn 2.8 words a day in the same time? Clearly not. Among the most robust findings of early bilingual language acquisition is, therefore, the result that there is a slight delay in simultaneous bilinguals building their lexicons and in their early grammatical development, when compared to monolingual children (Paradis 2009: 20). Their lower scores on standard-ized receptive and expressive vocabulary tests are hardly surprising. The receptive vocabulary consists of the words we understand and the expres-sive vocabulary of the ones we use. The former is always larger than the latter, during language acquisition at that age by a factor of 4 or 5, and among bilinguals the gap may be even wider. In both languages they can understand much more than they can say, but typically what they can say in either language is not the same. Because of this incongruence, they produce mistakes that differ from those of monolinguals, sometimes showing evidence of crosslinguistic interference (Nicoladis 2003).

Much depends on how these differences are handled. If the bilingual child's mistakes are ridiculed or disparaged, the burden gets heavier and the child may turn away from or develop an aversion to one of the lan-guages—in immigrant situations this would typically be the home lan-guage—with unforeseeable personal and social consequences.

Language is quintessentially social. Whenever we use it we interact with others, regardless of how many languages are involved in the process. Grosjean (1998) has observed that bilinguals typically adjust their behaviour depending on whether they interact with monolinguals or bilinguals. In a monolingual environment they tend to choose their interlocutor's language suppressing their other language(s) completely. In a bilingual situation they also tend to speak their interlocutor's pre-ferred language while keeping their other language(s) ready to be used if needed. Where speakers share their L1 and L2, the probability that they switch from one to another is much higher. What Gerhardie reports about 'the natural mode of expression' with his siblings—English peppered with Russian—is a case in point. Bilinguals, like speakers generally, adjust their behaviour to situation and interlocutor: With parents English, with siblings Russian; in the family Spaniolo, with the governess French, at school English and German; with friends Russian, at the lectern English; French, English, and German at work, Punjabi, Arabic, and Turkish at home; and so on. But the expectations for multilinguals to adjust differ from one society to another.

Thus, how children experience their multilinguality is strongly influenced by the society in which they grow up and by its ideology, which may include factors that lead to the valorization of languages. Two of our four polyglots report that they had French governesses, which is indicative both of their upper class upbringing and the prestige the French language enjoyed in Eastern Europe when they were young. In the meantime, the governesses and their language have gone out of fashion, but the prestige differential of languages has not. Today French parents and parents of many other non-English-speaking countries who can afford it are more likely to take in an English-speaking au pair or make arrangements for their children to spend a year abroad in an English-speaking country. The social stratification interacts with international power differentials and the appreciation of different languages associated therewith. In self-declared monolingual societies foreign languages are taught according to their perceived prestige and utility, while bicultural and bilingual minority groups are commonly stigmatized as socially inferior, as mentioned in Section 5.1, quoting Akerlof and Kranton (2010). This is particularly true of immigrants in Western countries (Williams 1994; May 2012), a topic we will discuss in Chapter 8. The linguistic biographies of our four protagonists show that a multilingual upbringing does not have to be a burden too hard to bear—if there is active support and appreciation for the task. Since this cannot be taken for granted, many children struggle to attain proficiency in two languages. It does not happen naturally, but requires dedication and patience, especially on the part of parents if the social environment is not conducive to bilingual upbringing.

Direct and indirect assimilation pressure that makes the overt presence of 'other' languages in other than professional or foreign language classroom settings undesirable makes the parents' burden of raising bilingual children harder to bear. This is a common plight for immigrant parents. A representative voice:

As a mother of American-born Korean children, I see how tremendously difficult it is to raise children bilingually in a mostly monolingual society. In an effort to help our children establish proficiency in Korean in an English-speaking environment, my husband and I have been trying to speak and read mostly Korean at home to our children....Despite what my husband and I have been trying to do to promote our children's acquisition of Korean at home, I worry that their future teachers might not value their heritage culture and language. I wonder if some of their teachers might forbid them from speaking Korean with other Korean children in the classroom. I worry that their teachers might convey to them directly or indirectly that speaking Korean is shameful and that 'real Americans speak English' (Shin 2005).

Growing up in an environment where linguistic diversity is normal certainly helps parents to raise their children to become proficient in two (or more) languages and children to develop a positive attitude to their languages. It is above all in countries committed to monolingual ideologies and policies that such environments are lacking. In cases where minority languages are not just tolerated but their use is encouraged and supported, it is as the result of struggles for the recognition of diversity. To summarize the discussion of this question, yes, a multilingual upbringing is a burden, for both children and parents, but the social environment is a decisive factor that can alleviate or aggravate it.

5.7 Conclusions

In this chapter we have looked at multilingualism from the point of view of the polyglot, the individual who has acquired and uses several languages in daily life. Self-reported observations by four prominent writers about their own multilingualism provided the prompts to introduce some of the issues where research has been concentrated in recent decades. Reviewing their cases and many others in the literature, we have explored the multifarious dimensions, skills, and significances of a life with multiple languages for the individual, which made us opt for a simple definition of the multilingual as a person who has the ability to use more than one language. We have addressed the questions of order of acquisition and dominance, and reviewed some of the research on the bilingual brain which can uncover differences and similarities between monolinguals and multilinguals more convincingly than preconceived notions of native speaker and mother tongue. It has become clear that individual multilingualism is a highly complex phenomenon defying easy and clear-cut typologies. The questions discussed in this chapter invariably led to answers with qualifications and caveats. Time and again, it was necessary to emphasize that most of the features and conditions associated with individual multilingualism are fuzzy, gradual, and probabilistic in nature, not definite, categorical, and causal. This holds particularly for the issue of how burdensome a bi- or multilingual upbringing may be, because individual multilinguality is socially conditioned and thus interacts with attitudes and ideologies as well as social divisions in terms of class, ethnicity, socioeconomic status, and migration; issues which will occupy us in subsequent chapters.

Problems and questions for discussion

1. If you are bilingual or know a bilingual person, how did you/that person become one?
2. Roman Jakobson was a pioneer of structural linguistics. The following lines are from his obituary. What do they tell us about the kind of polyglot he was?

   Dr Jakobson got his basic academic degree at the Lazarev Institute of Oriental Languages in Moscow, his master's degree from Moscow University, and his doctorate from Prague University. In all, he learned to speak six languages fluently—Russian, French, Polish, German, Czech, and English—and enough Norwegian and Finnish to lecture in them.

   In time, he also learned to read twenty-five languages, especially scholarly works. The languages spoken in his dreams, he said, were often a melange of all the tongues he knew. 'Jakobson is a peculiar man,' an envious fellow linguist once remarked. 'He speaks Russian fluently in six languages.'

   Actually, he said in an interview, he ordinarily thought about scholarly matters in English, domestic problems in Polish (his multilingual third wife was Polish), literature in French, and politics in Czech.[9]

[9] The *New York Times*, 23 July 1982. http://www.nytimes.com/1982/07/23/obituaries/roman-jackson-a-scholar-of-linguistics-is-dead.html (Roman Jakobson's misspelt name is in the link).

3. Why is it difficult to raise bi- or multilingual children? Name and discuss at least three reasons.
4. a. What is the relationship between L1 and dominant language?
   b. What does the notion 'adopted mother tongue' mean, and what role does it play in this chapter?
5. How did Vladimir Nabokov think (or think that he thought), and what can we learn from his introspection?

Further reading

Baker, Colin. 2011. *Foundations of Bilingual Education and Bilingualism*. Bristol: Multilingual Matters.

Grosjean, François. 2010. *Bilingual: Life and Reality*. Cambridge, MA: Harvard University Press.

Myers-Scotton, Carol. 2006. *Multiple Voices: An Introduction to Bilingualism*. Oxford: Blackwell.

6

Multilingual (international) institutions

This chapter looks at linguistic diversity of and in institutions. Ranging from the community level to that of international organizations, a great many institutions are faced with language management issues responding to the communication needs of multilingual clienteles. The multilinguality of the people served by and working together in institutions may include groups of speakers with languages at various levels of competence. For institutions providing public services that are expected to do so in a spirit of fairness, not disadvantaging any one group, on the one hand, and without compromising the goal of communicative integration, on the other, the general problem is designing a language regime that balances group interests and the common good. This is a complex task involving both tangible and intangible costs and benefits. Institutions differ in terms of size, objectives and the services they provide, while languages differ in terms of development and status, size of speech community, and perceived utility. Therefore, we cannot expect to find a universally applicable model for determining the optimal language regime, but some considerations are pertinent to a range of institutions. Four general questions are as follows:

- What is the cost of a language regime?
- Who bears the cost?
- Who benefits from it?
- What are the benefits?

We start by asking these questions of educational institutions and then move on to international organizations.

6.1 Bilingual education

In advanced industrial countries, formal education is predicated on mono-lingualism. Schools are administered in one language and teach all subjects in that same language which is assumed to be the pupils' mother tongue. This is the paradigm case and for a long time was an ideological cornerstone of compulsory education which, among other aims, was charged with advancing communicative integration in nation states. It is still the unmarked case in many places, even in multilingual countries. As an illustration, consider the elementary school of Egerkingen in the Swiss Canton of Solothurn which, in 2016, decided to require pupils who repeatedly speak a language other than German on the school premises to take classes in German at a cost of 550 francs to be borne by their parents.[1] In the event, one language is designated the sole 'legitimate language' while all others are illegitimized, in the sense of Bourdieu (1982), their use being made a punishable infraction. Penalty fees for speaking one's L1 are rare; yet the case at hand testifies to a deeply entrenched language regime and an ideology on the wane.

In response to decolonization, increasing population movement, international exchange, and increasing ideas of minority protection and democratization during the second half of the twentieth century, bilingual education has spread and is now more commonly promoted around the world. Realities and ideologies have changed to make the accommodation of multiple languages in educational institutions from nursery school (UNESCO 2008) to university level (Fabricius et al. 2017) more acceptable and give more languages a legitimate position in curricula and on school grounds. Consequently, 'bilingual education' has become a household word for many, although its meaning is not very

---

[1] *Switzerland's News in English*, 29 January 2016.

clear. The term covers a range of different schools. Some teach bilingual pupils, while others teach largely monolingual students to become bilingual and biliterate (*developmental bilingual education*). Still other schools or programmes are designed to help migrant pupils catch up with the dominant language without providing much instruction in or support for their L1 development (*transitional bilingual education*). Rather than educating pupils in both their home language and the dominant language, the main purpose of these schools is to facilitate migrant and other minority children's transition to mainstream schooling. By contrast, what Baker (2006: 131) called a 'strong' version of bilingual education refers to schools that teach most subject content through two languages with the aim of fostering fluency in both of them.

A related but conceptually different distinction is between bilingual education by choice and by necessity. Consider, for example, a bilingual (German-English) kindergarten in Munich which tries to attract clients by advertising 'an immersive bilingualism with an inquiry driven curriculum' which will inspire 'children to embrace their academic, cultural, physical, social and emotional learning potential in partnership with their peers, teachers and families within a stimulating and caring international environment'.[2] It charges monthly tuition fees of between €500 for 4 h/day and €850 for 9 h/day plus a €390 registration fee (reference year 2016). Who benefits? The fees as well as the wording of the advertisement make it clear that this institution caters to those who can afford it, starting from and contributing to reproducing a social divide. What are the benefits? Presumably, better career chances in an 'international environment' for the enrolled. The language that, supplementing the local language, is suitable for this purpose can only be English. No other could be marketed to the local German L1 clientele.

If we inspect the mission statement of the Turkish school in Amsterdam for comparison, instead of a 'stimulating and caring international environment' it promises to provide children and adults 'the opportunity to participate in the daily life of school, work and household chores'.[3] Dutch-Turkish bilingual education does not connote internationalism but competence-building that will pave the way to integration by mainstreaming minority children and helping them to become 'true Amsterdamers in a multicultural society'. Who benefits? Primarily the

---

[2] www.theikc.com/en/school-information/opening-times-tuition.
[3] http://www.turksonderwijscentrum.nl/indexnl.html.

migrants by receiving legitimate linguistic and cultural resources that will enable them better to function in the majority society; but also the majority society itself in that the school helps to reduce the risks of social rifts and conflicts.

The elitist kindergarten in Munich and the newcomer school in Amsterdam embody two maximally diverse kinds of bilingual education between which there is a wide range of institutions that function with and/or foster competence in two languages. The former is part of the global EFL/ESL industry that thrives on an evolving transnational labour market, assumed or real, while the latter is orientated to the local community and those trying to find a foothold, usually on the lowest rungs of the employment ladder. In the past two decades, various programmes were created to steer a middle course between global outreach and local community inclusion by emphasizing the advantages of bilingual education for the cognitive development of children. Wider recognition of the increased importance of community languages such as, for example, Spanish in the USA (Roca and Colombi 2003), as well as political changes that led to the provision of educational rights for minorities, such as Francophone Canadians in Canadian Provinces outside Quebec (Landry et al. 2007), and the shift towards multiculturalism in Australia (Lo Bianco 1988) have contributed to the spread of bilingual education programmes. Experience with and research about such programmes furthermore helped to publicize the insight that additive bilingualism is feasible and does not necessarily have ill effects on children's L1 development. Not to be left out of this trend, even dialect-speaking is nowadays subsumed under bilingualism and promoted as a good starting point for learning a foreign language (Figure 6.1). This amounts to a reversal of long-standing common knowledge still cherished by many politicians who believe that bilingual education produces semi-speakers and endangers social cohesion.

Schools, especially but not only in Western countries, have a long tradition of ostracizing dialects, and, with the same rationale, negative attitudes have long inhibited heritage language education, especially for impoverished and otherwise disadvantaged groups (Trifonas and Aravossitas 2014). However, the idea that unification and assimilation benefit both majority and minorities is slowly giving way to more accommodating approaches of tolerating and including diversity. Bilingual heritage schools have become a venue where, along with the community language, indigenous traditions and lifestyles are transmitted to the

Figure 6.1 'Teachers call for more dialect in schools.'

Source: Süddeutsche Zeitung, 29 June 2016: 'The Bavarian Teachers Association (BLLV) promotes more dialect in schools. Children from families where dialect is spoken possessed rich linguistic resources from which they could benefit in both school and future career, BVVL and the Association for the Promotion of the Bavarian Language declared. Dialects are a good basis for learning foreign languages. This kind of "bilingualism would also positively influence the development of social skills".'

younger generation, although many such schools are still limited to the elementary level. From there, the pupils move to the secondary level, which continues to function in the dominant language. A complete bilingual education from preschool to university is available only for minorities with a clear territorial base such as Wales and the Basque Country. It helps when the region is relatively rich, as is the case with the Basque Country (Cenoz 2008), which tops the list of per capita income in Spain. However, with public support, heritage language preservation can also succeed in economically less well-off regions such as Wales. Monolingual Welsh speakers had dropped to about 1 per cent of the region's population by the 1980s and Welsh was, therefore, all but pronounced dead (Wardhaugh 1987: 83). But then a carefully designed 'strong' bilingual education programme turned the fate of the language around, increasing the number of speakers to 562,000 or 19 per cent of the population of Wales, according to the 2011 UK census (Williams 2014).

It is rare for a declining language to regain its vitality, and language revitalization is not the aim of most bilingual education programmes. However, some lessons can be drawn from the case of Welsh. Where languages compete they almost never do so on an equal footing. There is invariably a prestige grading between the dominant language and the minority language, which the school has an important task to counter-balance, but the school alone is overcharged with such a task. What Fishman (1991: 398) called 'home-family-neighbourhood-community reinforcement' and Baker (2008: 105) 'usage or opportunity planning' is essential. Without official support for strong bilingual education across the whole age range and the creation of opportunities for language choice in public administration and in the private sector, the school cannot create social conditions that reduce prejudices about a language's 'inferiority' and low utility.

This is a general problem not concerning regional minority languages only but migrant languages, too. Because the prestige hierarchy of languages mirrors social stratification, language choice is entangled with value judgements, which is one of the reasons why bilingual education is often politically contentious (Bekerman 2005). Measured against the norm of monolingualism, it drains public coffers, reinforces social cleavages, and puts additional strains on pupils without contributing to the common good, or so the critics of bilingual education argue. To counter these charges, researchers in several disciplines have felt compelled to demonstrate that bilingual education not only has its advantages, but that its benefits outweigh its costs. Accordingly, pupils of bilingual schools have been shown to achieve proficiency in the dominant language on a level comparable to those of mainstream monolingual schools (Kaushanskaya and Marian 2009), but are more competent socially and in other respects (Franceschini 2011). Bilingualism furthermore promises longer disability-free life expectancy, as bilinguals develop dementia later than monolinguals (Alladi et al. 2013). Research has also suggested positive economic impacts of bilingual education. While the economic value of immigrant languages is generally low (Grin 2003), bilingual education might be an indirect asset under certain circumstances. Balanced bilingualism results in higher educational attainment, which in turn has a positive effect on earnings (Agirdag 2014). Other positive effects of bilingual education put forward in its defence include more tolerance for different viewpoints, minorities' higher self-esteem, empowerment, and more positive attitudes towards the mainstream society on the part of minorities.

Table 6.1 Potential costs and benefits of bilingual education; some examples.

	Benefits	Costs
Economic	Salary premiums, better employment opportunities, facilitates trade	Bilingual teacher training, more complex administration
Social	Fewer drop-outs, social harmony, minority empowerment, less discrimination	Heterogeneity, disorder, lack of unity
Intellectual	Creativity, more and diverse linguistic capital	Split identity, delayed L1 acquisition
Communication	Ability to speak with more people	More word-finding problems, risk of semi-lingualism

After decades of research, it should be possible to decide the case for (or against) bilingual education by means of an objective, incorruptible model that calculates the economic, social, and intellectual costs and benefits, as for example listed in Table 6.1. However, this ideal is far from any attainable reality. Even estimating the financial expenditures and returns of language teaching defies uniform calculation, as these depend on the languages involved, the distance between learners' L1 and the target language, individual aptitude, length of study, class size, number of learners, and home-background of learners, among other factors. Ginsburgh and Weber (2011) use econometric models to come to grips with the question of how the negative effects of too much linguistic diversity can be weighed against those of linguistic disenfranchisement (i.e. limiting the opportunity of minorities to use their languages in educational and other institutions). The models they present are sophisticated, incorporating a range of relevant variables, but their conclusion remains general and abstract: 'Diversity cannot be obtained or sustained for free' (Ginsburgh and Weber 2011: 203). This is true, but does not solve the problem of deciding on a language regime in any particular case. The variables that need to be taken into account are too numerous and diverse; and weighing the material costs and benefits of bilingual education against unobservable and intangible ones such as preservation of tradition, social harmony, intellectual flexibility, meta-linguistic awareness, etc. poses even more intractable problems.

What is more, it is notoriously difficult to control this kind of research for confirmation bias, or the tendency to report only on positive findings.

In this complex field of inquiry, it is not denigrating past research to raise the question whether a desire to make the case for or against bilingual education has not in some cases, albeit unwittingly, influenced the results. Do the research findings add up to a clear verdict in favour of bilingual education? Yes, if you are inclined to read them that way. Multifarious and comprehensive as they are, they can be used to justify a corresponding language regime, but they do not have to. Consider the case of 'mother tongue education' for migrants in the German federal state of North Rhine Westphalia where the 'development and promotion of multilingualism are taken as a point of departure of state policy' (Extra and Yağmur 2004: 93). A decade and a half after Extra and Yağmur's survey, the state government continues to devote considerable resources to this policy, paying the salaries of 860 additional teachers for twelve languages at an average cost of €60k per annum each (2016). What is interesting about this is not the cost, but that other German states allocate much smaller parts of their budget or nothing at all to mother tongue education of migrants. Within a single country where educational authorities are equally informed about relevant research findings and, presumably, equally committed to the common good, one federal state earmarks more than €50 million annually for mother tongue education and others nothing. At some 24 per cent, the proportion of North Rhine Westphalia's population with a migration background is relatively high, but at least five other German states have similar or higher percentages. Clearly then, neither research findings about positive or detrimental effects of bilingual education nor the prevailing social conditions can fully explain whether or not bilingual education is institutionally supported. More than anything else, it is a question of political priorities following the zeitgeist.

The intellectual climate is more favourable to multilingualism nowadays than it was a century ago, and in some parts of the world it is more favourable than in others. Differences of this sort can only partly be attributed to scientific progress. Intellectual currents, ideologies, and political exigencies are also important, if not more so. The European Schools (*Schola Europaea*[4]) exemplify this most clearly. These schools were established and are controlled by the governments of member states of the European Union. The mission of these schools is 'to provide a multilingual and multicultural education for nursery, primary and

---

[4] http://www.eursc.eu/.

secondary level pupils.[5] Fourteen European Schools in seven countries teach in various official languages of the European Union, working for the EU's language policy objective that 'every European citizen should master two other languages in addition to their mother tongue' (European Parliament n.d.). Generously funded by the EU, these schools are successful pioneers in providing a multilingual learning experience in a borderless Europe; in fact some of them are so successful and popular that they are coming apart at the seams and have to turn away students because of overcrowding.

Nevertheless, the European Schools contribute to the promotion of bilingual education, working like many other schools with the Common European Framework for Languages: Learning, Teaching, Assessment (CEFR), developed since the 1950s by an international task force set up by the Language Policy Unit of the Council of Europe. CEFR has absorbed recent research about, and pools much experience and insight into, methods and theories of language learning and teaching that have helped bilingual education to become more effective. Most importantly, rather than perpetuating the traditional view that takes distinct language systems as the point of departure, it puts the learners at the centre and the various modes of language contact, overlap, code-switching, and aggregate linguistic competence they experience. According to its guidelines, CEFR intends:

to encourage practitioners of all kinds in the language field, including language learners themselves, to reflect on such questions as
- what do we actually do when we speak (or write) to each other?
- what enables us to act in this way?
- how much of this do we need to learn when we try to use a new language?
- how do we set our objectives and mark our progress along the path from total ignorance to effective mastery?
- how does language learning take place?
- what can we do to help ourselves and other people to learn a language better?

(Language Policy Unit 2004: iv)

CEFR has helped bilingual education gain momentum in the EU, and the fact that it is available in forty languages[6] (including major

---

[5] https://www.eursc.eu/en.
[6] The languages are Arabic, Albanian, Armenian, Basque, Bulgarian, Catalan, Chinese, Croatian, Czech, Danish, Dutch, English, Esperanto, Estonian, Finnish, French, Friulian, Galician, Georgian, German, Greek, Hebrew, Hungarian, Italian, Japanese, Korean, Lithuanian, Macedonian Language, Moldovan, Norwegian, Polish, Portuguese, Russian, Serbian (Iekavian version), Slovak, Slovenian, Spanish, Swedish, Turkish, and Ukrainian.

non-European languages such as Chinese, Japanese, and Korean) is indicative of the worldwide recognition it has gained in the course of its development over more than a half-century. Notice, however, that the driving force behind it was politics rather than scholarship. Bilingual education became an object of scientific inquiry in advanced countries where political contradictions surfaced between notions of fairness and equity, diversity and unity. It is to these political tenets and constraints that we now turn by reviewing the language regimes of international institutions.

6.2 Language in international institutions

As Swiss linguist Ferdinand de Saussure put it

Presque toutes les institutions, pourrait-on dire, ont à la base des signes, mais ils n'évoquent pas directement les choses

[Nearly all institutions, one might say, are based on signs, which however do not directly evoke things.]

Cahier Ferdinand de Saussure, vol. 58, Le troisième cours. Geneva: Librairie Droz S.A. (2006: 89)

In modern society, the aims, values, rules, guidelines and legitimate procedures of institutions must be laid down independently of the actors involved. Institutions exist on various levels, forming a core element of states. As the result of the drawn-out process of state formation in Europe since the sixteenth century, states are understood as comprising a population, a territory, sovereignty (political independence), and a bureaucracy. Since the age of decolonization, these features have become universally recognized as essential to statehood. States are expected to provide their populations with security, a legal system, and an infrastructure of institutions. Political entities that do not fulfil these requirements are thought to be either in the process of nation building or considered as 'failed states'. The international political system, accordingly, consists of a relatively stable number of states, greatly different in size, population, and power, but nominally equal as actors on the stage of international law. States interact with other states, and to this end a system of international institutions has evolved which like other institutions cannot function without language.

Since states use one or a very limited number of languages for the purposes of administration, law, and exercising acts of official authority, the interaction between states and the cooperation of states in international organizations produces a coordination problem. Even the simplest situation illustrates that things can get quite complex. Assuming that the actors, states A and B that use different languages, are in agreement that they want to communicate with each other on an equal footing, four outcomes are conceivable (Figure 6.2). If A is fully competent in B's language, b, or B is fully competent in A's language, a, A and B could agree to use either (1) a or (2) b. Alternatively, they could (3) employ an intermediary who is competent in a and b, or they could (4) settle on a third language, c. (3′), a solution common in diplomacy, is for A and B to employ an intermediary (interpreter) each.

This is the simplest case under artificially idealized conditions that ignore the discrepancy between the normative equality of A and B and their languages and the factual inequality as well as any symbolic valuation of languages. If we allow any of these aspects to enter the picture and reckon with not just two speech partners but three or more it is obvious that coordination becomes very intricate and requires carefully planned decisions. A language regime must be decided on.

To avoid excessive ponderousness, some international bodies have a one-language regime, for instance NATO, English, and CIS, Russian. Others, such as the UN, have settled on more complex arrangements, trying to balance efficiency of communication with symbolic requirements of status and prestige. By far the most convoluted language regime ever evolved occurred in the course of the project of European integration after the Second World War. The next section describes the major aspects of institutional multilingualism in European institutions.

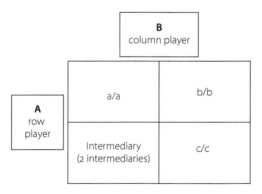

Figure 6.2 Simple coordination game between A, column, and B, row: Four options of language choice.

6.3 Unité dans la diversité: multilingualism in European institutions

Chosen as the winner of a contest, the phrase *unité dans la diversité* was proclaimed the motto of the European Union on 4 May 2000 at the European Parliament. The 1958 Treaty on European Union (TEU) as amended by the Treaty of Lisbon of 2007 states in Article 3: [The Union] shall respect its rich cultural and linguistic diversity, and shall ensure that Europe's cultural heritage is safeguarded and enhanced.[7]

In the same spirit as this most general statement, European Union institutions have on many occasions confirmed their attachment to the cultural diversity of Europe and the special importance they give to its languages (for overviews and discussions cf. Labrie 1993; Mamadouh 2002; Trim 2002; Strubell 2007; Extra and Gorter 2008). When the EU's predecessor, the European Economic Community was founded with the Treaty of Rome in 1958, a multilingual language regime was a matter of course, the first Council Regulation on 15 April 1958 determining Dutch, French, German, and Italian as 'official and working languages', without differentiating between these four. Their legal status was first set by the Treaties establishing the European Community and the European Atomic Energy Community that provided that the texts in each of the four languages were equally authentic. Since then the legal equality of Member States' official languages has been the basis of the Community's language regime and reaffirmed with each accession treaty, bringing the number of 'official and working' languages to twenty-four,[8] when Croatia joined the EU in 2013. The present EU language regime was never planned but evolved with the Community, the commitment of EU institutions to multilingualism being a direct effect of Community legislation (Athanassiou 2006: 6).

The main institutions to which this regime applies are:

- the European Parliament (legislative branch),
- the European Council (heads of state of all Member States),

---

[7] http://www.eudemocrats.org/eud/uploads/downloads/Consolidated_LISBON_TREATY_3.pdf.
[8] The official languages of the EU (2016) are: Bulgarian, Croatian, Czech, Danish, Dutch, English, Estonian, Finnish, French, German, Greek, Hungarian, Irish, Italian, Latvian, Lithuanian, Maltese, Polish, Portuguese, Romanian, Slovak, Slovenian, Spanish, and Swedish.

- the Council of the European Union (Member States' ministers of relevant portfolios),
- the European Commission (executive branch, headed by President),
- the Court of Justice of the European Union (judicial branch).

Setting aside the legal foundations of the language regime, the EU sustains linguistic diversity in its institutions as a political necessity underscoring the principle of equality between its citizens. Multilingualism is considered essential for guaranteeing democratic accountability, access to Community documents, the public's ability to invoke EU law, and the ability to communicate with EU institutions. Based on the above-mentioned treaties, the language regime provides that the Official Journal of the European Union, in which all legally binding documents are published, must appear in all official languages. Documents that member states or their citizens send to Community institutions may likewise be drafted in any of the official languages. While these principles hold for all of the above institution, there are many differences in detail.

The Rules of Procedure of the **European Parliament** provide that (Rule 158):

1. All documents of Parliament shall be drawn up in the official languages.
2. All Members shall have the right to speak in Parliament in the official language of their choice. Speeches delivered in one of the official languages shall be simultaneously interpreted into the other official languages and into any other language the Bureau may consider necessary.

In the EP all EU languages are equally important: all parliamentary documents are translated into all the official languages of the EU and every Member of the European Parliament has the right to speak in the official language of his or her choice.[9]

The right conferred on elected MEPs to speak and write in their own language has been reaffirmed with every accession because it is considered to 'lie at the very heart of Parliament's democratic legitimacy'.[10]

The **European Council** consists of all member states' heads of state or government and the President of the European Commission. Meetings use conference interpretation. From the point of view of interpreting, a meeting with a 24–24 language regime has 24 passive languages

---

[9] Fact Sheets on the European Union, Language policy: http://www.europarl.europa.eu/atyourservice/en/displayFtu.html?ftuId=FTU_5.13.6.html.

[10] SG.EL/01-125/def. Preparing for the Parliament of the Enlarged European Union—Steering Committee—Working Document No 9, On the Language Regime: additional options. http://www.europarl.europa.eu/meetdocs/committees/budg/20010912/DT9en.pdf.

(the language the members speak), and 24 active languages (the language the members hear); 552 language combinations in all. In European Council meetings this means that all the official languages are interpreted into all the official languages. Such a regime is called complete and symmetric. A team interpreting back and forth between all official languages requires at least sixty-nine interpreters, but if the active languages are limited to three, only a dozen or so interpreters are sufficient.[11] European Council Documents are drafted and can be requested in all official languages.

The **Council of the European Union** adopts as its 'default language policy' publishing all content in all official languages at the same time. This includes official documents in the Council's public register. On its website it differentiates between content published in all twenty-four official EU languages, content published only in (the de facto working languages) English and French, and content published in English, French, and any other relevant languages.[12]

The rules of procedure of the **European Commission** do not specify a language policy, but the Commission is bound by the general principle of publishing legally binding documents in all official languages. Many of its non-legally binding documents are published in one language only (usually English) or in three languages (English, French, and German). The same three languages dominate informal deliberations and are considered the working languages of the Commission (Forchtner 2014). Athanassiou observes that the choice of languages of internal deliberations is often influenced by custom. 'English tends to dominate where technical and economic matters are being discussed, while French prevails in areas of law and culture' (Athanassiou 2006: 20).

The Rules of Procedure of the **Court of Justice of the European Union** (Art. 29) provide:

(1) The language of a case shall be chosen by the applicant (subject to some exceptions). And
(3) The language of the case shall in particular be used in the written and oral pleadings of the parties and in supporting documents, and also in the minutes and decisions of the Court. Any supporting documents expressed in another language must be accompanied by a translation into the language of the case.[13]

---

[11] For more details about interpreting in EU institutions, see http://ec.europa.eu/dgs/scic/what-is-conference-interpreting/asymmetric/index_en.htm.

[12] http://www.consilium.europa.eu/en/about-site/language-policy/.

[13] Rules of Procedure, European Court of Justice: http://curia.europa.eu/jcms/upload/docs/application/pdf/2011-07/rp_cjue_en.pdf.

These provisions are deemed essential for the effective protection of the rights that citizens of EU Member States derive from Community Law. The Court's language regime differs from other EU institutions by allowing one of the involved parties, the applicant, to choose the language. However, the Court's internal deliberations are conducted in French only, which is also the language of its administration.

In addition to these institutions several others, including the Court of Auditors, the European Central Bank, and the European Environment Agency are also committed to the EU's multilingualism, but function in their day-to-day dealings in a limited number of working languages. They offer legally binding publications in all official languages, but may have a limited working language regime for their meetings and other publications. For instance, the European Union Intellectual Property Office (EUIPO), which is located in Alicante, Spain, has five working languages: English, French, German, Italian, and Spanish. In the event, the alphabetical order of listing coincides with that of frequency of use.

As a treaty-based organization, the EU is obliged to implement the language policy of recognizing all Member States' official languages as equally important, enshrined in Council Regulation No. 1 (OJ B 17, 6.10.1958), and its institutions have gone to great lengths to promote multilingualism not just as a precondition, but as an instrument of European integration. Yet, in practice, the proclaimed equality of the twenty-four official languages corresponds to a high degree of inequality in actual use in all EU institutions. Especially noticeable has been the advance of English since the accession of Britain and Ireland in 1973. By the early 2000s English had become the language in which the majority of all internal documents were drafted (Fidrmuc and Ginsburgh 2007).

Transparency and accessibility of EU legislation and policy to EU citizens has become even more crucial since the European Parliament was transformed in 1979 from an assembly of delegates of national parliaments into a directly elected body. Because of the demands of democratic legitimacy in a transnational polity, the EU language regime has become so complex that the huge language services of the Directorate-General for Translation and the Directorate-General for Interpretation are hard-pressed to sustain it. There is continuous tension between the requirements of efficient communication and symbolic respect for the Member States expressed by hoisting their flags and using their languages. Since these two exigencies are hard to reconcile, the language regime is considered a nuisance by many, albeit a necessary one that no national government has ever called into question. Yet, on other than very formal occasions, MEPs are increasingly likely to waive their right to speak their own language and will use one of the 'big' languages, the 'hypercentral language' English (De Swaan 2001: 185) having become the ever more likely choice.

Two major criticisms levelled against the EU language regime must be mentioned: its cost and its indebtedness to linguistic nationalism. With a staff of some 2,500 people in the DG Translation and a further 550 full-time interpreters plus 300–400 free-lance interpreters employed on a daily basis by the DG Interpretation, the European Commission operates the largest language service in the world. The total cost is no less than €1 billion annually, of which some €500 million are attributable to the Commission, about €200 million each to the Parliament and the Council and a somewhat smaller sum to the Court of Justice.[14] Warnings of mushrooming costs have been routinely met by two different counter-arguments. One downplays the expenditure on linguistic services by describing them as an insignificant fraction of the EU budget. Thus, all the conference interpreting, the DG Interpretation points out, costs the taxpayer a mere €0.25/citizen/year.[15] The second argument is more philo-sophical, emphasizing that linguistic pluralism and equality are European core values that must not be sacrificed on the altar of cost efficiency. Gazzola (2006) discusses a number of alternative language regimes for the European Parliament that would reduce cost, such as, *monolingualism* (using a single official language), *reduced multilingualism* (using only six official languages, like the UN), and *nationalization* (letting member states bear the cost of translation and interpretation), but comes to the conclusion that, for political reasons, cost reduction was not maximized. Rather, equality between languages was seen as a higher good.

In line with this reasoning the European Parliament and other EU institutions have repeatedly affirmed that 'the harmonious co-existence of many languages in Europe is a powerful symbol of the EU's aspiration to be united in diversity, one of the cornerstones of the European project'.[16] It is against this assertion that the second major criticism of

---

[14] According to information provided by Press Officer for Budget & Human Resources of the European Commission, 7/13/2016.

[15] http://ec.europa.eu/dgs/scic/about-dg-interpretation/index_en.htm#anchor3 (7/7/2016).

[16] European Commission. Languages: http://ec.europa.eu/languages/policy/linguistic-diversity/index_en.htm.

the EU language regime is directed. The core of the critique is that the commitment to fairness and linguistic pluralism is not genuine but derives from linguistic nationalism (May 2003). Wodak (2014: 135), therefore, speaks of 'hegemonic multilingualism', the ostensible hegemony being that of national languages. Focusing on the national language as an essential component of Member States' national identity, Strubell for the same reason sees an irony in the fact that countries, notably France, whose policy has 'been ferociously monolingual spearhead a multilingual aim for the citizens of the European Union' (Strubell 2007: 167). Europe's linguistic diversity, these and other critics argue, is not celebrated in its own right, but is intended to safeguard the privileged status of the national languages, on one hand, and stem the tide of English, on the other.

The problem at issue is that regional and other minority languages are the responsibility of the member states and thus beyond the jurisdiction of the EU. For managing institutional multilingualism, twenty-four languages are a large number, but these twenty-four are only part of a larger picture comprising more than sixty regional and minority languages spoken within the boundaries of the EU. The inclusion of non-European migrant languages, such as Arabic, Chinese, and Turkish, would further inflate that number. Not that the EU was unaware of or had not dealt with the issue of minority languages. The European Bureau of Lesser-Used Languages, set up in 1982, was funded by the European Commission and the European Parliament until 2010 and has since been replaced by the European Language Equality Network (ELEN), an NGO. The EU cooperates closely with the Council of Europe and supports the European Charter for Regional or Minority Languages,[17] but in its institutions it does not deal with minority languages. This results in a certain disproportionality if the number of speakers of a language is taken as the measure of its importance in the EU. To cite a prominent case that has been the subject of much debate for decades, Maltese, one of the twenty-four official languages, has some 400,000 speakers, is outnumbered more than twentyfold by Catalan, which is not an official language. The EU Charter of Fundamental Rights declares in Article 22: 'The Union shall respect cultural, religious and linguistic diversity.' It is generally understood that this diversity is not limited to the twenty-four official languages, but apart from the occasional resolution for the

---

[17] http://www.coe.int/t/dg4/education/minlang/default_en.asp.

protection of linguistic diversity[18] and the funding of various initiatives, such as the European Day of Languages on 26 September,[19] the EU has steered clear of intervening in the minority language issues of its member states.

In sum, the EU still interprets language equality in accordance with Council Regulation No. 1 that is concerned exclusively with national languages. The EU language regime can thus be seen as supporting the privileged status of national languages, which many member states continue to cultivate as a fundamental component of their national identity. By failing to recognize most of the EU's minority languages, multilingualism in the EU institutions is an extension at a supra-national level of the policies of monolingual nation states (Moratinos Johnston 2001: 57). Against this background, it is surprising that the equality of languages in the European Parliament is endorsed in the name of democracy as follows: 'If Parliament does not recognize their language, it is less likely that citizens will recognize it as being *their* Parliament' (Report of Secretary General, document PE 305.269/BUR/fin, 2001). This is surprising because the same argument fails to convince on the national level where, for the sake of convenience (though, it must be admitted, mostly correctly), it is assumed that minority language speakers are bilingual. The obvious question that arises, however, is this. If monolingualism on the national level does not compromise democratic government, why does the EU not act likewise, but burdens itself with twenty-four official languages? The answer has many aspects, but three stand out. (1) The present language regime rests on a history of treaties; (2) member states continue to embrace linguistic nationalism as an important part of their *raison d'état*; (3) the EU can afford it. Pragmatism and ideology work hand-in-hand. The EU allows itself the luxury of an unwieldy and expensive language regime because of the vested interest of its members.

6.4 Language management of other international institutions

A cursory look at other international institutions underscores the special nature of the European Union and the copious funding of its

---

[18] Specifically, the Arfé Resolutions 1981, 1983, and the Kuijpers Resolution 1987 concentrate on the promotion of minority languages in education and the media without, however, raising the issue of official status.
[19] http://edl.ecml.at/.

language regime. There are several regional international organizations, but none has a language regime that comes close to that of the EU in terms of complexity and cost.

Like the EU, the Association of Southeast Asian Nations (ASEAN) is a treaty-based organization. In 2007, it adopted the ASEAN Charter which commits its ten members, among others, to 'strengthen democracy, enhance good governance and the rule of law'. Art. 34 of the Charter tersely states: 'The working language of ASEAN shall be English.' The motto of the Association as stipulated in Art. 36 is 'One Vision, One Identity, One Community', which does not appear to be in conflict with the cited aims or the use of a single working language. Identity, democracy, one language, no problem.[20] Multilingualism in Southeast Asia is of a different dimension from Europe. In a region with more than one thousand languages and each one of the member states grappling with its own linguistic diversity and history of mutable language regimes, the nexus of multilingualism and democratic legitimacy/transparency is not a controversial issue. That most ASEAN members are still considered developing countries and that the EU's GDP per capita is about ten times that of ASEAN can be mentioned in passing to highlight the differences in the financial constraints of language regimes. Another point worth noting is that English is not indigenous to the region and hence not associated with an unfair advantage for some of the parties involved, although it is widely used in some ASEAN countries.

The African Union (AU), founded in 2001 as the successor of the Organisation of African Union, brings together fifty-four countries. According to the Agenda 2063, a strategic framework for the socioeconomic transformation of the continent over fifty years, it seeks to build 'an Africa with a strong cultural identity, common heritage, values and ethics,... good governance, democracy, respect for human rights, justice and the rule of law'.[21] AU maintains its website in English, French, and Arabic. Article 11 of the Protocol to the AU Constitutive Act, lists 'Arabic, English, French, Portuguese, Spanish, Kiswahili and any other African language' as official languages of the AU and all its institutions. Article 25 of the Constitutive Act addresses the issue of working languages as

---

[20] The question of how firmly entrenched democracy is in ASEAN countries has often been raised (e.g. Peou 2016), but cannot be discussed here.

[21] Agenda 2063, http://www.au.int/.

follows: 'The working languages of the Union and all its institutions shall be, if possible, African languages, Arabic, English, French and Portuguese.' The caveat 'if possible' betrays the dilemma of a pan-African language regime as perceived by those concerned. There is a desire to rely on African languages, which however, to date, cannot be realized. The Rules of Procedure adopted 2004/2011 by the Pan-African Parliament stipulate that (Rule 39) 'The working languages of Parliament shall be the working languages of the Union.'

MERCOSUR/MERCOSUL is a South American trade block of eleven members and associated members founded in 1991. The Parliament of MERCOSUR 'guarantees transparency and access to all projects and documents' and to this end designates as its official languages Spanish, Portuguese, and Guaraní. It attaches equal importance to all official languages, and Parliamentarians are entitled to speak in the official language of their choice.[22] On its website MERCOSUR presents itself in Portuguese and Spanish only; however, the inclusion of Guaraní is symbolically important, as it is the only indigenous language of South America accorded official status. Along with Spanish, Guaraní is one of the official languages of Paraguay, one of MERCOSUR's member states. A comparable situation obtains in the East African Community where indigenous Swahili enjoys official status along with exogenous English and French.

Other international organizations focused on economic cooperation, such as APEC, CARICOM, and COMESA, typically make do with a small number of working and/or official languages, linguistic transparency and legitimacy not being an issue. In many organizations, pragmatism overrides status considerations and official multilingualism does not mean that all official languages are used equally frequently or that no other languages are used. Yet, official status is both symbolically important and indicative of many organizations' history. For instance, the six official languages of the UN are the languages of the five major victors of the Second World War and Arabic, added in 1973, while Japanese, German, and Italian are conspicuously absent, although Japan, Germany, and Italy are the second, fourth, and sixth top contributors to United Nations budgets. This is because the designation of the three countries as enemy states to the United Nations in the UN Charta has never been revoked. In organizations such as the IOC, IPU, and OECD,

---

[22] https://www.parlamentomercosur.org/innovaportal/v/152/1/secretaria/lenguas-oficiales.html?rightmenuid=146.

French enjoys equal status with English, reflecting conditions at the time of their foundation. Most striking, perhaps, in the overview of some of the more important international organizations (Tables 6.2 and 6.3) is the overwhelming preponderance of a small number of prominent European languages. The complete absence of any Asian languages save Chinese from world organizations and the presence of just one African and South American indigenous language each in major regional organizations bespeaks the long shadow cast by European colonialism, on one hand, and organizational path dependence, on the other. Just like language hierarchies on the national level mirror power differentials, the distribution of languages in international organizations can be understood as a reflection of political influence in the world. Every language regime of an international organization requires detailed analysis of both its legal framework and actual practice; however, in the light of the synopsis in Tables 6.2 and 6.3, the general picture leaves

Table 6.2 Official (o) and working (w) languages of major international organizations.

Language	Arabic	Chinese	English	French	Russian	Spanish	Interpretation
IGO	A	C	E	F	R	S	
Common-wealth of Nations			o				
ICC	o	o	o, w	o, w	o	o	
ILO			o	o		o	
IMF			o				A, C, F, R, S, Japanese
IOC			o	o			A, R, S, German
IPU			o	o			A, S
ITU			o	o		o	
OECD			o	o			
UN	o	o	o	o	o	o	
UPU			w	o			
WB			o				A, C, F, R, S
WHO	o	o	o	o	o	o	
WTO			o	o		o	

Abbreviations: IGO Intergovernmental Organization, ICC International Criminal Court, ILO International Labour Organization, IMF International Monetary Fund, IOC International Olympic Committee, IPU Inter-Parliamentary Union, ITU International Telecommunication Union, OECD Organisation for Co-operation and Development, UN United Nations, UPU Universal Postal Union, WB World Bank, WHO World Health Organization, WTO World Trade Organization

Table 6.3. Official (o) and working (w) languages of major regional international organizations.

Language IGO	Arabic A	Chinese C	English E	French F	Portuguese P	Russian R	Spanish S	Interpretation, other
ASEAN			w					
APEC			o					
AU	o		o	o	o			
CARICOM			o	o				Dutch
COMESA			o	o	o			
CIS						o		
Council of Europe			o	o				
EAC			o	o				Swahili
Mercosur					o	o		Guaraní
NATO			o	o				
OAS			o	o	o		o	
Unasul			o		o		o	Dutch

Abbreviations: IGO Intergovernmental Organization, ASEAN Association of Southeast Asian Nations, APEC Asia-Pacific Economic Cooperation, AU African Union, CARICOM Caribbean Community, COMESA Common Market for Eastern and Southern Africa, CIS (CHГ) Содружество Независимых Государств (Commonwealth of Independent States), EAC East African Community, MERCOSUR Mercado Común del Sur (Common market of the south), NATO North Atlantic Treaty Organization, OAS Organization of American States, Unasul Unión de Naciones Suramericanas (Union of South American Nations).

little room for doubt about the hegemony of European languages and the West in the world.

The ascent of English as the preeminent lingua franca of the world is but the latest expression of the domination of the West, notwithstanding the fact that it is supported by many non-Westerners. For international understanding it serves a function that has its apologists (e.g. Pennycook 1994; Van Parijs 2007) and its critics (e.g. Phillipson 1992); however, the fact remains that it is not a neutral language, but one that accrues advantages to some more than to others and of which, in spite of the indigenization of English in many parts of the world and the discourse about globalization, some claim property rights. This is why interpreters are employed in international institutions, to neutralize any imbalance. The problem has been

Historical digression: The language issue in the League of Nations

After the devastation of the First World War with over 17 million deaths, serious efforts were made to secure peace. On 10 January 1920, the first international organization dedicated to the promotion of world peace was founded, the Société des Nations (or League of Nations, Sociedad de Naciones). The first council meeting convened in Paris on 16 January 1920 and the first General Assembly representing forty-two states gathered on 15 November 1920 in Geneva where the League would be based until its dissolution on 31 July 1947.

When the League of Nations was created as part of the Traité de Versailles (Treaty of Versailles) that concluded the Paris Peace Conference, French and English, the languages of the treaty, were used; however, there was from the beginning an awareness of the divisive potential of languages. The first Assembly recognized Spanish as third official language, but the Italian delegate reminded the Assembly that other delegations had national languages too, a point also emphasized by the Japanese delegate Inazō Nitobe:

It is a mere platitude to assert that there is no barrier between nations harder to overcome than language. It is a barrier that does not stop at the tongue, as it strikes its root in the manner of expressing thought and often in the very spring of thought itself. The difference in language was identified with that of race and was regarded as a just reason for enmity, as is hinted in such terms as Babel, barbarian, balbus, etc. This linguistic barrier is now increasing with the rise of new nationalities. In Europe alone forty-nine languages are in actual use. Suppose each desires to be heard! Hence the urgent need of a common language is more than ever felt. (Nitobe 1921)

Nitobe attended the 13th World Congress of Esperanto in Paris in August 1921 as the head of the delegation of the League of Nations and wrote an extensive report about the congress from which the above paragraph is quoted. As a result, a formal motion was made to adopt Esperanto as the working language of the League, which was accepted by the majority of delegates, but vetoed by France. A member of the Académie française since 1897, the French delegate Gabriel Hanotaux (1853–1944) argued that French *was* the international language of diplomacy and no other working language was needed. At the time, French was the leading language of international relations and retained this position in the League of Nations, especially when it became clear that, although President Woodrow Wilson had called for the new international body to be created, the USA would not become part of it.

Yet, Nitobe addressed a number of issues that, considering the fact that he wrote his report a century ago, appear strikingly modern. He pointed out that the language question of the League was discussed 'from the point of view of the practical working of the League on the one hand and of economy on the other'. The former led to the adoption of French and English as working languages in practice, 'without officially excluding any other tongue'. In view of the fact that member states 'speak twenty-eight languages exclusive of some important dialects', he furthermore remarked:

Apart from the general argument which makes the international aspect of the language problem devolve upon the League, we must remember that the bi-lingual arrangement of the League places a heavy handicap on some nations and thus evokes a question of justice (Nitobe 1921).

What specifically the question of justice entails he explains as follows.

The most unselfish person will hesitate to expose himself and his nation, as long as he is a national delegate, to the chance of indignity and ridicule by presenting his case, however excellent, in broken French or English! (Nitobe 1921)

The risk of 'indignity and ridicule' involved in having to use a language without perfect command on the international stage, that is an immaterial, symbolic consequence of the language regime the League had given itself, was to Nitobe a noteworthy defect which, however,

cannot be radically overcome by the mere adoption of an auxiliary language, which would probably be based on Western (European) linguistic systems without any reference to those of the Orient. I do not believe, however, that the Orient will raise any objection on this score. (Nitobe 1921)

A key argument in favour of an auxiliary language for international communications was of material rather than symbolic nature. As he explained, 'from the view-point of world economy no linguistic device is more reasonable and cheaper than the adoption of a common tongue' (Nitobe 1921). This was the more urgent, as 'there is every evidence that national languages are growing in number' (ibid.).[23]

---

[23] Nitobe (1921) explicitly mentions 'the Irish delight in reviving Gaelic', the Czechs and their 'once great language', and Flemish, which among others caused the 'Towers of Babel multiplying'.

known and addressed long before the UN with its six-language regime emerged as the centrepiece of a wide network of supranational organizations after the Second World War, as a historical digression may illustrate.

The national languages did grow in number as did nation states, and it is sobering to realize that, a century on, the problematic issues of the language regimes of international organizations are fundamentally no different. In addition to considerations of practicality, which in the context of concerted efforts to replace belligerent by peaceful means of international conflict resolutions had priority, Nitobe mentioned prestige, justice, cost, new nationalisms, and Western dominance as important issues that beset the search for a stable international language regime. The hope he placed in Esperanto was frustrated by linguistic nationalism, and the matter of justice ('a heavy handicap on some nations') is still as pressing as it was when the dust of the Great War had just settled. As long as languages play any role in the political partition of the world and in international institutions some languages (or one) have to be selected to the disadvantage of others, a language regime that does not produce its discontents is unlikely to emerge.

6.5 Conclusions

Compulsory education and democratic institutions awaken and foster expectations of fairness and equality that have often proved difficult to reconcile with linguistic pluralism, because both evolved against the backdrop of the monolingual ethos of the nation state. When it comes to multilingual institutions, financial constraints and the requirements of efficient communication further aggravate tensions between justice and practicality. In this chapter, we have seen what kinds of challenges this tension pose at the micro level to educational institutions, and to intergovernmental institutions at the macro level. In both cases, considerations of the advantages and drawbacks of supporting multilingualism play a role, although cost–benefit analysis in a strict sense is not feasible. Extant legal frameworks, political preferences, values and sentimental attachments inevitably enter the equation, and the interests of individuals and/or minority groups have to be weighed against those of all parties concerned.

While attitudes to bilingual education nowadays have become more favourable and more respect is accorded to lesser-used languages, such languages are rarely used in formal education or in international institutions.

The dominant position of European national languages for the purposes of schooling in Europe and beyond has proved hard to eliminate by decree. On the international scene, declared commitments to linguistic pluralism often do not guarantee parity of languages in actual use. Caught between statutory frameworks requiring the respect and equal treatment of all languages and limited means to implement such requirements, pragmatism often prevails. This holds even for the EU, the intergovernmental organization with the largest number of languages recognized as official and working languages. Since this multiplicity also makes for the costliest language regime any organization has ever had, the EU's commitment to multilingualism can hardly be called a lip service, but it is unmanageable and therefore often undercut in practice. Although a multilingual language regime is justified by noble principles such as equality, fairness, and democracy, persistent status differences between national and minority languages at the state level raise questions about the nexus between language and participatory government in supranational organizations, too. A review of other such organizations revealed that, rather than objective criteria of 'best practice', language regimes of multilingual institutions reflect the historical conditions of their creation. Once again this illustrates the importance of analysing multilingualism as a socially embedded practice.

Problems and questions for discussion

1. The European Parliament justifies its policy of multilingual communication maintaining that the right of its members to speak in their own languages 'lie at the very heart of Parliament's democratic legitimacy'. What are the implications of this principle for the relationship between language(s) and democracy, in Europe and elsewhere?
2. Is there or was there a public discussion in your country about bilingual education? If so, how are the assumed advantages and disadvantages pitted against each other?
3. Communication efficiency and respect for linguistic diversity are two language policy goals. Can they be balanced in international organizations?
4. Why did Esperanto not become the working language or the League of Nations?
5. How many language combinations for interpretation result from the EU regime of official and working languages?

Further reading

Ammon, Ulrich. 2006. Language conflicts in the European Union. On finding a politically acceptable and practicable solution for EU institutions that satisfies diverging interests. *International Journal of Applied Linguistics* 16(3): 319–38.

European Parliament. 2012. Multilingualism in the European Parliament. http://www.europarl.europa.eu/aboutparliament/en/007e69770f/Multilingualism.html (accessed 7 January 2017)

Franceschini, Rita. (2013). History of multilingualism. In: C. A. Chapelle (ed.), *The Encyclopedia of Applied Linguistics*. New York: Blackwell Publishing. doi: 10.1002/9781405198431.

McEntee-Atalianis, Lisa. 2015. Language policy and planning in international organisations. Multilingualism and the United Nations: Diplomatic baggage or passport to success? In: U. Jessner-Schmid and Claire J. Kramsch (eds), *The Multilingual Challenge: Cross-Disciplinary Perspectives*. Berlin: DeGruyter, 295–322.

7

Talk of the town

Language in super-diverse cities

7.1 Cosmopolis

Brussels, the centre of EU institutional multilingualism discussed in Chapter 6, is at the same time a focal point of globalization, a *cosmopolis* that brings together not just people from all walks of life, but from all continents, nations, creeds, ethnic groups, and languages. It is not a mega-city like Tokyo or London; yet it is a space of interaction between citizens from diverse backgrounds that characterizes the dynamics of urban life today. The convergence of mobility, domestic and international migration, postcolonialism, transnationalism and technology in the centre of an officially trilingual country make Brussels an exemplar of contemporary urban pluralism. To develop the themes to be discussed in this chapter, we therefore start with a brief look at multilingualism in Brussels.

In the Belgian capital multilingualism has long been part of the social fabric. The country has three official, territory-bound languages, French in the south, Dutch in the north, and German in a small area in the East, but in the Brussels Capital Region, an administrative unit consisting of nineteen municipalities, only French and Dutch have official status. This means that inhabitants have the right to be served by civil offices in the language of their choice and that many official functions are offered in the two languages only. Numerous other languages have a strong presence in the city. Tens of thousands of well-to-do foreign professionals from other EU countries working for EU institutions and NATO have made English a widely spoken language in Brussels. Adding to the mix, Eurocrats, diplomats, consultants, lobbyists, and interpreters bring other languages with them: German, Italian, Spanish, and Portuguese, among others. Living in the elegant green suburbs, they can afford to send their children to international schools and feel comfortable in what, notwithstanding the advance of English, is today a largely French-speaking metropolitan environment (Janssens 2007).

At the lower end of the social hierarchy, extra-European languages are spoken, heard, and seen in the street: Moroccan Arabic, Berber, Turkish, Lingala, Wolof, among many others. Verlot et al. (2003) list fifty-four languages from Afrikaans to Zweeds (Swedish) spoken by pupils in Brussels' elementary schools. Other statistics list as many as 104 home languages spoken in Brussels (EurActiv.com 2013) where, however, they receive little support for mother tongue education. 'The municipality provides almost no financial means for maintaining and developing allochthones cultural features including allochthone languages' (Verlot et al. 2003: 7). In Matong, a district named after an area of Kinshasa, African languages are resonant of Belgium's former colonial possessions from 1885 until 1962 in the current Democratic Republic of the Congo, Rwanda, and Burundi. Another inner-city neighbourhood, Molenbeek, is home to a community of Arabic speakers, mostly of Moroccan origin, whereas many Turkish immigrants have concentrated in Schaerbeek in the north of the city.

The Brussels Capital Region stands apart from Francophone Wallonia and Dutch-speaking Flanders. It has a long history of immigration and has absorbed more migrants than any other part of the country. While Brussels accounts for about 10 per cent of the total population of Belgium, a full third of all non-Belgian nationals and more than 40 per cent of non-EU residents of Belgium live there. In the 1920s, a first wave of Italian labour migrants moved to northern Europe and consequently formed the biggest group of non-nationals, also in Brussels. Since many of them were later naturalized, this is not revealed in official statistics

(Verlot et al. 2003: 2). A continuous influx from neighbouring France has also left its mark on the city; nowadays the French constitute the second-largest identifiable group of non-Belgian nationals after Moroccans. Immigration from former colonies and other sub-Saharan countries where French has official status has further contributed to the French-ification of Brussels, a development which has been going on since the nineteenth century, much to the dismay of the Flemish community whose activists would prefer it to be the mainly Dutch-speaking city it once was. Language conflict is a constant in Belgian politics and has brought down more than one national government (Nelde 1994; Mettewie and Janssens 2007; Vogl and Hüning 2010). In Brussels, the French–Dutch competition is part of the background noise to a multi-lingual chorus of voices that, if not always harmonious, is played out without too much dissonance, English playing a peculiar role in the concert. To mention one example, in 2013, the Flemish minister for education Pascal Smet proposed that English be made an official lan-guage of Brussels, citing the importance of diplomacy and tourism in the city as material reasons (EurActiv.com.2013). Knowing about the perennial competition between Dutch and French in Belgium, the defensiveness of French speakers vis-à-vis English, and that Dutch has been on the retreat in Brussels for years may, however, help to appreci-ate some of the unspoken reasons of the minister's proposal.

What distinguishes the multilingualism of Brussels from other cities is the special mix of languages. Three highly standardized European languages that are the national languages of neighbouring countries are spoken side by side by large population groups. Bilingualism in any of these languages is widespread, 95 per cent of the population report high proficiency in French, 33 per cent in Dutch, and 33 per cent in English (Janssens 2007: 4). For the purposes of education, French and Dutch enjoy equal status in Brussels where both language communities have the right for their children to be taught in the language of their choice. While this language regime is supported by both communities, there is also some discontent with what in effect amounts to a segregated educational system. Many inhabitants of Brussels, especially among the more highly educated, would prefer bilingual education instead of French and Dutch being taught as second language in Flemish and Francophone schools, respectively (Mettewie and Janssens 2007: 123). In addition to the two endogenous language groups, speakers of other

European languages form sizeable groups, among which Italian, Spanish, Portuguese, and Romanian stand out, suggesting, perhaps, a Romance language-affinity to French. Bilingualism in any two of the three top languages has high economic utility in Brussels, whereas bilingualism involving other languages counts for little. There is a pronounced attitudinal gap between the languages taught at school, above all the two official languages and English, but also German, Italian, and Spanish, which command high prestige and utility, on one hand, and migrant languages such as Turkish, Moroccan Arabic, and African languages, which have low prestige and little utility, on the other. Not surprisingly, therefore, the vast majority of more than 95 per cent of migrant language speakers are convinced that bilingualism including one of the prestige languages is indispensable to secure employment (Janssens 2007: 6).

As a favoured destination of domestic and international migration, Brussels has become one of the most multicultural cities of Europe. At the beginning of the twenty-first century, 31.7 per cent of its inhabitants were born abroad, 8.4 per cent in Flanders and 10.1 per cent in Wallonia, in all more than half the population. As a result, there were then forty-five different nationalities with more than 1,000 inhabitants in Brussels (Deboosere et al. 2009), many of them forming concentrated settlements of immigrant communities. Migration continues to be the most important demographic factor, making the population composition of the city ever more diverse and relatively young, because it is primarily young people who are on the move in search of change, employment opportunities, and a better life. To summarize, the face of present-day multilingual Brussels has been shaped by internal migration, immigration from former colonies and labour exporting countries around the Mediterranean, as well as by the freedom of movement of EU citizens enshrined in Article 45 of the Treaty on the Functioning of the European Union. Two official languages, the international lingua franca, and a great number of European and other migrant languages make for a complex linguistic arrangement that overlies social stratification and spatial segregation (Bolt 2009; Musterd et al. 1998) between poorer districts, mixed neighbourhoods, and exclusive quarters inhabited by well-paid expats. Similar geopolitical dynamics have been at work in many other European cities and around the world, forming a challenge for an integrative theoretical approach to urban multilingualism as well as for social policy makers.

7.2 Urbanization and language

Brussels is one of the world's 524 cities with one million inhabitants or more, thirty-four of which are in Europe compared to 105 in China. The UN (2014: 1) has reported that:

Globally, more people live in urban areas than in rural areas, with 54 per cent of the world's population residing in urban areas in 2014. In 1950, 30 per cent of the world's population was urban, and by 2050, 66 per cent of the world's population is projected to be urban.

For these calculations and projections, the UN relies on national definitions of cities and/or urban settlements, which differ widely. For instance, China's cities are categorized into four tiers based on population size, development of administrative services, infrastructure, and cosmopolitan nature (Cartier 2002). In the UK, a city is any large town which has a cathedral, whereas the US Census Bureau defines cities as urban areas having a population of 50,000 or more. In Japan a settlement is called a city (*shi*) if it has at least 30,000 inhabitants. In India, the population of an urban agglomeration (UA) should not be less than 20,000 as per the 2001 census, which further distinguishes 'Million Plus UAs/Towns' (of which there were fifty-three in 2011). In the Netherlands and some other European countries, towns or villages were granted 'city rights' in medieval times and continue to call themselves cities, even though some of them have just a four-digit population. In Germany, a city with more than 100,000 inhabitants qualifies as a *Großstadt* or 'big city'. In view of such diversity of categorization, the European Commission and the OECD have proposed a new classification of urban centres based solely on population size (Table 7.1).

Table 7.1 The OECD–EC definition of cities according to population size.

Urban centre sizes in population	
S	between 50,000 and 100,000
M	between 100,000 and 250,000
L	between 250,000 and 500,000
XL	between 500,000 and 1,000,000
XXL	between 1,000,000 and 5,000,000
Global city	of more than 5,000,000

Source: http://ec.europa.eu/regional_policy/sources/docgener/focus/2012_01_city.pdf.

The number of large cities with more than 1 million inhabitants has increased spectacularly by a factor of 6 since 1950, but the majority of urban dwellers live in medium-sized cities of up to 500,000 inhabitants. In any event, the crucial difference between city and countryside is quite clear, and it is also apparent that the large-scale population shift from rural to urban areas is a modern phenomenon associated with industrialization (Poston and Bouvier 2010: 279). Urbanization has been an intrinsic part of other social transformations, notably the concentration of economic activity and trade, higher levels of literacy and education, better health, and longer life expectancy. And it has many social implications concerning the relationships between people. As Simmel (1903) remarked at the beginning of the twentieth century, the intimacy of personal small-circle relationships of rural life is superseded by abstract, depersonalized, market-mediated relationships prevalent in the metropolis. The modern city puts rationality and rationalization over religion and magic, engineering over cultivating, technology over nature, perpetual change over uniformity of habit, and—particularly important in the present context—mobility and diversity over constancy and similitude. Urbanization cannot progress by natural population growth alone, it is mainly driven by migration which brings greater diversity, be it domestic or international migration. To borrow Simmel's words: 'For the metropolis it is decisive that its inner life is extended in a wave-like motion over the broader national and international area' (Simmel 1903 [2002: 17]). This is still true today as economic processes transform villages into mushrooming cities in the course of a few decades.

Consider the city of Shenzhen in southern China. A fishing village called Baoan County until the mid-twentieth century, its population stood at 314,000 in 1979 when it was renamed Shenzhen (深圳市, literally: 'deep drains city', referring to a feature of the natural environment). By 2014, it was approaching 10 million, an increase that could not have happened without redrawing administrative boundaries and massive immigration. As Tang (2016) explains, one third of the migrants originated from neighbouring Guangzhou and other Cantonese-speaking areas, another third from surrounding provinces where various southern Chinese dialects are spoken, and the rest from Mandarin-speaking areas in the north. 'Given this multilingual setting, what to expect when young people with these varied backgrounds interact?' (Tang 2016: 145). The 'multilingual setting' that Tang speaks of has been brought about by strong incentives for migrants to move to the city. Mandarin is more widely spoken in Shenzhen than elsewhere in southern China without having marginalized Cantonese. In this important entrepôt business people and public service employees also speak English. Shenzhen is a showcase of urban growth propelled by domestic development and globalization; however, economic growth is coupled with urbanization everywhere, and in China it has progressed at breath-taking speed for a generation, inevitably producing the linguistic diversity that provokes Tang's above-quoted question. Migrants from the countryside, where they rarely heard other tongues in their daily life, suddenly live in close proximity with speakers of various languages and dialects with whom they can and to some extent have to interact. How will the new city dwellers, their speech behaviour and their languages be affected by these relocations? The deep-reaching linguistic changes and reorganizations of speech communities brought about by mass migration and social mobility have become the preeminent theme of Chinese sociolinguistics, which Xu (2015) calls 'linguistic urbanization'.

In the Western world, urbanization happened earlier, and it is not by coincidence but in response to the concomitant social changes that the study of urban multilingualism originated in the West. The very discipline of sociolinguistics was first conceived by researchers of, and for investigating language use in, the most highly urbanized societies, because the population density of cities leads to linguistic differentiations not found in the countryside. Early on, attention focused on city dialects/sociolects of national languages that were diagnosed to be indicative of social stratification. This was in keeping with 'methodological nationalism', which subsumed society under the nation state (Beck and Sznaider 2006) and characterized the social sciences generally. Today it is time for a cosmopolitan outlook, as social stratification increasingly intersects with national and ethnolinguistic diversity within the city limits whose inhabitants Simmel (1903 [2002: 12]) judiciously characterized as 'creatures reliant on difference' (*Unterschiedswesen*). The individual and group differences found in today's cities call long-established dichotomies into question: national/international, authentic/made-up, pure/hybrid, internal/external, and also native/foreign with regards to language.

It is in cities rather than in the countryside that new language configurations constantly emerge as an inevitable consequence of population movements, framed but not wholly determined by national language regimes. Together with the acceleration of urbanization, such configurations have become a prominent element of urban social reality posing a challenge to social analysis. As an object of scientific investigation, multilingualism is essentially an *urban* phenomenon, that is, the linguistic face of urbanization. Until quite recently, the tenet that national cohesion required linguistic assimilation was rarely questioned, and research on urban multilingualism was about a transitional phenomenon, the expectation being that within a generation or two immigrants would give up their language of origin and make their children speak the majority language. Many immigrants did just that. In New York City, for example, where bilingualism is pervasive, an empirical study found that 'all ethnolinguistic groups are experiencing shift to English by the third generation' (Garcia 1997: 15). Generally speaking, the smaller the migrant group or ethnolinguistic community in a city, the faster the shift to the dominant language. It is in this sense one has to understand Chríost's (2007: 2) remark that 'the city is the birthplace of the most outstanding linguistic innovation but also a cemetery of languages'. The basis of this kind of thinking is that languages are objects that can be kept or lost. It inspired a great deal of research pursuing questions such as how languages end up on the urban graveyard; how communities differ in this regard, being characterized by varying degrees of 'language loyalty' (Fishman 1966); and how social structures, culture, and religion influence the process and relative velocity of language shift. Meanwhile the focus of scholarly attention has shifted from languages to speakers, and assimilationist policies are no longer uncritically accepted in many places. There is consequently a greater willingness to accept and to study multilingualism as a more stable phenomenon. As such it forms part of the interdisciplinary research agenda of transnationalism, for globalization crucially depends on the intermediate role that cities play as the principal stage and steppingstone of boundary crossing dynamics (Smart and Smart 2003). The fact stated in the 2014 UN report, mentioned at the start of this section, that more than half the world population live in cities underscores the need to build a theory of a 'globalising sociolinguistics' (Smakman and Heinrich 2015) that extends beyond the social reality of Western countries and the methodological nationalism that informed the early development of the study of language in society.

Urban life is already the reality of more than 50 per cent of humanity and is destined to spread further. Not only are cities becoming the dominant form of social life around the globe, the globe at the same time makes its presence felt in the city. The percentage of immigrants in cities is invariably higher than the national average. To integrate the ensuing dimensions of urban variety and transcend the limitations of conceptualizing city life in terms of majority and minorities as methodological nationalism would suggest, Vertovec (2007) introduced the notion of 'super-diversity'. He originally used this notion to refer to a condition that 'is distinguished by a dynamic interplay of variables among an increased number of new, small and scattered, multiple-origin, transnationally connected, socio-economically differentiated and legally stratified immigrants who have arrived over the last decade' (Vertovec 2007: 1024). Vertovec's principal focus was initially on England where mass immigration not only meant more numbers but also more motives for migration and categories of migrants in terms of countries of origin, qualifications, and intentions of stay. The notion of super-diversity turned out to be an apt label for the widely shared feeling that, driven by globalization or as a part of it, migration patterns have taken on a new quality that impacts cities around the world.

Many cities, especially those that, in the public imagination, used to typify the nation state where they are located—Paris, London, Rome— no longer do so in a stereotypical way, but as centres of multiculturalism and concentrations of differences. Sometimes before their inhabitants knew it or were ready to acknowledge it, cities had become 'multilingual cities' and were as such made the object of large-scale surveys: Athens, Brussels, Dublin, Gothenburg, The Hague, Hamburg, Kiev, Limassol, London, Lyon, Madrid, Melbourne, Montreal, Osijek, Oslo, Ottawa, Rome, Sophia, Strasbourg, Toronto, Utrecht, Vancouver, Varna, Yaoundé. This alphabetically ordered list comprises the 'multilingual cities' investigated in three major projects, (1) the 'Multilingual Cities Project' begun in the European Year of Languages, 2001, (Extra and Yağmur 2004), (2) the LIMA project about 'Linguistic Diversity Management in Urban Areas' (Redder et al. 2013), and (3) the LUCIDE network 'Languages in Urban Communities: Integration and Diversity for Europe' (King and Carson 2016). These are just three relatively prominent research programmes among many others that have investigated urban multilingualism in recent years. At first glance the cities on the list do not reveal any common features distinguishing them from monolingual cities. Some of them, for instance Hamburg, London, and Toronto, intuitively correspond more closely to the image of a multilingual metropolis than others, and there clearly are manifest differences in degree of multilinguality between these cities.

The language arrangements in cities are very distinctive, calling for detailed description and analysis. At the same time, the fact that the list includes cities that do not immediately come to mind when thinking about multilingualism is indicative of a change not only of facts, but also of perspective.[1] The 'monolingual city' is an idea that veils actual diversity, while the 'multilingual city' bespeaks a new approach, a changed lens through which to consider it. There is diversity in any large concentration of people, but under the auspices of 'super-diversity' it is more likely to be recognized, examined, and described for what it is than under conditions of normative monolingualism and methodological nationalism. Because they thrive on migration, cities are internally diverse, some more so than others and, determined by varying attitudes and language policies, some more openly than others. For instance, the Swiss city of Fribourg/Freiburg celebrates every year on or around 26 September *la Journée du bilinguisme/den Tag der Zweisprachigkeit* or 'bilinguism day', while the city of Basel, just an hour and a half away by train, represents a configuration Lüdi (2007) calls 'monolingual and heteroglossic'. In spite of their evident presence, as a matter of policy Basel does not acknowledge multiple languages. Thus language policy is yet another factor to be reckoned with in any systematic attempt to understand multilingual cities; one of many. What then are the elements of urban multilingualism that combine to form different types of multilingual cities? Section 7.3 discusses this question.

7.3 City language profiles

Cities can be described in terms of variables such as geographic location, population size and density, ethnic composition, the local economy, per capita productivity, collective wealth and disparity of wealth, public transport, waste management, and crime rate, among other elements. A language profile including relevant information about the city's linguistic resources is another such variable. Regarding the data to

---

[1] For a map of migration to European cities, see http://www.citylab.com/work/2015/02/4-maps-crucial-to-understanding-europes-population-shift/385293/(accessed 7 Janaury 2017).

be encompassed in such a profile, a rough distinction is between social and linguistic elements which have a bearing on different types of urban multilingualism. In describing different cities, making a first assessment of the social variables, then of the linguistic ones, and finally of the interaction between the two enables us to identify commonalities and differences and on this basis make meaningful comparisons (Table 7.2).

S_1, population size, is a variable in any study of urbanism, and it should be relevant for research about urban multilingualism. That linguistic diversity increases with population size seems intuitive; however, historically big cities have also played an important role for the promotion of standard languages, such as, for example, Parisian French. Moreover, it is not difficult to think of examples that do not fit the equation 'the bigger the more diverse'. Tokyo, the biggest metropolitan agglomeration in the world, is remarkably homogeneous linguistically. There is no place where another language is spoken to the exclusion of Japanese and where monolingual speakers of Japanese would be lost.

Table 7.2 Urban language profiles with social and linguistic variables.

Social variables	Language variables
S_1 Population size	L_1 Default language(s) −national, official, dominant
S_2 Social stratification	L_2 Number of languages and their demographic strengths
S_3 Age structure	L_3 Language policy −legal status (national/municipal)
S_4 Migration patterns −historical −postcolonial −recent	L_4 Language hierarchy −official −school −recognized/protected minority −non-recognized minority −home
S_5 Settlement patterns −social class −ethnic segregation	L_5 Communication practices −lingua franca −language contact −multi-ethnolect
S_6 Temporary inhabitants −expats, foreign students, tourists	L_6 Visual manifestation −presence in linguistic landscape
S_7 Level of education, academic achievement	L_7 Bi-/plurilingualism
S_8 Attitudes −cosmopolitan −provincial −xenophobic	L_8 Multilingualism hierarchy −cosmopolitan −ethnic

This is because since Japan's modernization in the late nineteenth century the spread of standard Japanese was realized effectively (Heinrich 2012), and because Japan pursues a restrictive immigration policy. On the other hand, there are any number of mid-sized cities with a fraction of the population of Tokyo, such as, Duisburg, Germany (488,000), Southampton, UK (250,000), and Montreuil, France (105,000), that have foreign-born population shares of 33 per cent, 15 per cent, and 25 per cent, respectively, and are linguistically quite mixed. There does not seem to be a linear correlation between population size and linguistic diversity. Geographic location, economic structure, immigration policy, and other factors intervene.

Yet the relationship between population size and number of languages (S_1/L_2) is part of the language profile of any multilingual city, whereby the number of languages is to be calculated relative to a defined threshold number of speakers, for instance 1,000, as in the case of Brussels cited in Section 7.2. If we take the population of languages with more than 1,000 speakers divided by the 1.1 million inhabitants of Brussels, we get a language diversity index of 0.0409 (Brussels: 45,000/1,100,000). By comparison, Tokyo (the city's 23 wards) with a population of 9 million and 13 languages[2] with more than 1,000 speakers would have a language diversity index of 0.0014, which means that Brussels is more than 40 times as diverse as Tokyo. This is a very rough index that does not differentiate between languages, saying nothing about them except that they have no less than 1,000 speakers. However, this index would be just one of several language-related data that make up a city's language profile, and it can be useful for comparing cities with each other.

S_2, social stratification, involves differences in material wealth and life chances. How these inequalities relate to linguistic varieties is the classic question of sociolinguistics. Under conditions of urban multilingualism this question is to be extended to cover languages. Are there any noticeable correlations between indicators of social class, such as per capita income, wealth, and level of education and language, where 'language' is a proxy variable for the group that speaks it as a first or home language? For most cities the dominant/default language (L_1) is easily

---

[2] This is actually overstating the case; 13 is the number of languages Backhaus (2007: 73) identified on a sample of signs he collected for his analysis of the linguistic landscape of Tokyo.

established, for instance, 'the language used when asking for directions'. However, in cities with large migrant populations the spatial concentration of language groups can be so intense that in some places the dominant language is reduced to a minority position. How does the social stratification of such neighbourhoods compare to the city at large? Are there any differences in terms of social stratification between L1 speakers of the default language and other languages spoken in the city? Are there any differences in this regard between the non-dominant languages of the city? Many general statistics are available, but classifications of people according to their ethnic origin, foreign-born or immigration background do not necessarily allow any conclusions about their language preferences and proficiency. Because of the growing number of people with mixed ethnic origins, the many bilinguals, and the various degrees of proficiency in dominant and non-dominant languages, suitable research instruments to answer these questions are not readily available but need to be tailor-made separately for every city.

Upon arrival, immigrants typically find themselves on the lower rungs of the social ladder. This is well known from 'classical' immigrant cities such as New York, Sydney, and Toronto. Less information is available about the social stratification of ethnic and linguistic groups within cities in terms of the linguistic majority and amongst groups. How does the demographic strength of a linguistic minority (L_2) come into play and how does it interact with the prestige of the language? Ethnic languages, national languages, and international languages clearly differ in this respect, but it is not easy to conceptualize this difference relative to a specific urban environment. In a sense, English, Italian, and Berber (Tamazight) form language groups in Brussels, but intuitively these are groups of a different nature. In Brussels as well as in the wider European or international context, the three languages are unequal in terms of total number of speakers, number of L2 speakers, average per capita income of their speakers, and prestige. These four measures vary across cities. For instance, the prestige of Italian and the per capita income of Italian speakers in Buenos Aires, where they number several hundred thousand, may not be the same as the corresponding values in Brussels as well as relative to other languages spoken in Buenos Aires. Accordingly, the position of Italian in the language profiles of the two cities will differ on these counts. Comparisons along other dimensions will then reveal the extent to which this is due to the relative demographic strength of Italian in the two cities. Ordering a city's languages by demographic

strength is a piece of the mosaic of its linguistic resources to be comple-
mented by others, in particular the statistics of first and second/foreign
language speakers.

S_3, the age structure of the city population, may be relevant in connection with S_4, migration patterns. Rather than forming a uniform
group, migrants are of various kinds, such as, immigrants from former
colonies, immigrants coming to stay, follow-up migrants (family reuni-
fication), political refugees with an uncertain future, temporary expats,
Labour migrants (contract workers, guest workers), cross-border labour,
foreign trainees, and returned migrants. Under certain conditions mass
migration, especially labour migration, implies that a migrant group's
age structure differs markedly from the rest of a city's population, for
example by having a lower average age, by having few elderly members,
or by having few children. The latter would imply, for example, that the
city education authority does not have to make any arrangements for
the linguistic needs of the children of this group. In conjunction with
other variables, the age structure of language groups may have a bearing on
the *language hierarchy* of the city (L_4), which finds expression, among
other things, in the public services it makes available in some but not in
other languages. Another aspect of the hierarchy is status ascription.
A city may have official languages, recognized minority languages, non-
recognized but tolerated minority languages, and forbidden languages.
Cutting across these categories are literary as opposed to unwritten languages. The latter will not typically find a place in a school curriculum,
although the status of an unwritten vernacular may be a matter of dispute. Maghrebi Arabic, for example, rarely written and lacking a unified
standard, is the variety of Arabic spoken by many immigrants from
North Africa in France. Some of them would prefer their children to
learn Maghrebi Arabic, while others favour Standard Arabic. Parisian
authorities and the French Ministry of Education have to take a position
in accepting one or the other as 'an optional subject' at the *baccalauréat*.
The situation is further confounded because Algerian, Moroccan, and
Tunisian migrants lobby for their own sub-varieties of Maghrebi Arabic
(Caubet 2008).

The case of the capital of highly centralized France illustrates the general principle that a city's language policy (L_3) is embedded in the legal
framework of a national policy (to be further discussed in Chapter 8). It
can deviate from the national policy, for example in granting recognition and protection to languages that do not enjoy such privileges on

the national level. A municipal language policy may be wider than the national one; however, if it were more restrictive it could be successfully challenged under national law. The Japanese city of Kawasaki provides a pertinent example. While the website of the Japanese Ministry of Health, Labour, and Welfare provides information about labour law, health insurance, pension system, etc. in Japanese and English, the website of Kawasaki offers all sorts of legal advice and practical information in two varieties of Chinese, Korean, Portuguese, Spanish, Filipino (Tagalog), and Thai in addition to Japanese and English.[3] Kawasaki is an industrial city with a relatively large foreign population that has for many years pursued a policy of inclusion. It offers interpretation services in several languages for consultations of newcomers and has established a Representative Assembly for Foreign Residents,[4] granting foreign residents a degree of participation in local government that goes far beyond official immigration policies at the national level.

L_3, language policy, consists of deliberate efforts by the authorities, elected officials, and bureaucrats to regulate the language behaviour of citizens and residents in various domains of social life. The issues to be dealt with at the municipal level are concrete and specific: education, public service, information, and signage. The city has an obligation to respond to the needs and desires of its inhabitants—for 'cities are made of desires', Calvino (1993)—and accordingly in many cases balance particular interests and the common good. It can accommodate migrants by providing information in languages other than the dominant language spoken by numerically relevant groups. It can offer language courses in the dominant/legitimate/national language, or place a duty on immigrants to attend such courses.

City officials tend to decide on pragmatic grounds to what extent information is made available in multiple languages about the city, industry and jobs, housing, public transport, medical and welfare services, childcare and education, environment and rubbish disposal, emergency preparation, etc. At the same time, symbolic considerations may also play a role. Multilingual image-building strategies catering to temporary rather than long-term residents (S_6) are a case in point. Tourism has become a huge industry and a source of income for cities the world over. To project an international image is, therefore, in the

---

[3] http://www.city.kawasaki.jp/index.html (accessed 7 January 2017).
[4] http://www.city.kawasaki.jp/en/page/0000037241.html (accessed 7 January 2017).

民　政　總　署
INSTITUTO PARA OS ASSUNTOS CÍVICOS E MUNICIPAIS

Figure 7.1   Institute for Civic and Municipal Affairs, Macau.
© Florian Coulmas.

interest of many. Consider Macau (Figure 7.1). In the shadow of cosmo-politan Hong Kong with more than ten times the population, Macau vigorously exhibits its colonial past as a brand.

Some 0.7 per cent of the population of Macau are estimated to speak Portuguese.[5] The vast majority of the Macanese people speak Cantonese, although Mandarin has become more common in recent years. Portuguese is retained as one of Macau's official languages, the rationale after the return to China in 1999 being its importance in legal matters. The other official language named in the special administrative zone's Basic Law is Chinese without any specification as to whether this should be Mandarin or Cantonese. There are some newspapers and a radio and a TV channel in Portuguese, and the Universidade de Macau appeals to foreign students with a Chinese-Portuguese-English trilingual image, but on campus English is rapidly crowding out Portuguese. The decorative

[5] Exact statistics are not available. The Macau Statistics Bureau lists ethnicity, but not language. http://www.dsec.gov.mo/SearchEngine.aspx?SearchKeyword=Portuguese+langu age&SearchGUID=7e2408be-e887-4d8c-b87b-8d69d0473d99 (accessed 7 January 2017).

aspect that the former colonial language has taken on is evident from the fact that it is much more visible in central districts frequented by tourists than in residential areas at the periphery.

L_6, the visible manifestation of languages in the linguistic landscape, is another important datum in the language profile of multilingual cities. A city's linguistic landscape represents what Simmel (1903), quoted in Section 7.2, called 'the inner life of the city [which] is extended in a wave-like motion over the broader national and international area'. Meanwhile, the structuration principles of the linguistic cityscape, how it reflects power differentials, the competition, collaboration, and inter-mixing of different groups, and the governing functions of public bodies, have become the subject of a new branch of sociolinguistics and a substantial research literature (Gorter 2006; Backhaus 2007; Shohamy and Gorter 2009). The linguistic landscape is an important aspect of the public sphere (Coulmas 2009) where social facts are reflected and created. This includes official signage as illustrated in Figure 7.2, advertisements, billboards, shopfronts, public announcements, election posters, among others. As a general rule, the legibility of the multilingual city only involves languages with an agreed-upon written form, although on notice boards, graffiti, and in other public spaces both sub-standard varieties and languages that are not usually used in writing sometimes appear. The visual display of multilingualism is variously motivated by commercial, political, and cultural reasons, and it relates to language hierarchies and social stratification in the city.

On the trilingual sign in Hohhot, Inner Mongolia (in Figure 7.2), Chinese is the national language and Mongolian is the recognized regional language which is displayed largely for symbolic reasons to demonstrate the government's policy of accommodating minorities. The dominant language of the city is Chinese rather than Mongolian. Roman letters are employed for the benefit of tourists who are not expected to read either Chinese or Mongolian. The bilingual street signs in Macau are a manifestation of the city's policy of bilingualism serving both practical and symbolic functions. Tourists unable to read Chinese can at least make out the Portuguese. In New Delhi, according to The Delhi Official Languages Act, 2000 (Delhi Act No. 8 of 2003), Hindi in Devanagari script is the official language of the Capital Territory of Delhi, English may be used for administrative and legislative purposes, and Punjabi in Gurumukhi script and Urdu in Persian script are second official languages of the city. In the event, a question arises whether

Figure 7.2 Multilingual street signs in four cities: Hohhot: Mongolian, Chinese, Mandarin Pinyin; Macau: Chinese, Portuguese; New Delhi: Hindi, English, Punjabi, Urdu; Nanjing: Chinese, English, Japanese, Korean.

© Florian Coulmas.

'Mahatma Gandhi Marg' should be considered English, for *marg* (मार्ग) 'road' is not an English word. In Nanjing, by contrast, 寺 of 灵谷寺 (líng gǔ sì) is translated as 'temple', rendering this part of the sign unmistakably English. The other two languages, Japanese and Korean, are, like English, for the benefit of tourists only, because there are no sizeable Korean- or Japanese-speaking communities in Nanjing, but the temple is a major tourist attraction.

Signage in public places is usually publicly authorized and funded, but it is not always uncontroversial. Rather, the linguistic landscape is frequently contested territory. If two or more languages are displayed, which one comes first? Shall they all be the same size, the same colour? What font should be used? What if the directions of scripts are not the same? None of these questions are too petty to make it on a city council's agenda. Because writing is associated with authority, detached from any individual author and, in contradistinction to speech, permanent, it is a more potent manifestation of a community's presence than the spoken language. Community unrest has therefore often found expression in vandalism and protest directed against signage. Defacing bilingual road signs or calling for the removal of a language from public spaces is a favourite pastime of nationalists, chauvinists, and others who engage in ethnic strife. After the break-up of Yugoslavia and the subsequent wars, anti-Cyrillic protests were a frequent occurrence in Croatia, especially in the war-torn city of Vukovar.

In the Balkans, biscriptality, defined as 'the simultaneous use of two (or more) writing systems (including different orthographies) for (varieties of) the same language' (Bunčić 2016: 54), is part of the history since the earliest days of Christianization. The Latin and Cyrillic alphabets that spread with Roman Catholicism and Orthodoxy, respectively, came to be associated with ethnic divisions, and eventually served as a means of claiming language status for intercommunicable varieties of South Slavic (Yugoslavian), Bosnian, Croatian, Montenegrin, and Serbian. Bunčić (2016) introduced the term 'orthographic pluricentricity' to describe this situation, which he analyses in great depth. In the present context it must suffice to mention this region as an example of the politicization of orthography and how conflicts are acted out in the linguistic landscape. Of course, the general acceptance of bi-/multilingual signs by citizens of multilingual cities is not unusual. However, where language rights are contested and different ethnolinguistic communities are on a collision course, public signage offers itself as an arena for expressing discontent.

While the public display of a language in a city functions as an acknowledgement of its speakers' presence and is, therefore, usually welcomed by them, the contents of the message may have an influence on how much it is appreciated, as the admonition in Figure 7.3 may illustrate.

Warnings against transgressions (fare dodging), petty crimes (pickpocketing), and public nuisance (loud music) given in languages that are not otherwise used by the authorities can be a touchy issue as they may be considered discriminatory. In any event, conclusions can be drawn from the languages the authorities use to communicate with the public about their speakers' standing in the city and the local government's policies and attitudes towards them. When it comes to the really important things in life, language must not be a barrier. The citizens of Düsseldorf are thus informed about the rules of bulky waste collection in five languages (Figure 7.4).

Multilingual announcements in the public sector are indicative of the relative demographic strength and/or perceived importance of the language groups in question, although they may not reveal much information about their geographic whereabouts. In the commercial sphere this is different. Here the spatial distribution of languages on signs of various sorts is directly related to patterns of settlement (S_5) and economic activity. And it is not just bakeries, greengrocers, and hardware stores that advertise their products in the languages they expect their customers to read. While public announcements are top-down reflecting the dominant culture, commercial signs, community fliers, private notices, help-wanted ads, job announcements, inscriptions on vehicles, etc. are bottom-up, giving expression to multilingualism as it is lived: various languages used side by side, competing for space, influencing each other, being adapted to local circumstances and interacting with the local hegemonic language which, in some places may be pushed into the background. In London, for example, Bengali, Gujarati, and Polish are spoken by more than 100,000 speakers each (King and Carson 2016: 165). Where their speakers live in relatively compact communities, these languages have a visible presence that goes beyond the occasional shop sign. How is the demographic strength of a language reflected in the linguistic landscape? Who are the writers, and how are their messages keyed to what readership? Do texts conform to, or violate, standards? Do they exhibit evidence of language contact?

L_5, communication practices, are the subsection of the language profile to which these questions refer. They are familiar from the sociolinguistics

Figure 7.3 Prohibition signs at a park in Tokyo. A more appropriate translation of the Japanese text that supplements the pictograms and captions would be: 'In addition, please refrain from any activities that may disturb others.'

© Tobias Söldner.

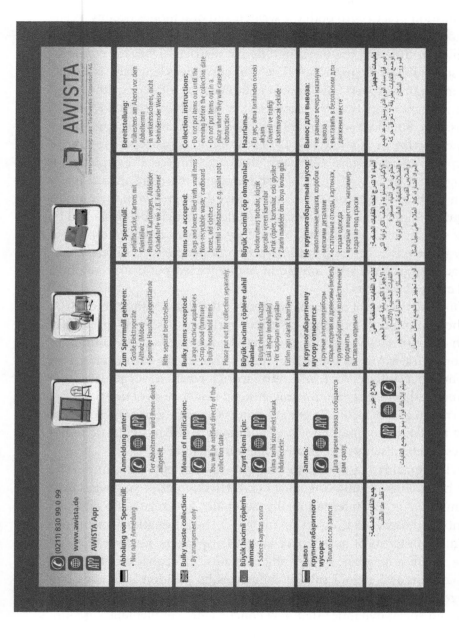

Figure 7.4 Information about bulky waste collection in Düsseldorf in German, English, Turkish, Russian, and Arabic.

Note: Instructions about 'How to separate rubbish correctly' are made available in 12 languages: German, English Russian, Turkish, Arabic, Italian, Japanese, Albanian, Armenian, Croatian, Polish, and Serbian.

Source: https//www.awista-duesseldorf.de/de/content/Downloads/Downloads.htm (accessed 7 January 2017).

of speech, but they are equally relevant for the written dimension of urban multilingualism (Reh 2004). In the city language profile, communication practices in both the written and oral modes occupy a central position. Is there an uncontested lingua franca, or is this function fulfilled by different languages in different districts? Does the commercial sector follow its own rules? 'Use your customer's language' is a strategy marketing experts have known to be effective for a long time (Swift 1991). To mention but two examples, in a study of the Old City of Jerusalem, Spolsky and Cooper (1991) observed Arabic-speaking shopkeepers acting in this way, and Li (2009) found shopkeepers in Trier, a 'sleepy' town in western Germany, studying Chinese, the explanation being that it is the birth place of Karl Marx and therefore attracts many Chinese tourists. In a similar manner, cities differ greatly in their multilingual composition, urban communication practices being shaped by very specific local conditions. What they all share in common is that they involve the meeting and interaction of people with different language backgrounds who mingle in highly varied political, economic, and cultural contexts.

One occurrence of particular interest to the study of multilingualism is the coming into existence of urban varieties of speech that reflect such encounters and embody the intent and ability to make communication work across boundaries. These varieties are characterized by phonological interference, innovative word formation, vocabulary from a range of languages, and unconventional sentence structures. Widely referred to as *multi-ethnolects* with a term Clyne (2000) coined in contrast to *ethnolect*, these innovative additions to urban linguistic repertoires will be discussed at greater length in Chapter 10.

What remain to be mentioned here, however briefly, are attitudes (S_8) and hierarchies of multilingualism (L_8). Hierarchies of languages exist on multiple levels, internationally, nationally, and relative to cities, as mentioned earlier in this section under S_3. The international status of a language in terms of numbers of L1 and L2 speakers, number of countries where a language enjoys official status, its economic utility and recognition as a school subject influences its position in a city's language hierarchy. However, super-diverse cities have their own language mix and social dynamics that may concur with, supplement, or counteract the international or national language system. As King and Carson (2016: 143) observe, some languages are more visible than others in city life, and some have greater market value than others. There is likely to be a correlation between these two parameters, but how the relative visibility and economic utility of languages interact is to be determined empirically for each city. The same holds true for social attitudes towards a city's languages and the kinds of bilingualism found in the city.

It is not just with regards to visibility and utility that languages differ. The coexistence of multiple languages on every level, from the world to the individual, means inequality. From this it follows that multilingualism will not usually be appreciated or rejected as such. It is necessary to conceptualize bi-/multilingualism as a capacity with different aspects and valorizations relative to the languages bilingual speakers or groups of speakers command. Just as languages are valorized differently, so are different kinds of bilingualism (L_7). The relative utility of languages is an important factor in this regard, as proficiency in some languages improves employability and is hence regarded as a valuable component of human capital which in turn translates into attitudes towards various kinds of bilingualism. To mark a major divide, Jaspers and Verschueren (2011) proposed a distinction between 'prestige multilingualism' and 'plebeian multilingualism'. Prestige or upmarket multilingualism typically involves European languages, especially those that were carried to all continents in the wake of Europe's colonial expansion, English, French, Portuguese, and Spanish in particular. In stark contrast, languages that migrants carry from other continents to Europe and North America, with the possible exception of Japanese and Chinese, enjoy little or no prestige. Bilingual competence encompassing these languages, for instance, Akan, Filipino, and Sindhi, does not imply any gain in prestige, but is more likely to be perceived as a threat to the extant language regime. The market value of languages and bilingual proficiency involving them also tends to relate to their speakers' level of education (S_7), competence in European languages being acquired at school, while community languages are often spoken by migrants who have a relatively low level of education.

Attitudes towards multilingualism are additionally shaped by cultural traditions, deliberate policies, and how they are implemented by municipal authorities. By responding as a matter of course to the linguistic needs of newcomers and other minority groups and embracing diversity as a positive asset, a city government can contribute to an atmosphere of openness, tolerance, and inclusion; whereas an assimilationist policy of integration by subordination to a monolingual regime or neglect of immigrant languages are likely to foster nationalist and xenophobic attitudes.

Whatever their origin and gestation, language attitudes are a factor of language hierarchies and are therefore an important element of cities' language profiles. These profiles are embedded in national legal provisions and educational policies; however, being the crossroads of migration flows, many cities design and implement their own language policies which are more tolerant of linguistic diversity than national language policies. This may be considered an effect of globalization and an indication of the growing importance of worldwide relations on the sub-national level. Most cities are subject to superordinate national law and national policies, but in some, such as Singapore, there is no difference or potential tension between municipal and national policies. As we will see in Chapter 8, they exemplify the growing importance of cities in global networks especially well.

7.4 Conclusions

A city is a place of encounter and perpetual motion. It dies when it stands still. And, as long as it is alive, the talk of the town will be in different voices adjusting to changing circumstances. After two centuries of linguistic nationalism and a system of general education largely committed to it, the idea that linguistic heterogeneity is not necessarily detrimental to social cohesion has been slow to take root in Europe. Cities have been the place where this notion first gained acceptance, because diversity is more pronounced in cities than in the countryside, and municipal authorities have to deal with the concrete issues of the growing multiethnicity of contemporary societies.

In this chapter we have looked at the multilingual city as a social reality and as an object of investigation. Since it is the task of the social sciences to unravel the complexity of social phenomena, the latter—the investigation—seems to be a logical consequence of the former—the reality. However, while the increasing urban multilingualism certainly calls for investigation, the increasing willingness to answer this call is in response both to factual and ideological changes. It would surely be premature to say that nationalism is on the wane as an ideology, but methodological nationalism is, and this means, among other things, that cities as the indubitable pioneers of the coexistence of large agglomerations of people of different ethnic backgrounds, languages, nationalities, and social strata have become an object of research in their own right, not just in urban studies, but in the sociology of language too. Urban space is where linguistic innovation occurs, where meanings are made visible in the linguistic landscape, communication across language boundaries is practised, and language groups compete for social recognition, status, and economic advantage. The language profile introduced in this chapter offers an approach to investigating the interaction of the social and linguistic variables which shapes different types of urban multilingualism that mirror and are part of the social inequality that characterizes all cities.

Problems and questions for discussion

1. Which linguistic groups can you identify in your city? Calculate the language diversity index of your city or any other city of your choice!
2. Does your city have a language policy? Is the use of languages as medium of instruction in publicly financed schools regulated by official decree? Are the language requirements of the city's linguistic groups met? If not, why not?
3. Are there in your city any job advertisements that specify languages? If so, which languages are required for what kinds of jobs?
4. Is there a social stratification of linguistic groups in your city?
5. What is linguistic urbanization?

Further reading

Extra, Guus and Kutlay Yağmur (eds). 2004. *Urban Multilingualism in Europe. Immigrant Minority Languages at Home and School.* Clevedon: Multilingual Matters.

García, Ofelia and Joshua A. Fishman (eds). 1997. *The Multilingual Apple. Languages in New York City.* Berlin, New York: Mouton de Gruyter.

King, Lid and Lorna Carson (eds). 2016. *The Multilingual City. Vitality, Conflict and Change.* Bristol: Multilingual Matters.

Shohamy, Elana and Durk Gorter (eds). 2009. *Linguistic Landscape. Expanding the Scenery.* New York and London: Routledge.

8

Multilingual (multiethnic) countries

8.1 Background

All multilingual countries are different. What unites them is that, implicitly or explicitly, they have to define a relationship between language and governance. This chapter reviews a number of examples and discusses the relevant factors that distinguish different types of multilingual countries. It considers the question of what has become of the nineteenth-century ideology of linguistic nationalism and the European ideal of the unity of state, nation, and language in the twenty-first century where minority rights have augmented if not replaced the call for ethno-cultural self-determination current before and after the First World War. The language regimes of two very different countries, one in Asia and one in Europe, are reviewed in detail. The chapter discusses the notions of national, official, and minority language and looks at how language groups are accommodated in various states, where conflicts arise, and it probes the role of national affluence for creating the conditions for a conflict-free coexistence of different language groups in one state. Since populations change and languages change, conflict avoidance in the age of nation states is a permanent task.

8.2 Community relations

As we move from urban to national multilingualism, we may pause and take some time to tour Singapore, for Singapore is a city and a state. The city's language policy is not constrained by superordinate national law, for the city's language policy is the country's language policy. Because of the densely populated compact territory of the island (700 square kilometres, 7,697 inhabitants/km²), there is no need for regional adjustments to the country's basic legal framework and no potential for any divergence of national and municipal policy goals. The principles underlying the city state's language policy were established by a leader who embraced multilingualism for pragmatic rather than sentimental reasons. Singapore is today, in many ways, a showcase for the successful institutionalization of multilingualism. Given that language rivalries were already an issue in colonial times and that outright hostilities were part of the reason why Singapore, somewhat unexpectedly, became an independent country, this could hardly have been predicted when the new state was founded.

A Crown Colony since 1946, Singapore achieved independence from British rule through its inclusion in the Federation of Malaya in 1963, which on the occasion was reconstituted as Malay*si*a, the 'si' in the name being Singapore. However, political differences between the city government and the federal government almost immediately surfaced, in which community relations played a major part. Singapore had to leave the Federation to become an independent republic in 1965.

At the time, community relations couched in race, language, and to some extent religion were tense. The principal reason for Singapore's break-away/expulsion from the Federation was political differences between Chinese and Malay elites who represented the two largest ethnic groups on the Malay Peninsula. Through the separation of Singapore, a new political entity with a large Chinese majority of some 75 per cent of the total population came into existence. Prior to Independence, anticolonial sentiments ran high, and the ideological association of language and nation was taken for granted the world over. No one outside Singapore would have been surprised, therefore, had Chinese been put at the apex of the postcolonial language hierarchy as the new country's national language. As many leaders of the Chinese community saw it, such a policy would only have corrected the marginalization of the Chinese language under White rule—although, at the time, Mandarin was not the majority language among Singapore's Chinese.

Surprisingly, and largely due to a farsighted leader, this is not what happened. Lee Kuan Yew, who had been involved in educational policy before Independence, faced down vociferous demands by the Chinese Chamber of Commerce for Chinese to be made the national language and instead embarked on a distinct policy of multilingualism. An English educated 'Straits born' Chinese, Lee was keenly aware of the explosive potential of language and the risk it posed for a new state that was aspiring to become a nation. His view, which reflected his own upbringing and proved him a pragmatic politician, was that a nation does not have to be anchored in a language and, in the case of Singapore, could not be. No matter how large the Chinese majority, Singapore was a multiethnic polity, and care had to be taken to circumvent the perils of community strife. A policy of sidelining minorities could not be in the interest of the common good, Lee thought, citing Sri Lanka's language policy as a cautionary example.

'I do not want a Ceylon[1] position where with one stroke of the pen, they abolished English, made Sinhalese their official language, crippled the Tamils who had learnt English well. Endless trouble thereafter' (Lee 2011: 33). The path Lee Kuan Yew adopted instead was a policy of multilingualism with English as the pivot: 'English will be our working language, and you keep your mother tongue. It may not be as good as your English but if you need to do business with China or India or Malaysia or Indonesia, you can ramp it up' (Lee 2011: 292). 'Ramp it up' was what Lee himself did, first with his Hokkien Chinese and then Mandarin, in order to be a credible politician.

In Lee's words this sounds simple. In actual fact institutionalizing a bilingual education system without alienating any of the groups involved was a remarkable political achievement. Lee had been Singapore's Prime Minister before Independence, since 1959, and continued in that role until 1990. The two main pillars of his education and community policies were meritocracy and multiracialism, that is, the recognition of distinction coupled with the promise of equality. Four 'races', nowadays called 'ethnic groups', were recognized in Singapore and thus, in a sense, assembled. In census reports, school enrolment surveys, and other documents the

---

[1] Sri Lanka, a British Crown Colony from 1802 until 1948, was then known as Ceylon.

following four groups are distinguished: Chinese, Malay, Indian, and Other.[2] The last one is obviously an administrative formation, however, and to some extent this is also true of the other three, for the Chinese, the Malays, and the Indians do not form internally homogenous groups. Externally, that is, in relations with each other, these categories are intuitive and hence acceptable; nevertheless, accentuating 'race' as an element of national policy was not without its problematic. PuruShotam (1998) has analysed in great detail the tensions that arise from having a (constructed and officially promoted) racial identity and yet being fully equal in terms of status and opportunity, as required by a meritocratic social policy. For wherever the concept of race had been a determinant of politics, it was used to legitimize inequality, if not domination. This was certainly so during colonial times and was still a valid view in the mid-twentieth century when the wave of decolonization gained momentum.

A policy of racial recognition and separation grounded in the imperative of equality was both new and ambitious. Part of the equation was the dissociation of race and language. The four racial categories meant that Singapore's Chinese were Chinese, but not all of them spoke (standard) Chinese; the Malays were Malays, but not all of them spoke (standard) Malay; and, more obviously perhaps, the Indians were Indians, but not all of them spoke Tamil. As Lee Kuan Yew put it in an address to Senior Civil Service Officers at the Regional Language Centre, on 27 February 1979: 'Language has nothing to do with race. You are not born with a language. You learn it.'[3] Strong words that helped to demystify language without diminishing its importance for social life.

Under Lee's guidance, Singapore institutionalized a policy of multilingualism based on the recognition of Chinese (Mandarin), Malay, Tamil, and English as official languages[4] with Malay retaining the status

---

[2] Current statistics count 74.3% Chinese, 13.3% Malay, 9.1% Indian, and 3.2% Other (Singstat 2015).

[3] http://news.asiaone.com/News/Education/Story/A1Story20090227-125024.html (accessed 7 January 2017).

[4] Article 153A of the Constitution of the Republic of Singapore provides:
  (1) Malay, Mandarin, Tamil, and English shall be the 4 official languages in Singapore.
  (2) The national language shall be the Malay language and shall be in the Roman script: Provided that—
      (a) no person shall be prohibited or prevented from using or from teaching or learning any other language; and
      (b) nothing in this Article shall prejudice the right of the Government to preserve and sustain the use and study of the language of any other community in Singapore.

of national language[5] and English continuing to function as the primary language of education and administration. Since 1967, all pupils have been required to study their mother tongue as a school examination subject, in addition to English. The 'mother tongues' of the ethnic majority and the two major minorities are constructs associated with the officially recognized 'races' which PuruShotam (1998: 56) calls 'bureaucratic simplifications'. For the administration which had to deal with the mundane issues of curriculum design and organizing public services acceptable to all in a multiracial city, such classificatory measures were inevitable.

One of the consequences of the 'simplifications' was that, like it or not, by virtue of the quadrilingual policy every Singapore citizen is assigned a race, associated with which is a 'mother tongue' officially recognized and valorized as the vehicle of transmitting its culture—Mandarin for the Chinese, Malay for the Malays, Tamil for the Indians, and English for Others. In line with the status of these four languages, Art. 44 of the Constitution of the Republic of Singapore determines the ability to read and write at least one of them as one of the qualifications for membership of Parliament.

The ad hoc categorization of races and their languages created problems, for the vast majority of Singapore's Chinese came from homes where non-Mandarin varieties of Chinese were used, notably Cantonese and other Yue dialects, Hokkien and other Min dialects, and Hakka dialects. Similarly, the Malay race encompassed speakers of a complex array of vernacular and formal varieties of Malay, as well as Boyanese, Bugis, Javanese, and Minankabau. Other than Tamil, the languages spoken by Indians included Gujarati, Hindi, Malayali, Punjabi, Sindhi, Singhalese, and Urdu, among others (Khoo 1980). And even the speakers of English did not speak one English (see below in this section). In 1979, the Government confronted this situation in its *Report on the Ministry of Education*, acknowledging unsatisfactory school performance and ineffective bilingualism due mainly to the fact that 'the languages of instruction (primarily English and Mandarin) were not spoken at home by some 85 percent of school children'[6] for whom the policy of bilingualism actually meant trilingualism (English, Mandarin, and a dialect). This was a direct consequence of the segmentation of the population into four 'races'

---

[5] That is, the status it had in the Federation of Malaya.
[6] Report on the Ministry of Education 1978, prepared by Goh Keng Swee and the Education Study Team. Singapore: National Printers, 1979.

and the artificial mother tongue ascription. As a result, not all Singaporeans learnt their 'mother tongue' sufficiently.

A related criticism of Singapore's language policy was directed against the annual Speak Mandarin Campaign (SMC) that was first launched in 1979 in order to create a bond between all Chinese Singaporeans (Ng 2011). The campaign achieved its purpose in that it successfully promoted Mandarin, which as a result replaced Hokkien as the most widely used Chinese language in Singapore. However, SMC thereby also created a majority language that, by sheer weight of numbers, came to occupy a position which was hard to reconcile with the egalitarian concept underlying the choir of Singapore's many voices. If Mandarin gained in importance in the educational system, the possibility of Malay and Indian students interacting with their Chinese peers would be reduced and social cohesion threatened. The obvious solution was the further advance of English among all ethnic groups as a supplement to SMC. There is much evidence to suggest that this process has been going on for decades and still continues, ever more turning English into the country's lingua franca (Myers-Scotton 2006: 97–100; Singstat 2015), although not quite as expected by the government. In any event, that English was made the medium of instruction in all schools in 1987, while 'mother tongues' are taught as L2s helped the process along.

In view of this development, the allegation that SMC has devaluated Chinese dialects and hence amounts to a denial of genuine linguistic diversity in Singapore (Bokhorst-Heng and Silver 2017) has to be taken with a grain of salt. Making the country's multilingualism manageable by associating ethnic group and language in a straightforward way and thus reducing (officially recognized) diversity was one of the purposes of the campaign, with the same reasoning as affording Tamil a privileged status over Hindi, Punjabi, Guajarati, Malayali, and other Indian languages. Singapore's leaders tried to mould the diversity of races and languages into a unique trait anchored in Singapore, rather than China or India (Lee 2012), simplifying or overgeneralizing both categories in the process. Call it pragmatic or opportunistic, Lee Kuan Yew's language policy was realistic and motivated by a concern for the wellbeing of the Singaporeans, and in this regard very successful.

However, there is never a guarantee for a one-to-one correspondence between a policy goal and its outcome. As in other policy fields, unanticipated consequences of a language policy cannot be excluded. A case in point is the expansion of English referred to above. The kind of English that has been spreading and which Singaporeans increasingly adopt as their home language is a distinct variety known as 'Singlish' (Alsagoff 2010, Leimgruber 2011). Because it incorporates many elements of local languages and also differs phonologically from standard British English, it is not appreciated by the educational authorities who see English as an asset that allows Singapore to hold its own in the international market place. In their view, universal reach is what counts rather than the local touch, hence the 'Speak Good English Movement' (Rubdy 2001). The government's promotion of standard English is reminiscent of the attitude underlying SMC; Chinese shall be Mandarin, and English, British English.

That Singlish plays a much bigger role today than it did in colonial times is an illustration of the unforeseen consequences of a language policy as well as of the fact that social language arrangements keep changing, and not always in a predictable way. A language profile of contemporary Singapore compiled along the lines discussed in Chapter 7 is markedly different from what its counterpart at the time of Independence looked like. In the mid-twentieth century, the administrative language of the Crown Colony was English and in addition there were more than 30 language groups with 1,000 speakers or more. Meanwhile, Singapore has four official languages and, reflecting the city state's increased economic standing, some new immigrant languages have materialized, notably Japanese, Korean, and Thai. The most substantial change is the adoption of Mandarin and English as home languages by many Chinese Singaporeans and the corresponding retrogression of other Chinese dialects.

Because Mandarin-speaking grandchildren allegedly no longer easily converse with dialect-speaking grandparents, the SMC-induced shift to Mandarin has been criticized for impeding communication across generations within families, but Zhao and Liu (2010) have shown that the spread of Mandarin must not be equated with the disappearance of Chinese dialects as home languages. The situation is more complex, as there is hardly a family in Singapore whose children are not routinely exposed to several languages. Home language use has been and continues to be a controversial issue of Singapore's language policy; other such issues include language recognition, status allocation, language use in the media, language combinations of bilingual education, and teacher training. For some of them, perhaps, better solutions could have been found. However, the government of the new state was called upon to act, while pursuing, at the same time, the intricate task of nation building. Since Independence, Singapore has been a testing ground of national multilingualism challenged with balancing diversity and equality without compromising the material wellbeing of all.

The last-mentioned aspect is of utmost importance, reminding us of the fact that language policy is a distinct, but not an isolated policy field. Singapore's spectacular rise within a half-century from colonial backwater to one of the most affluent countries in the world benefited all groups. GDP per capita increased from US$427 in 1960 to US$56,284 in 2014[7] and, equally significant and related to material wealth, Singapore's schools rose to the top of the OECD's global student assessment ranking.[8] These achievements contributed to reinforcing confidence in government policies, including language policy, a great deal of criticism notwithstanding.

Singapore has something other than language to be proud of. Yet, balancing equality and racial distinctness remains a permanent challenge for policy makers. While the four groups and the four officially recognized languages are a manifest and widely accepted aspect of the country's social reality, many Singaporeans remember that societal language arrangements and identities are not hewn in stone. Ever the clearheaded realist, Lee Kuan Yew (2011: 291) pointedly said that 'identity varies with circumstances', and when asked whether the question of which language(s) should be used in Singapore was settled, he bluntly replied:

No, language usage in the world will always evolve and shift. In the next 50 to 100 years, for us, the dominant languages will be English and Chinese in that order. But who can tell what languages are dominant in the world in 200 to 300 years? Latin was the language for Europe.... Gradually Latin disappeared. No one can say English will be dominant forever' (Lee 2011: 256).

8.3 Countries, nations, languages

Countries are difficult objects to compare. The 193 member states of the United Nations (2017) are polities of very diverse kinds, ranging in

---

[7] Index Mundi: http://www.indexmundi.com/facts/singapore/gdp-per-capita (accessed 7 January 2017).
[8] Programme for International Student Assessment (PISA) 2014: http://www.oecd.org/education/bycountry/singapore/.

population size from less than a million to more than one billion; in geographical size from some tiny islands to a subcontinent; and in per capita income from some $500/year (Somalia) to more than $140,000/year (Qatar). Countries differ widely with regard to ethnic, linguistic, and cultural fractionalization, African countries heading lists of the most diverse countries, whereas European countries generally rank close to the bottom.[9] And countries differ in terms of age, in how long they have existed as a sovereign polity. China has existed as a nation for four and a half millennia; the Republic of South Sudan became a state in 2011. Singapore is the prototype of a young country, that is, a new polity that lacks any historical or at least mythical past on which to base its claim to nationhood. Multiracialism and multilingualism were built-in from the start.

Switzerland is a counterpart to Singapore. The Confederation of Localities—nowadays called 'cantons'—looks back on a history of some 700 years as a more or less autonomous state. Remarkably, the Confederation withstood the nineteenth-century political drive to linguistic monoculture in Europe that was already firmly established when Max Weber referred to it a hundred years ago when he observed,

Today, in the age of language conflicts, a shared common language is pre-eminently considered the normal basis of nationality. Whatever the 'nation' means beyond the mere 'language group' can be found in the specific objective of its social action, and this can only be the *autonomous polity* (Weber 1978: 359).

As this quote shows, Weber was keenly aware of the risks inherent in using language as a principal criterion of political autonomy, perceptively characterizing his/our age as that of language conflicts. The matter-of-factness with which the principle of the national language is still taken for granted in the Western world is illustrated by a little episode set in present-day London.

The teacher explained that our grade was going to stand up on the stage, and one by one we were to say 'Welcome' in our mother tongues. When the teacher asked me to speak in Pakistani, I certainly didn't know what to say (Rahman 2014: 213).

In England people speak English, in France French, in Portugal Portuguese, and in Pakistan—well, what if not Pakistani. In this regard, Switzerland almost looks like the exception that proves the rule. While

---

[9] Alesina et al. (2003) and Fearon (2003) have compiled lists of ethnic and linguistic fractionalization by country, based on data gathered and categorized by the Encyclopaedia Britannica.

discrimination on grounds of language, race, religion, and nationality are hardly unknown, in Switzerland people are more aware of national linguistic diversity, and managing its official multilingualism has been relatively free of conflict.

Three major European cultural languages, German, French, Italian, along with Rhaeto-Romansh are Switzerland's national languages.[10] The percentage of the speakers of each language in the population is given in Table 8.1.

The four national languages are eulogized in the country's new national anthem (see the text box) which embodies the commitment to multilingualism in a single hymn.[11] There are two main reasons why language has never been the cause of serious community friction in Switzerland. First,

Table 8.1 Permanent resident population by main language(s), 1970–2014, in per cent.

	1970	1980	1990	2000	2014
Total	6,011,469	6,160,950	6,640,937	7,100,302	8,041,310
German/Swiss-German	66.1	65.5	64.6	64.1	63.3
French	18.4	18.6	19.5	20.4	22.7
Italian	11.0	9.6	7.7	6.5	8.1
Romansh	0.8	0.8	0.6	0.5	0.5
Other languages	3.7	5.5	7.7	8.5	20.9
Total in %	100	100	100	100	115.5*

Note: * Because many people who took the survey mentioned more than one main language, the total exceeds 100 per cent.
Source: Statistik Schweiz 2014.

[10] The Swiss constitution in Article 4 declares: Les langues nationales sont l'allemand, le français, l'italien et le romanche [the national languages are German, French, Italian, and Romansh]. And the Federal Law on the National Languages and Comprehension between the Linguistic Communities 441.1 of 5 October 2007 specifies:
   Art. 5, Langues officielles
   1 Les langues officielles de la Confédération sont l'allemand, le français et l'italien.
   Le romanche est langue officielle dans les rapports avec les personnes de cette langue.
   2 Les autorités fédérales utilisent les langues officielles dans leur forme standard.
[11] Translation: White cross on red ground, our sign for the federation: Diversity, independence, peace. Let us be strong and united, that the concord may enlighten us. Liberty for everyone, And equality for all. The Swiss flag, symbol of peace and unity.

Swiss multilingualism is based on the territoriality principle, and second, socioeconomic disparity is moderate and does not run parallel to language divisions. Historically the territoriality principle was a division between German in the east and French in the west of the country, Italian in the south being added in the nineteenth century, and eventually Romansh. Most cantons have a single official language; in seventeen cantons it is German, in four French, and in one Italian. Romansh enjoys co-official status in the trilingual canton of Graubünden, together with German and Italian, and, as specified in the 2007 language law (footnote 9), Romansh speakers have the right to communicate in their language with the authorities. The three cantons of Bern, Fribourg, and Valais are officially German-French bilingual. The territoriality principle means that schools use German as language of instruction in Zurich, French in Geneva, and Italian in Bellinzona. An official language other than the canton's language is typically learnt as an L2, although the advance of English in recent decades has undermined the policy of prioritizing the teaching of Swiss national languages for this purpose (Zustand...1989; Grin and Korth 2005), so much so that Watts and Murray (2001), referring to English, ask: 'the fifth national language?'

> *In September 2014, the Swiss, true to their tradition of direct democracy, chose a new national anthem through a process of online voting. Its special feature is not reproducible in the English translation: it unites four languages in one stanza:*
>
> > Weisses Kreuz auf rotem Grund, unser Zeichen für den Bund:
> > Vielfalt, Unabhängigkeit, Frieden.
> > Soyons forts et solidaires,
> > que l'entente nous éclaire.
> > Per mintgin la libertad
> > e per tuts l'egualitad.
> > La bandiera svizzera,
> > simbolo di pace ed unità.

The most conspicuous figures in the statistics given in Table 8.1 are those indicating the increase within four decades from 3.7 per cent to 20.9 per cent of 'other languages' that survey respondents mentioned as their 'main language'. From the statistics it is not clear to what extent the 20.9 per cent of 'other languages' in the 2014 survey account for the 115.5 per cent of the total; or whether multiple answers to the question of main language were not admissible in earlier surveys. Yet, there can be no doubt that a new element has entered the neat arrangement of four national and three and a half official languages.

A further dimension of complexity is added in German-speaking Switzerland, where a diglossia of spoken dialects (*Schwyzertütsch*, Baur 1983) vs. written standard German (*Schriftdeutsch*) obtains. Some of the dialects are as distinct phonologically from High German as are Chinese dialects from Mandarin and hence cause problems for Francophone and Italophone Swiss having learnt (High) German as an L2 at school. This occasionally provokes animosities if not linguistic chauvinism on both sides, however these are not embedded in a nationalistic discourse, but rather in a discourse about Swiss confederate cohesion. L2 instruction is meant to secure unhindered bilingual discourse: in a mixed setting, everyone speaking their L1 is certain of being understood by the others, but what they speak should not be too far removed from what the others have learnt as L2. However, maintaining clearly distinct Swiss German varieties, as opposed to German German is a crucial feature of the linguistic culture of the German-speaking cantons. It can be understood as an expression of local patriotism which, however, is mitigated by the national commitment to multilingualism. Although Swiss multilingualism is strictly territorial and there are, accordingly, many Swiss citizens who use but one language in their everyday lives, a monolingual ethos is much less deeply entrenched in Switzerland than in neighbouring countries, notably France and Germany.

The contrast between an old tradition-bound landlocked European confederation and a new postcolonial insular Southeast Asian republic could not be starker; yet, in regards to multilingualism there are some conspicuous parallels between Switzerland and Singapore (Table 8.2). Both countries take part in several major literary languages that serve as national languages elsewhere and which, therefore, are divorced from linguistic nationalism. In both countries, the language arrangement of the largest group is characterized by a pronounced diglossia involving a standard variety based in another country—China and Germany—and in both countries the presence of 'other languages' has made itself felt in recent decades, while the advance of English exerts pressure to change established patterns of language use.

In terms of population size and dynamics the two countries are also in the same league, and, most importantly, in terms to societal wealth. According to one projection, Singapore and Switzerland, together with

Norway, will be the wealthiest countries in the world by 2040.[12] Not surprisingly, therefore, both countries have a net migration surplus. While the two countries exemplify that linguistic diversity is not necessarily an impediment to affluence, it is also a fact that national wealth greatly facilitates managing official multilingualism (Liu 2015: 86). Running a multilingual administration and setting up a multilingual school system involve additional expenditures for textbook production, teacher training, administrative coordination, etc., and although economic parameters are not the only determinants of an effective bi-/multilingual education programme, it helps when budgetary limitations do not interfere. Note as an indirect indication the positive correlation between literacy rates and national wealth.[13] That richer countries have higher literacy rates shows that education is key for national wealth and that sufficient funding is a precondition for quality education. And note also that rich countries can afford to be generous to minorities. Whether they actually provide sufficient funding for minorities, for them is a political rather than an economic question.

Another important issue is the impact of the languages of schooling on economic performance. Official multilingualism in Singapore and Switzerland involves highly developed languages adjusted to all domains of use that enable access to a wide range of information and therefore have utility in the labour market. This is why these two countries are rare exceptions to Pool's (1972: 213) finding that 'there are almost no highly linguistically diverse, prosperous countries'. For where the linguistic fractionalization of a country involves a multitude of unwritten

Table 8.2 Switzerland and Singapore, some social indicators.

Indicator	Switzerland	Singapore
% of world population	0.11	0.08
Net migration 2016	+ 50,000	+ 60,000
Fertility rate	1.53	1.24
Median age	42	40
Nominal GDP per capita 2040 (estimate)	$173,423	$214,757

[12] Citigroup, Global Economics View. http://www.willembuiter.com/3G.pdf (accessed 7 January 2017).
[13] Cf., e.g., Unesco's literacy data at http://www.uis.unesco.org/literacy/Pages/data-release-map-2013.aspx (accessed 7 January 2017).

languages, this often works as a brake on economic development. Note in passing, however, that Liu (2015), analysing Indonesia's development since independence, argues convincingly that the potentially negative economic effects of a country's linguistic heterogeneity can be counteracted by a language regime that puts no group at an advantage. In Indonesia the lingua franca of the archipelago, the common Malay of trade among merchants, is the national language, rather than the language of the largest group, Javanese.

8.4 Formative factors of national multilingualism

So far in this chapter, we have considered two officially multilingual countries from which, although they are by no means typical, several lessons can be drawn about the factors that distinguish types of multilingual countries.

8.4.1 Age of country

Singapore is young and Switzerland old. While this is obviously a graded criterion, since many states have in the course of history changed their form of government, their territory, and the composition of their population, age is a factor to be taken into consideration, not least because it relates to the level of traditions and national histories and myths built up over time. The linguistic diversity that obtains in old countries such as Italy and France where an indigenous language was cultivated over several centuries and gradually dispersed throughout the whole territory, differs from that of young countries like the Democratic Republic of the Congo and Senegal that became states after the Second World War II by virtue of external political dynamics and with little regard for the indigenous languages. The political map of Africa is revealing by itself. About 44 per cent of all national borders are straight lines arbitrarily cutting across language territories and ethnic groups. Virtually all of the countries that were established within these frontiers are young states that had to deal with a multilingual populace from the start.

This is not to say that old nations, such as, for instance, China, Iran, or Greece are monolingual, but in their recent past they did not experience the (forced) adoption of an exogenous language, initially brought by foreign rulers and retained after self-rule had been achieved. A country's age, especially if it relates to a colonial past, thus has a bearing on the nature of its multilingualism and how it is managed.

8.4.2 Official status of language(s)

An important aspect of the legacy of the colonial period is the use of European languages in education and government. In twenty-two of the fifty-four African UN member states, French is the sole or a co-official language, in twenty-one countries it is English, in six Portuguese, and in one Spanish. Arabic is the official or co-official language in twenty-six countries. In some African countries, more than one European language has official status, for instance in Equatorial Guinea (Spanish, French, and Portuguese) and the Seychelles (English and French). In a few countries, African languages are accorded co-official status, notably Swahili in Tanzania, but an African language being the sole official language of the country, as Amharic in Ethiopia, is the odd exception. Some countries have a whole array of official languages, for example South Africa, eleven, and Zimbabwe, sixteen. Since European languages are invariably among them—in the said cases, English—their position tends to be strengthened rather than diminished by the large number.

These arrangements have various implications. First, legal acts, statutes and other official documents are published in what for large parts of the population is a foreign language. By the same token, access to higher education presupposes a good command of a language that differs from that of home and everyday pursuits (Zsiga et al. 2014). From the point of view of European linguistic monoculture this may seem taxing, but to Africans—and not just Africans—it is the normal state of affairs that official and quotidian activities require different languages.

European colonialism on the other side of the Atlantic was quite different, but its linguistic footprint is similar. Without exception, European languages fulfil the function of official language: Spanish in eighteen South and Central American countries, Portuguese in Brazil, and Dutch in Suriname. All countries and several dependent territories in the Caribbean are administered in English, Spanish, French, and Dutch. Indigenous languages are recognized as co-official in some countries, for instance, Quechua and Aymara in Peru and Bolivia where Guaraní also has official status, as it has in Paraguay. No indigenous language enjoys sole official status in any American country.

Canada is officially bilingual, its Constitution providing that English and French have equality of status and equal rights, while provincial and municipality laws grant various degrees of protection to minority languages (Foucher 2007). In the USA, the question of a national or official language has been contentious for a long time (Sullivan and Schatz 1999). In 2006, the US Senate voted to designate English the national language of the United States. However, the US Voting Rights Act requires states to conduct elections in minority languages if the minority group constitutes more than 5 per cent of the electorate. English is the official language of many States where it is used in nearly all governmental functions, although some States accord co-official status to Native American languages. The State of Hawaii has designated Hawaiian as an official language, largely for symbolic reasons, as it is spoken by only a very few speakers. In New Mexico and Louisiana some public services are provided in Spanish and French, respectively, giving these languages quasi-official status. In view of the fact that, according to the US Census Bureau, 20.8 per cent of the US population speak a language other than English at home (Ryan 2013), authorities at the state level have to be more pragmatic and accommodating than the federal government which drafts, deliberates, and enacts all legislation in English only.[14]

In Oceania, European languages dominate officialdom. Seventeen countries use English as the official language, three use French, and in five countries local languages enjoy (co-)official status, such as Filipino in the Philippines, Nauruan in Nauru, and Māori in New Zealand.

The situation in Asia is more complex: almost fifty indigenous languages have official status in the countries of the continent. However, Portuguese persists as an official language in Timor Leste and Macau, as English does in Hong Kong and in several major countries, notably Philippines, Pakistan, and India where it serves functions that were fulfilled by other languages in the past. As Chaudhary (2001) explains:

In each age, along with many other languages, there has been a prestige language discharging prestigious functions like medium of administration, diplomacy, education, literature, science, etc. It was Sanskrit once upon a time, followed by Prakrit, Pali, Apabhramsa/Magadhi, then Arabic-Persian, English, and Hindi. But none of these so

---

[14] See especially Fig. 5 of the report, 'Percentage of people five years and over who spoke a language other than English at home': 2011. http://www.census.gov/prod/2013pubs/acs-22 .pdf#page=12&zoom=auto,-14,316 (accessed 7 January 2017).

called 'prestige languages' have ever been the mother tongue of a sizeable group of people in India. (Chaudhary 2001: 143)

Chaudhary then continues, quoting himself (1968):

... for something like two thousand years no language spoken naturally by any section of the population of India has been the common language of the country's politics or culture. The languages actually current, as such over that period, have been three— Sanskrit—a synthetic language, Persian and English, both languages of foreign rulers. (Chaudhary 2001 (1968))

Incomplete as it is, this short circumnavigation of the globe suffices to show the overwhelming impact of the European expansion on national multilingualism around the world, especially with regard to official language status. For distinguishing types of multilingual nations, the official status of European languages in countries outside Europe is thus a significant criterion.

8.4.3 Demographic strength of languages

Official status does not imply demographic strength. A language may be official in a country where it is spoken by a minority of the population only. Such is the case in many countries where European languages have continued to serve official functions after decolonization, but non-European languages also come to mind. For example, Pakistan's official and national language is Urdu which, however, is the first language of just 7.5 per cent of the population.[15]

Since Urdu, in principle, is learnt at school by all pupils and promoted as the country's lingua franca, it would be misleading to characterize it as a minority language on the basis of its relatively low percentage of L1 speakers (Mansoor 2009). Punjabi has five times as many speakers in Pakistan, but lacks the prestige of Urdu. What is more, while Punjabi is heavily concentrated in the province of Punjab, Urdu has no geographic centre in Pakistan, which in the event is an advantage for allocating it official status, as its regional neutrality is less likely to incite resentment.

---

[15] Population by Mother Tongue. Pakistan Bureau of Statistics 1998. http://www.pbs.gov. pk/sites/default/files/tables/POPULATION%20BY%20MOTHER%20TONGUE.pdf (accessed 7 January 2017).

The incongruity of demographic strength and official status is a common occurrence. By way of conceptualizing the interaction between these factors of multilingualism, Srivastava (1984: 101) proposed a two-dimensional matrix (Figure 8.1). According to its relative political power and demographic strength, each one of a nation's languages falls into one of the four quadrants, A Majority, B Janata, C Elite, and D Minority (where Hindi *janata* (जनता) means both 'folk' and 'public'). English would be A in Britain, but C in India. An example of B would be Creole in Haiti where French is C. The vast majority of all languages of the world fall into field D which thus requires further differentiation (Section 8.4.4). The reference unit of the matrix is the country. Relative to it, a language's position in the matrix may both change and differ. Consider, for example, Chinese in Japan. In the pre-modern state, (written) Chinese was C, being used for administrative and other power-related functions. Nowadays, Chinese is a minority language in Japan in the sense of D, that is, of small demographic strength and divested of power. Status planning in Indonesia at the threshold of independence was directed at shifting Indonesian (Bahasa Indonesia) from D to A, an exceptionally successful endeavour of postcolonial language planning, it may be noted in passing. In Macau, Portuguese is currently moving from C to D. Generally speaking, in many countries, the processes of modernization and democratization brought with it a drive to establish a language regime of intersecting fields A and B and the phasing out of C. D could not be spirited away however.

Population dynamics may cause the demographic strength of a language to change; modern immigrant countries can provide many examples. When Canada was founded in 1867, some 50 per cent of the population spoke French. Within a generation's time this was down to less than 8 per cent, without turning French into a minority language in

Quantum	+ Power	–
–	A Majority	B Janata
+	C Elite	D Minority

Figure 8.1 Matrix for classifying languages in terms of political power and demographic strength.

Source: Srivastava 1984.

the sense of D because it retained its status with regard to power as laid down in the Constitution.

Australia is another example of demographic change brought about by migration. Since the mid-twentieth century some seven million people have migrated to Australia, forcing the country to change its once rigid Anglophone outlook to embrace multiculturalism (Clyne 1991). A 2010 policy statement by the Australian Government declares:

Today, one in four of Australia's 22 million people were born overseas, 44 per cent were born overseas or have a parent who was and four million speak a language other than English. We speak over 260 languages and identify with more than 270 ancestries. Australia is and will remain a multicultural society.[16]

The same policy statement also speaks of 'Australia's First Peoples—the Aboriginal and Torres Strait Islander Peoples' to which the Australian Government pledges 'wide ranging support' which, however, comes late in the day. While the demographic strength of immigrant languages such as Turkish, Greek, Italian, but also Chinese, Japanese, Indonesian, Korean, and Vietnamese continued to grow, most Aboriginal languages have been driven to extinction, the few remaining ones counting their speakers in two or three digit figures.[17] They fall without exception into the D quadrant of the matrix in Figure 8.1, 'minus quantum' and 'minus power'.

Over time, then, and a very short time at that—the first white settlers having arrived in 1788—migration flows have twice fundamentally changed the demographic strengths of language groups and the linguistic profile of Australia. The Australian Government in the quoted policy statement maintains that multiculturalism 'gives [Australia] a competitive edge in an increasingly globalised world' to which, however, the Aboriginal and Torres Strait Islander Peoples will contribute little. For in contradistinction to the international migrants, they have no links to anywhere outside Australia.

This brings us to the next factor to be dealt with in differentiating kinds of multilingual nations, minorities.

---

[16] *The People of Australia—Australia's Multicultural Policy.*
https://www.dss.gov.au/our-responsibilities/settlement-and-multicultural-affairs/publications/the-people-of-australia-australias-multicultural-policy (accessed 7 January 2017).
[17] For detailed information refer to the Australian Institute for Aboriginal and Torres Straits Islander Studies at http://aiatsis.gov.au/collections/about-collections/languages (accessed 7 January 2017).

8.4.4 Minority languages

Numbers are important, but there is more to minorities and minority languages than numbers. A common differentiation among minority languages is between indigenous languages—Welsh in the UK, Breton in France, Sorbian in Germany—and immigrant languages—Punjabi in the UK, Arabic in France, Turkish in Germany. Both kinds of groups face a dominant majority and in many ways cannot avoid defining themselves in relation to, and being defined by, the majority. They may also compete with each other, as has been happening in the UK where of late more people speak Polish than Welsh (Figure 8.2).

Since immigrants put themselves into a minority position, whereas indigenous peoples have been incorporated into a state dominated by a majority against their will or at least without their doing, it is sometimes assumed that there is a greater willingness on the part of nation states to

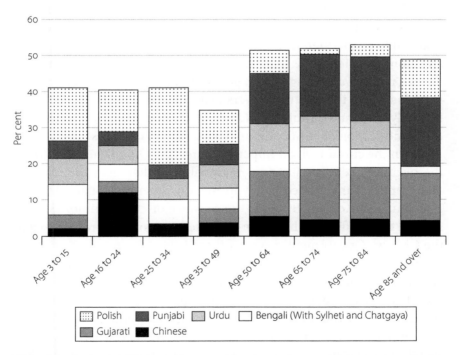

Figure 8.2   England and Wales, residents aged 3 and over whose main language is not English.

Source: http://www.ons.gov.uk/peoplepopulationandcommunity/populationandmigration/populationesti-mates/bulletins/2011census/2013-05-16#main-language (accessed 7 January 2017).

make concessions for indigenous groups than for immigrants. This is not necessarily the case though, as illustrated by the example of the Australian Aborigines, among many others. Rather, it is the zeitgeist or the ideology that has changed. Rigid assimilation and discrimination policies were thought less offensive in the nineteenth century than nowadays, when White supremacy is no longer (openly) taken for granted and individual self-realization, subnational identities, language rights, and diversity are cherished.

As mentioned above, the Aborigines have no kin outside Australia, a lot they share with thousands of groups in many other countries, such as the Native Americans in the USA, the 180-plus ethnic peoples in Russia, and the sixty odd groups covered by the European Charter of Regional and Minority Languages in various European states. Given what was said above in Chapter 3 about the difficulty of counting languages, it comes as no surprise that in many countries the number of indigenous minority languages has proved hard to establish in a non-arbitrary way. In countries where many unwritten languages are present, this problem is particularly acute. Since a life without letters has become all but impossible in the modern world of nation states, the availability of a written form is often taken as a criterion of recognizing an idiom as a language. Alternatively, language recognition and the development of a writing system go hand in hand, as has been the case in China where the Central University of Nationalities (中央民族大学, formerly 'Central Institute for Nationalities') has since 1953 worked on the identification of ethnic minorities and their languages.

When the curtain fell on Imperial China (the Qing Dynasty) early in the twentieth century, just four nationalities other than the majority Han were ever mentioned in any formal documents: Mongol, Tibetan, Manchu, and Korean. By 1979, the number of ethnic minorities had swelled to fifty-five that had been identified and formally recognized by the Chinese Government, many of them having been provided with a writing system for the first time (Sun and Coulmas 1992). It is worth emphasizing that all of these 'new' minorities, of course, did not come out of nowhere. They had been there before, but the authorities had never occupied themselves with surveying them and compiling lists. The modern state has to take stock of what it has and what it is, and is, therefore, averse to fuzziness and white spots on the map. Just as it does not tolerate any territories without defined land rights, it tends to classify people in various ways, citizens and non-citizens, adults and minors, and ethnic groups, among others. Participatory government and the rule of law presuppose a clearly delimited populace. In this sense, China's fifty-five ethnic minorities are a product of the modern classificatory state. Most of them are indigenous minorities, but some are not. China's ethnic Koreans are more properly described as a national or cross-border minority that is akin to the dominant ethnicity of a neighbouring state. With regard to national multilingualism this is an important distinction. National minorities whose language is the official or national language of a titular state are usually in a stronger position and have a better chance of being recognized and getting support for their language than indigenous or immigrant minorities.

Finally, the lattice of national borders has created transnational minorities that are dispersed over several countries but do not form a majority in any of them, such as the Basques in Spain and France, the Roma across Central and Eastern Europe, and the Kurds in the Middle East.

The four types of minorities described in Table 8.3 may not be exhaustive; some minority languages do not fit into any of them, but the categories are wide enough that most do. Some of the exceptions are of interest mainly because they expose the conceptual and methodological weaknesses of language assignment. Take, for example, Latin, Sanskrit, and other liturgical languages that are conventionally regarded as dead

Table 8.3 Types of minorities in modern states.

Type of minority	Definition	Examples
Indigenous minorities	Ethnic groups whose homeland is entirely incorporated into a state dominated by another people	Australian Aborigines, ethnic groups in China, Ainu in Japan, Welsh in UK, Romansh in Switzerland
Immigrant minorities	Recent (post-Second World War) immigrants with or without citizenship	Moroccans in Netherlands, Punjabis in UK, Turks in Germany, Brazilians in Japan
National (or cross-border) minorities	Ethnic groups who live in a state, but are kins of and speak the language of another, often neighbouring nation	Koreans in China, Russians in the Baltic Republics, Hungarians in Romania, Romanians in Italy
Transnational minorities	Ethnic groups whose homeland stretches across national borders, but who do not form a state of their own	Kurds in Turkey, Syria, Iran, Iraq; Berbers in Tunisia, Algeria, Morocco, Mali; Catalans in Spain, France, Italy

languages. Latin is one of the official languages of the State of Vatican, spoken fluently by many members of the Roman Catholic clergy, though not as a native language. Sanskrit was still claimed as a mother tongue by some 14,000 speakers in India from Delhi to Bangalore, according to the 2001 census. Sanskrit enthusiasts therefore submitted a writ petition to the High Court of Punjab for declaring it a minority language. But there is something peculiar about Sanskrit in that it shows wide demographic fluctuations over successive census surveys, rising from 6,106 speakers in 1981 to 49,736 in 1991 and then falling back to 14,135 speakers in 2001. How is that possible in ten-year intervals? Ganesh Devy of the People's Linguistic Survey of India offers the following explanation. 'This fluctuation is not necessarily an error of the Census method. People often switch language loyalties depending on the immediate political climate' (quoted from Sreevastan 2014). This is an aspect of the interaction of individual and national multilingualism worth keeping in mind. Against the background of the ideological European concept of mother tongue/national language of which there can be only one and an 'either/or' mind-set, this statement is astounding. However, it is congruent with Lee Kuan Yew's remark quoted at the end of section 8.2 that identity varies with circumstances, reminding us once again that when it comes to language we are not only dealing with fuzzy categories and perennial change, but also with different attitudes some of which may be at variance with received views.

Other minority languages that are difficult to assign to any of the four categories are those that do not exist for the authorities. Max Weber's dictum about 'the age of language conflicts' refers not just to border-crossing minorities that may give rise to international territorial conflicts, but also to contentious status allocations within one state. Italy, home of nineteenth-century irredentism, nowadays prides itself on a liberal language regime that guarantees protection to twelve regional and minority languages.[18] Venetian is not among them because, according to the Italian authorities, it is a variety of Italian and as such does not need special protection. The Regional Council of Veneto has

[18] These languages are: French (120,000 speakers), Occitan (50,000 speakers), Franco-Provençal (70,000 speakers), German (295,000 speakers), Ladin (28,000 speakers), Friulian (526,000 speakers), Slovene (85,000 speakers), Sardinian (175,000 speakers), Catalan (18,000 speakers), Arberesh (a variant of contemporary Albanian; 100,000 speakers), Greek (3,900 speakers), and Croatian (1,700 speakers), as listed by National law—482/1999 'Norme in materia di tutela delle minoranze linguistiche storiche' (Law governing the protection of historical linguistic minorities), adopted on 15 December 1999 (quoted from Sierp 2008: 304).

adopted a different stance, passing a law in 2007 to the effect that Venetian *is* a language.[19]

In sum, because minority status may be contentious and because of shifting loyalties and ethnolinguistic affiliations, it is not always possible to answer the question of how many languages are spoken in a country with exactitude.

8.4.5 The wealth of nations

A final factor that has a bearing on how national multilingualism is institutionalized and lived is the relative wealth of a country. Generally speaking, nation states, compulsory education, and capitalism have been bad for minor languages. If market forces are left unchecked, many minor languages will cease to be spoken as their speakers turn to bigger languages that offer better economic opportunities. In a nutshell this is the reason why minority protection is necessary, assuming that it is in the interest of the minority or of the common good to maintain its language. This is a modern idea that has gained ground with increasing affluence. Whereas in the nineteenth and early twentieth centuries assimilationist policies or more or less benign neglect were the norm, the second half of the twentieth century has seen a marked shift towards tolerance for and appreciation of diversity. The rich countries of the West, in particular, adopted more minority-friendly policies.

The prime example of an indigenous minority language that benefits from national affluence is Romansh in Switzerland. Spoken by just 0.5 per cent of the population, it enjoys the status of national language and partly-official language. It is advantaged in territory allocation, that is, even communities with a Roman population share below 50 per cent can be designated Romansh-speaking. The Canton of Graubünden maintains a translation service and provides bilingual textbooks up to high school level. Romansh can be studied at the Universities of Zurich, Freiburg, and Geneva. There is a radio station, a TV programme, a news

---

[19] Art. 2—Lingua veneta

1. Le specifiche parlate storicamente utilizzate nel territorio veneto e nei luoghi in cui esse sono state mantenute da comunità che hanno conservato in modo rilevante la medesima matrice costituiscono il veneto o lingua veneta [The speech forms historically used in the territory of Veneto and in places where the same have been preserved to a significant degree constitute Venetian or the Venetian language].

agency, a daily newspaper, and a publishing house (Chasa Editura Rumantscha). The language society *Lia rumantscha* is subsidized by the government which also funds other activities for the benefit of Romansh, such as nursery school teacher education and the compilation of an idiomatic dictionary.[20]

These measures and the overall policy of supporting Romansh must be seen as part of Switzerland's quadrilingual language regime and its eternal balancing act of avoiding German-language dominance or the collapse of the system by the incursion of English. Within this context, Romansh benefits from conditions that few other indigenous minorities can even dream of. And yet, all actions aimed at securing its survival may amount to no more than an attempt to square the circle, as one of the renowned experts in the field puts it (Solèr 2008). Romansh exists in three different spoken varieties which, since the sixteenth century, developed five written forms. Corpus planning resulted in the compromise variety Rumantsch Grischun in 1982, which is promoted by the authorities although it is not much liked by anyone. All speakers of Romansh are at least bilingual, many speaking both German and French, the languages they use for all purposes of communication that go beyond the concerns of the inner community. Rumantsch Grischun is intended to give the language the modern appearance that the local varieties lack and thus help it survive. However, as Solèr argues, this well-meant policy may be counterproductive, as Romansh speakers prefer local varieties and use other standard languages for modern purposes anyway. Romansh serves a function in a habitat (in the Bourdieu sense) of tradition and community life, and if that habitat disappears, Romansh will disappear. It does not take much imagination to see that many indigenous minority languages that were bypassed by industrialization, modernization and, today, globalization face a similar catch twenty-two, without however receiving the generous support from a benevolent and wealthy society that enables Romansh to persist. Switzerland can afford to pay much attention to its indigenous minority and treat it well. Less affluent countries often have other priorities.

---

[20] For a detailed account of the present situation of Romansh, see *Romansh. Facts & Figures*. 2004. Chur: Lia rumantscha [second revised and updated edition], a publication made available in Romansh, German, French, Italian, and English.

8.5 Conclusions

There is hardly a state that is not in one sense or another multilingual, and many of the factors that have an influence on national multilingualism are very particular and result from a country's history. However, some that have been discussed in this chapter are of a more general nature and cannot be ignored in any description and analysis of multilingual countries. The age of a country as a sovereign polity plays an important role, especially with regard to the colonial history (European expansion) that led to the transplantation of European languages to all continents. The colonial legacy is conspicuous when we direct our attention to the languages which are accorded official status. That European languages are employed for official and educational purposes in countries outside Europe where they are the L1 of a small section of the population at most is a characteristic feature of young postcolonial states, while relative proximity of official/national language and the majority population's L1 characterizes 'classical' nation states. The absolute and relative size of the majority is a variable and hence the demographic strength of the languages present in a state territory which does or does not coincide with their speakers' relative power. It is, therefore, necessary to distinguish several kinds of linguistic minorities. In fact, multilingual countries differ from each other most significantly in the kinds of minorities they encompass and how they are accommodated in the language regime. The geographic distribution of languages in a state territory as well as language recognition and the ascription of language to ethnic group were shown to be further important factors that are subject both to legal provisions and economic conditions. In conclusion, at the state level multilingualism is above all a matter of relations between a majority and minorities and should be understood in terms of diverging or converging interests of minorities and their reference majorities.

Problems and questions for discussion

1. What is the territoriality principle, and what does it mean for managing linguistic pluralism? Give some examples.
2. What kinds of linguistic minorities can you think of? Make a list and describe any differences you deem important.
3. Try to apply the quantum/power matrix (Fig. 8.1) to languages in your country.

4. Why could the capitalist economic order be a problem for linguistic diversity?

5. According to India's national census, Sanskrit had 6,106 speakers in 1981, 49,736 speakers in 1991, and 14,135 speakers in 2001. What do these figures tell us?

Further reading

Fearon, James. 2003. Ethnic and cultural diversity by country. *Journal of Economic Growth* 8: 195–222.

Heller, Monica. 2011. *Paths to Postnationalism: A Critical Ethnography of Language and Identity*. Oxford: Oxford University Press.

Judt, Tony and Dennis Lacorne (eds). 2004. *Language, Nation, and State. Identity Politics in a Multilingual Age*. New York: Palgrave Macmillan.

Lim, Lisa and Ee-Ling Low (eds). 2009. Multilingual, globalizing Asia. Implications for policy and education. *AILA Review* 22.

9

Diversity in cyberspace
The multilingual internet

9.1 Offline

Imagine a life offline! No, try again, imagine a life where the term and the concept of offline do not exist! This is a life without apps, chat rooms, and emails; no smileys, emoticons, or emoji; a life without Facebook, Line (ライン), Weibo (微博), Islamic Social Network (الاسلام تاج الاجتماعي شبكة التواصل), and Odnoklassniki (Одноклассники); a life without text messaging, cyberbullying, and blogposts in the electronic information loop. There are no tweet storms, no Flickr, no Instagram, no YouTube, no WeChat (微信), no e-commerce, and no customer tracking. Wikipedia is unknown, and so is WikiLeaks, not to mention League of Legends. There are no data monsters like Google and NSA; big data is beyond imagination, and online dating science fiction. The e-book is yet to be invented, and students know no more about CMC, CAT, and CAI[1] than their teachers do. No spam, no hacking, phishing, or malware. Digitalese

---

[1] Computer-mediated communication, computer-assisted translation, and computer-assisted instruction, respectively.

181

is no one's jargon, and textisms have yet to irritate the first newspaper reader who associates a cookie with a cup of coffee. Google maps does not help you find your way about, or shower you with personalized ads; you cannot spend hours surfing in your bedroom, belong to a hashtag community, or skype with your friends. You cannot lose money on fake pay sites or buying bitcoins. No stories or pictures go viral, nobody is bothered by trolls, and, just think of it, no one indulges in the narcissistic pleasures of posting selfies. No one has thought of netiquette, a cloud is a meteorological phenomenon, 'office' means a room with a desk, 'friend' means friend, 'to chat' means moving your lips, and 'cut and paste' means using scissors and glue. Nobody exploits personal information on a massive scale for profit, and nobody makes a living developing new search engines, text processing software, or plagiarism checkers. Virtual communities do not exist and are, therefore, no more common in one part of the world than in another. Although Canadian media guru Marshall McLuhan already thought of the world as a 'global village' in the 1960s, his vision did not even hint at the digital divide that separates those for whom all of the above is still true from the rest of us in the networked world today.[2]

For readers born in the right, that is, the northern hemisphere, say, after Edward Snowden set foot on this planet in 1983, this is a world long past and hard to envisage. Because of the novelty of the internet and all of the technological innovations of hardware and software it brought in its train, there is wide agreement that for the past few decades we have all been engulfed in a communications revolution on a par with that instigated by Gutenberg half a millennium ago in Europe. Indeed, to call the internet and the World Wide Web 'agents of change' in analogy to Eisenstein's 1980 book about the printing press sounds like a gross understatement, given that the internet changes not just communication, but pretty much everything from business, commerce, and banking, to politics and population dynamics, interpersonal relations, education, religion, and literature.[3] Since we are still in the middle of it all, the transformations that are effected—on the macro level of social structure and on the micro level of norms and conventions of individual

---

[2] The International Telecommunication Union keeps track of the digital divide most reliably: http://www.itu.int/en/ITU-D/Statistics/Documents/facts/ICTFactsFigures2016.pdf (accessed January 2017).

[3] Cf. for business, Castells 2002, for politics, Dutton 2013, migration, Greschke 2012, education, Wegerif 2013, interpersonal relations, Barnes 2001, religion, Enstedt and Pace 2015, literature, Browner et al. 2000.

behaviour—cannot yet be assessed comprehensively, but there is no denying that our ways with words are no longer what they used to be.

The extent to which the internet pervades our lives and whether or not the indispensability of computers for participating in social and economic life is socially desirable are issues much too big to address in passing (Castells 2010; Zuckerman 2013; Keen 2015). Nor can we tackle in this chapter the intriguing questions of how mobile communication and online tools impact the way we organize our everyday activities and create digital institutions (Hodgkin 2017). In the context of this book, we have to focus our attention more sharply. We will concentrate on exploring some of the implications of digital communications technology on language choice, on societal and individual multilingualism, and on the multiplicity of languages in the world. In particular, we will discuss the relative prevalence of different languages on the internet, the prominence of writing in online communication, language contact in social media, and the role the internet may play for vanishing languages.

9.2 Online

As discussed in Chapter 1, the world's languages differ widely in demographic strength and in their spatial distribution. In earlier chapters we have looked at cities, countries, and organizations as communication spaces that are characterized by municipal, national, and organizational rules, regulations, and conventions fashioned by social conditions and economic expediencies. With the birth of the World Wide Web in 1991, computer-mediated communication opened up a completely new, global communication space that changed the ways in which people use language and how languages coexist (Jones 1995). Cyberspace is a field of language use with its own physical conditions, political settings, and social conventions to which it is assumed that by the mid-2020s the vast majority of adults on the planet will have access (Keen 2015: 13). While the rules of oral and visual communication are not invalidated in cyberspace, there are characteristic differences, restrictions, and extensions which, if we were to analyse them adequately, would require that the traditional tools of grammar and discourse analysis in the analogue world be adjusted. Internet linguistics has consequently emerged as a research field in its own right (Androutsopoulos 2006; Warschauer et al. 2007; Baron 2008; Crystal 2011; Danesi 2016). Theoretically, this new field is concerned with *language* in online communication rather than with any particular languag*e*s, but only theoretically. In actual fact, research about online language use is heavily focused on English (Tagg 2015: 100), which in itself may be seen as an indirect indication of the relative frequency of occurrence of languages used online. Before deliberating any particulars of digital communication, we therefore have to take a look at how the diversity of the world's languages is reflected in cyberspace.

9.3 The prevalence of different languages on the internet

First, we have to be clear about what we are talking about. Language use on the internet can be measured in different ways, such as counting the languages of websites, the amount of email traffic by country, and the number of internet users by language (Table 9.1). All of these approaches cover certain aspects, but cannot present a comprehensive picture of linguistic diversity on the internet.

The figures listed in Table 9.1 that underlie the graph in Figure 9.1 give the impression of exact measurements which, however, is quite misleading. As the caption tells us, the statistics refer to just one day and are, therefore, indicative of a trend at best. Similarly, that the data quoted in Table 9.1 are indexed to a single month in 2016 is not a matter of pedantry or over-exactness, but only reflects the still ongoing dissemination of the electronic technology which does not allow for more lasting statements. These statistics are nevertheless worth mentioning, especially the column of user growth in Table 9.1, which reveals the dynamics of the expansion. Because the technology that drives it was first developed in the United States, English was in the vanguard of online communications which began at a time when the ascent of English as global lingua franca was already far advanced. The prevalence of English was, therefore, assumed to be further strengthened by the internet, while most other languages would be marginalized if not wiped out. English was branded a 'killer language', and its functions in the globalizing world became one of the most widely (and most emotionally) discussed topics in sociolinguistics and adjacent fields of study (Ceramella 2012), as the dominance of English on the web was perceived as a threat to linguistic diversity.

For instance, EnglishEnglish.com announced in 2003 that 80 per cent of home pages on the web were in English. German came in a very

Table 9.1 The ten most widely used languages on the internet in millions of users, June 2016.

Top ten languages used on the web–30 June 2016

(Number of internet users by language)

Top ten languages on the internet	Internet users by language	Internet penetration (% population)	Users growth in internet (2000–2016)	Internet users % of world population	World population for this Language (2016 estimate)
English	948,608,782	67.8%	573.9%	26.3%	1,400,052,373
Chinese	751,985,224	53.1%	2,227.9%	20.8%	1,415,572,934
Spanish	277,125,947	61.6%	1,424.3%	7.7%	450,235,963
Arabic	168,426,690	43.4%	6,602.5%	4.7%	388,332,877
Portuguese	154,525,606	57.9%	1,939.7%	4.3%	266,757,744
Japanese	115,111,595	91.0%	144.5%	3.2%	126,464,583
Malay	109,400,982	37.8%	1,809.3%	3.0%	289,702,633
Russian	103,147,691	70.5%	3,227.3%	2.9%	146,358,055
French	102,171,481	25.9%	751.5%	2.8%	393,892,299
German	83,825,134	88.3%	204.6%	2.3%	94,973,855
Top 10 languages	2,814,329,132	56.6%	848.4%	77.9%	4,972,343,316
Rest of the Languages	**797,046,681**	33.7%	1,141.0%	22.1%	2,367,750,664
World total	**3,611,375,813**	49.2%	900.4%	100.0%	7,340,093,980

Source: http://www.Internetworldstats.com/stats7.htm.

distant second with 4.5 per cent, and Japanese ranked third with just 3.1 per cent. But what can be learnt from data such as these? They must be seen in the context of the number of internet users. In 1995, there were about 16 million in all. At the time, Asia was practically not on the map of the digital world (Figure 9.1). In the course of the next five years, the number of internet users multiplied by a factor of 25 reaching 414 million by 2000, and the growth continued at a similar rate. At the time of writing this book, in autumn 2016, the number was close to 3.5 billion and eleven of the top twenty countries with highest numbers of internet users were in Asia. The number of Chinese internet users had reached 688 million, just topping 50 per cent of China's total population (CNNIC 2016: 49), or more than twice the population of the USA.

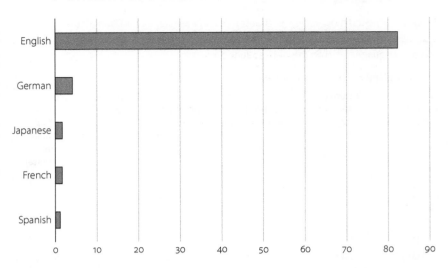

Figure 9.1   Languages used on the internet by number of speakers, 1997 (in per cent).
Source: Data from Internetworldstats.

Accordingly, the Chinese language has made major progress if we look at the number of speakers (Figure 9.2), but as a content language of websites it still lags far behind English and several other European languages as well as Japanese (Table 9.2).

A wealth of internet statistics is now available; however, while big data offers new information it also raises new questions. How reliable are language statistics? Are internet search engines equipped to cover all relevant language differences? These and similar questions are the subject of new research fields (Zuckerman 2013: 136) driven especially by the sprawling marketing industry (Khang et al. 2012). One study (Vaughan and Thelwall n.d.) that investigated a possible bias of search engines relating to language found that US sites were much better covered than sites of Chinese-speaking countries (China, Taiwan, and Singapore). Examining the possible causes of the bias, the study concluded that language preference could be discounted, but that US sites had a cumulative advantage due to the density of links. In the event, language turned out not to be the cause of the bias, but the effect on measuring the magnitude of different languages is the same. Part of the problem is that the state of the web is anything but stable. It 'is continuously expanding, moving, and transforming itself. The World Wide Web is in flux' (Lévy 2001: 140). Consider Google's book digitization project.

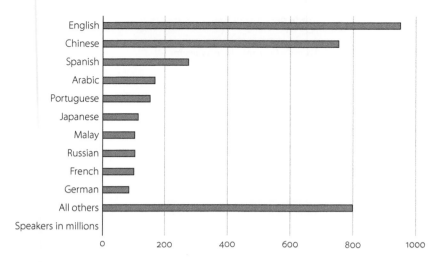

Figure 9.2 Languages used on the internet by number of speakers, 2016, in millions.
Source: Data from Internetworldstats.

How much of a language bias is there, not out of ill will or negligence, but simply because the project is far from complete (Aiden and Michel 2013)? The same holds for UNESCO's *Digitization of Old Books, Manuscript, and Other Documents.*[4] This continuing project uses ISO 639-3 for coding languages (see Chapter 1), which functions as a filter (Pariser 2011) that is not controlled by ISO itself, but by the Summer Institute of Linguistics (SIL), a faith-based organization. ISO standards are periodically adjusted, and ISO 639-3 may not distort the general picture, but for groups whose language falls through the net it makes a difference.

'The presence of languages on the internet' thus means different things to different people and in different contexts, while exact estimates of language shares remain elusive. However, the uncertainties, ambiguities, possible biases, and imprecisions of gauging comparative linguistic presence in cyberspace notwithstanding, the observation reported by Pimienta et al. (2009: 32f.) was undoubtedly correct and must be assumed to continue. They diagnosed 'a growing bias in favour of English for the most generic of search engines', but at the same time

---

[4] http://www.unesco.org/webworld/mdm/czech_digitization/doc/digitiz.htm (accessed January 2017).

Table 9.2   Languages of websites 2016.

Usage of content languages for websites, September 2016	
English	52.9%
Russian	6.4%
Japanese	5.5%
German	5.5%
Spanish	4.9%
French	4.0%
Portuguese	2.5%
Italian	2.2%
Chinese	1.9%
Turkish	1.7%

Source: W³Techs.com[5]

found a steady decline of the share of English language content websites from 75 per cent in 1998 to 45 per cent in 2005. Anything else would be surprising, however, since the technology extended further to non-English-speaking countries. The situation is, in this regard, comparable with the advent of the printing press five centuries ago. That the 42-line Bible, the first book Gutenberg printed with moveable type, was in Latin did not bolster the position of Latin in Europe; quite the opposite. By reducing the cost of books[6] and making them potentially available to a wider readership, the printing press provided an incentive to produce texts in vernacular languages and thus contributed to turning them into literary languages that would eventually challenge the monopoly of Latin.

The reported decline of English is in proportion to the total, whereas the absolute number of English language websites continues to increase, driven not least by the worldwide lead of English as a foreign language, which was already an established fact in pre-internet times. The situation is in flux, and the overwhelming incidence of English language content is still regarded as a problem by some researchers who perceive a connection between language and democratic participation and the potential threat English poses to lesser-used languages (Garfield 2016; see section 9.5).

[5] https://w3techs.com/technologies/history_overview/content_language (accessed January 2017).
[6] Irony of history, the 42-line Bible is today considered the most expensive book in the world.

If maximization of efficiency were the only determinant of digital communication, the dominance of English would likely be irreversible. However, myriads of new websites that go online every day in various different languages suggest that this is not a foregone conclusion. Because we are venturing into uncharted waters where technological innovation and social dynamics interact in novel ways, it is hard to predict how the web will evolve, other than that it will involve the entire population of the globe before long. With regard to the overarching question of this chapter concerning the relative strength of different languages on the internet, predictions are particularly difficult. Statistics capture just snapshots of a situation that is rapidly changing, and they are never all-inclusive. One thing they do make us see, however, is the enormous increase of written communication; we will now take a closer look at this aspect.

9.4 Writing in cyberspace: online literacy and quasi-orality

At the beginning of the millennium, Steven Vertovec—who popularized the notion of super-diversity (Chapter 7, section 7.2) in a much noted paper (Vertovec 2007)—argued that the falling cost of telecommunication was the key factor in the formation of global links and enhanced migrant transnationalism (Vertovec 2004). At the time, he was referring to cheap international telephone calls. However, according to one estimate (www.radicati.com), as early as 2004, 77 billion emails were sent and received every day. A decade later that number had almost tripled to reach 205 billion. Even if 90 per cent of this figure were spam, this would still make 20 billion emails daily. Since the World Wide Web went live, written communication increased by leaps and bounds transforming what used to be a heavily lopsided medium, where few wrote and many read, into an interactive channel used by sections of the population that a generation ago would have set pen to paper only for special occasions, if at all. Since a large part of online communication is machine-generated, it is impossible to estimate the total amount of written online communication between people, but it is undeniable that more people write and that literacy plays a much more important role in their lives than ever before in human history. Literacy thus obtains new social functions and has new effects on language as well. The bulk of research about online communication, accordingly, deals with writing.

189

As more people write, languages are written differently and more languages are used in writing. These include dialects, which used to play a marginal role when writing was associated with formality, a high level of education and relatively clearly defined notions of correctness. However, nowadays 'dialect is increasingly employed for written personal communication, in particular in computer-mediated communication (CMC)' (Siebenhaar 2006: 481) on social network platforms and for email. The role of written language for defining and upholding standards is changing and new standards keyed to CMC arise that merge features of the spoken and the written, as formerly understood. In online chat rooms, large amounts of spontaneous, unedited text are exchanged giving rise to a style that has been called 'written discourse' or 'quasi-orality' (Coulmas 2013: 146). At the same time, the immediacy of online contact has resulted in several contrivances compensating for the absence of face-to-face co-presence, such as emoji, emoticons, spelt out paralinguistic signals (haha), hesitation signs (mmmmmm), and typographical means such as using case (THANKS), numerals (see u l8er), punctuation, and so on...for signalling emotions that have become the object of what Androutsopoulos (2006: 420) called the 'first wave of linguistic CMC studies'.

Many case studies have been conducted on emerging online codes focusing on internet jargon in various languages, such as contractions, abbreviations, the integration of loan-acronyms (especially from English), other forms of language contact, such as code-switching and code mixing, and destandardization, the deliberate use of stigmatized forms of writing to indicate identity, forms of participation, and attitudes towards language use, among others (e.g. Wright 2004; Danet and Herring 2007; Androutsopoulos and Juffermans 2014). In the early years of such research, linguistic features that had to, or could, be attributed to the new medium played a central role, not least because its limitations were in plain view.

In the beginning, the appearance of languages other than English was rare and limited to European languages. For a while the proliferation of even these languages in cyberspace was slow and beset with problems, the main reason being the constraints of the ASCII (American Standard Code for Information Interchange), which did not provide for the coding of characters that are not part of the English alphabet. Françoise Sagan, Jürgen Habermas, and Stanisław Lem were thus temporarily robbed of their cedilla, umlaut, and stroke and miserably reduced to

Francoise, Jurgen, and Stanislaw. Scholars named König or Téné, if they wanted to be quoted, had to acquiesce to being called Konig or Koenig and Tene. Languages written in other alphabets, be it Cyrillic, Greek, Arabic, or Hebrew, and non-alphabetic scripts such as Chinese, could be represented in a romanized variety only.

Greek in the Latin alphabet, known as Greeklish or Latinoellinika, was among the first languages studied from the point of view of a romanized default representation (Koutsogiannis and Mitsikopoulou 2003; Androutsopoulos 2009). Initially used mainly in diasporic communities, Greeklish was widely perceived as compromising the integrity of the Greek language and it was a hotly debated issue among Greek intellectuals.[7] Similar feelings were expressed about Arabish or Arabizi, which likewise first appeared in diasporic contexts, hence also known as Franco-Arabic (Ghanem 2011). Such romanized spellings were often ad hoc, deviating from official transliteration schemes and exhibiting the influence of the spelling conventions of the dominant language in the diaspora/migrant environment, that is, typically English or French. Androutsopoulos (2006) used the term 'trans-scripting' to describe the practice of using the spelling conventions of one language to write another. First coming into currency out of necessity, these varieties became part of the repertoire of many online writers who use them for expressive purposes, as for example, in 'Urdish', that is, Urdu written in Latin script with a heavy admixture of English words and phrases (Mukud and Srihari 2012). The spontaneous, unregulated writing in Latin script of languages conventionally written in their own script is not without peculiarities, notably the lack of a standard. Ironically, the ensuing unsystematic variation turns the automatic normalization of texts thus generated on social media platforms for purposes of data mining and analysis into a difficult task, as Kaur and Singh (2015) have shown for romanized Punjabi.[8] These examples, among many others, demonstrate that in CMC, language contact has acquired a new meaning. As compared to its traditional Gurmukhī script, Punjabi in Latin

[7] Meanwhile several conversion services for converting Greeklish to Greek as well as other internet gadgets for Greeklish are available online, for instance at http://www .greeklish-to-greek.gr/Start_en.aspx (accessed January 2017).

[8] The same holds for other languages. Androutsopoulos (2009) observed that spelling variation is the hallmark of Greeklish, and it has been shown that the number of variable Greeklish spellings of words increases geometrically with their length (http://www. greeklish-to-greek.gr/Statistics_en.aspx (accessed January 2017).

script facilitates the incorporation of English words. The same holds for many other Indian languages, so much so that, early on in the internet revolution when most electronic communication devices did not support Indian scripts, CMC was viewed as leading to their demotion and eventual replacement by the Latin alphabet in its English guise.

However, the original ASCII was soon expanded and eventually superseded by Unicode which is comprehensive enough to code most of the world's writing systems.[9] Today, it is a matter of course that information can be exchanged in Chinese or Korean or Tamil, or any language you care to write, but it is good to remember that this is a recent accomplishment and that, therefore, the situation of linguistic diversity online is still quite unstable. Not all coding problems have yet been solved for all software programs and all languages, but, from the initial difficulties of mapping accented letters to ASCII equivalents to the internationalization of search engines, applications, and the World Wide Web enabling the online representation of hundreds of scripts, it has been a quantum leap.

In 2016, Google unveiled a new code, called Noto, designed to sideline Unicode and further expand Google's dominance of global online communications. The name is short for 'no tofu' where 'tofu' does not refer to bean curd, but is internet slang for empty white boxes (or a black diamond with a question mark ◆) that appear on the screen in place of undisplayable characters. Noto is a big typographic project that is said to bring an end to this problem by providing fonts for more than 800 languages. Whether the problem will be solved by making displayable all scripts that so far could be displayed as image files only or not at all, or by setting a new universal standard that pushes all others into oblivion remains to be seen. After all, online fonts are an extension of printing technology that reduces handwritten characters to stylization. For example, the Nüshu syllabic script created early in the Qing Dynasty (1644–1911) by women in Hunan Province, China, has never been used in other than handwritten form. The same is true of the huge cuneiform literature for which several different electronic fonts are now available.[10]

---

[9] Just to explicate the order of magnitude of the difference between the two, the original ASCII defines 128 characters, while Unicode defines 2^{21} characters covering some 135 historic and modern scripts.

[10] Cf., for example, http://www.hethport.uni-wuerzburg.de/cuneifont/ (accessed January 2017).

For research these are wonderful tools, but it should not be overlooked that such tools also shape the object of research. The medium does make a difference, as these fonts inevitably reduce graphic variation, as writing generally reduced linguistic variation in the pre-digital age. In the long run the new fonts are likely to delimit popular conceptions of the universe of languages.

The technical problems and solutions of devising and applying fonts for displaying a multitude of languages in CMC shed light on the greatly increased role of visible language. The fleeting nature of words exchanged on internet platforms notwithstanding, making them visible means giving them a permanent, potentially standardized form. At the same time, much of what floats through the net is meant to undermine and bypass the standards of traditional writing, and it is this overstepping, violating, and ironicizing of the rules of 'proper' writing that internet linguistics has been studying most attentively.

The writing of non-standard varieties used to be rare if not severely stigmatized in most literary cultures, but in cyberspace it has seen a huge surge anywhere between Switzerland (Siebenhaar 2006) and China (Liu 2013). As Fiorentino (2006) observed for Italy, dialect writing in CMC can be spontaneous by way of code-switching in chat rooms, or deliberate in dialect forums. And Miola (2015), surveying the Lombard language online, even sees internet literacy as a force of dialect resurgence. Many substandard forms of written languages that formerly did not get past the gatekeepers of print culture are effortlessly presented to an online readership, and often with a purpose. For instance, African marabouts in France use a derided form of non-standard French to manifest their Africanness, rather than out of incompetence (Vigouroux 2011). Deliberately misspelt words, cryptolects, and cant languages are also commonly observed on social media platforms. Circumventing filters, for instance for vulgarities, and contesting social norms are some of the functions of internet slang such as Russian Olbanian (Gorham et al. 2014), Chinese river crab language (Wang et al. 2016), and French Verlan, a youth jargon named after one of its prominent features, l'envers, 'the reverse'. Verlan has been around since the 1980s, but has spread widely during the digital revolution. It consists of playfully changing the appearance of words by transposing the order of syllables—for example Verlan *vénère, auch, cimer* for standard French *énervé* (nerved), chaud (warm), *merci* (thanks), respectively, and by incorporating memes or internet buzzwords, often of foreign languages, especially English. It also has a social aspect, testifying to its origin in disadvantaged suburbs of Paris. Messili and Ben Aziza (2004: 31) thus speak of 'the pleasure of abusing the official French learnt at school, the French of adults, the company's French of those who belong to society, which somehow means taking revenge for the exclusion through a hermetic language by those who are strangers to the group'.

The aspect of a little rebellion against the authority of standards can be detected in CMC jargons of many languages.[11] The internet facilitates, even promotes, code-switching, code-mixing, and the use of substandard forms and non-words to an extent never seen in print culture (Crystal 2006: 128f., Androutsopoulos 2013), thereby functioning as a stage for centrifugal forces that erode standards and broaden the spectrum of written communication. One can see in this development a second phase of vernacularization—the process of developing written forms of spoken vernaculars—echoing the transition from Latin to Europe's national languages and from Classical Chinese to national languages in East Asia, associated with the process of modernization. Of course, like printing technology, the internet also offers the tools for validating and upholding standards, for instance by making reference works universally available. What is more, it can be used for boosting the prestige of a language or variety by establishing its presence in cyberspace and thereby supporting a claim to a standard.

Online communication changes many things, but it also renews established traditions. Arguably, two kinds of reference works, dictionaries and encyclopaedias, embody the essence of societal literacy. These works are quintessentially a product of the art of writing that detaches author from content, and as monuments of print culture represent the authority of standards in its most highly developed form. This authority, however, has been thoroughly undermined by the internet, as dictionary makers were forced to adjust to the fast-paced evolution of digital communication (see Chapter 2, fn. 3), and professional encyclopaedists were pushed off their pedestal, purportedly in the name of 'swarm intelligence', by

---

[11] See, for instance, for Japanese: http://www.fluentu.com/japanese/blog/japanese-internet-slang/; Chinese: http://www.revolvy.com/main/index.php?s=River%20crab%20(Internet%20slang)&item_type=topic; Russian: https://eagleandthebear.wordpress.com/tag/olbanian-language/; Dutch: http://www.sms-taal.nl/; German: http://www.chatiquette.de/abkuerzungen.htm; Italian: http://italian.about.com/od/vocabulary/a/aa053106a.htm; French: http://monsu.desiderio.free.fr/curiosites/verlan1.html; English: http://www.internetslang.com/ (all accessed January 2017).

collaborative writing. Not only can everyone contribute to Wikipedia, but new Wikipedias can be launched for any language. Since 2001, when Wikipedia was founded in English, based on the idea that no central authority should control editing,[12] dozens of Wikipedias in other languages have been created every year, while the number of English language articles continues to grow almost exponentially.

Thus, yet another way of determining the online vitality of languages is by looking at active Wikipedia pages. Wikipedia maintains a meta page that lists all languages for which Wikipedias have been created (https://meta.wikimedia.org/wiki/List_of_Wikipedias). By September 2017, it encompassed 299 languages of which 288 had active pages. The remaining eleven had been removed for further improvement. The life expectancy of individual entries on this site is short as it is regularly updated and overwritten by editors, setting limits to totally anarchic mushrooming. Accordingly, the excerpted data in Table 9.3 only serve for illustration and to demonstrate that statistics of this kind must be used with circumspection. Table 9.3 is ordered for the number of wiki articles available in the respective languages, encompassing the thirteen languages with more than 1,000,000 wiki articles. A comparison with the ranking of languages in Table 9.1 reveals some conspicuous differences. That, as in Table 9.1, English tops the list in Table 9.3 comes as no surprise, but what follows is unexpected. Swedish ranks second and Cebuano third. The former is the language of just 9.2 million L1 speakers compared to some 400 million L1 speakers of English, and of the latter it is safe to assume that the vast majority of the readers of this book have never heard the name. Like Wary-Wary further down the list on rank 10, Cebuano (locally known as Binisaya) is an Austronesian language spoken by some 20 million speakers in the Philippines.

The discrepancy between English and Swedish in demographic strength is one indication among others in the same list that demonstrates the absence of any correlation between size of speech community and magnitude of Wiki. Dutch ranks higher than Spanish, Russian, Japanese, French, and Italian, all of which have much larger speech communities. Or take Hindi with a speech community of some 180 million

---

[12] Internet critics have pointed out that this ideal has been compromised by a new generation of gatekeepers of the Wiki world, which, as noted by Anne Perkins, 'is the world according to young white western male with a slight personality defect' (quoted from Keen 2015: 155).

speakers. In the full list of the quoted website it ranks 55, below Latin (rank 49) which has no L1 speakers. These statistics are partly due to the fact that the collaborative enterprise of Wiki-writing is still quite new and, like the penetration of the internet, unevenly distributed across countries. Yet, finding Cebuano and Waray-Waray among the top ten languages is puzzling. Both outrank Tagalog (Filipino, rank 70 with 65,480 articles), the national language of the Philippines, by a large measure which raises the question whether this is indicative of the relatively low degree of diffusion of Tagalog, or of any ulterior motives for redacting Wiki articles in these two languages. Considering the fact that the full list also includes five artificial languages—Esperanto (32), Volapük (53), Ido (98), Interlingua (108), and Interlingue (183)—this may well be so, for the speakers of all of these languages are at least bilingual and would, for the purposes of gathering information, usually turn to sources in established standard languages with a good corpus of literature. Thus, providing information in the form of a reference work may not be the only motivation for creating Wikis. A status thing is at play as well which, however, embodies a contradiction of sorts. Celebrating the 'democratization of knowledge', Wikipedia has made the gilt-edged leather-bound twelve-volume showpiece of the drawing room library obsolete,[13] but the prestige associated with an encyclopaedia is gladly exploited to enhance the standing of a language.

In political circles and among the general public, deciding whether a variety is a language or dialect is often contentious, and in discussions about this issue writing plays an important role. Non-linguists are usually more inclined to recognize a variety as a language if it can be shown to have a written form. For that, creating a Wikipedia is a good start and much easier than persuading a publisher or raising the funds necessary to bring out a book. Wikipedias have, therefore, become a favoured arena of language activists.

---

[13] This is not because Wikipedia is better than conventional encyclopaedias as a source of knowledge, but because the latter have been driven out of the market and transferred to online publishing themselves. For studies assessing the quality of Wikipedia entries compared to other encyclopaedias, see, for instance, Casebourne et al. (2012).

Table 9.3 The languages in which more than one million Wikipedia articles were written by October 2016.

№	Language	Self-named	Articles	Total	Edits	Admins	Users	Active Users	Depth*
1	English	English	**5,256,928**	40,437,467	852,091,160	1,281	29,225,609	121,429	944
2	Swedish	Svenska	**3,538,863**	7,167,254	37,336,772	67	512,400	2,895	5
3	Cebuano	Sinugboanong Binisaya	**3,029,650**	5,592,044	10,722,721	4	30,072	132	1
4	German	Deutsch	**1,984,606**	5,719,733	163,456,637	205	2,495,029	18,193	101
5	Dutch	Nederlands	**1,876,971**	3,676,944	48,678,291	48	792,562	3,617	12
6	French	Français	**1,800,257**	8,342,495	132,833,611	161	2,615,145	14,875	210
7	Russian	Русский	**1,346,118**	5,000,072	93,509,824	90	1,975,101	9,751	138
8	Italian	Italiano	**1,305,586**	4,555,384	88,946,763	112	1,415,074	7,420	121
9	Spanish	Español	**1,288,375**	5,623,446	93,817,675	71	4,368,466	15,987	189
10	Waray-Waray	Winaray	**1,261,787**	2,872,467	6,289,734	2	29,939	87	4
11	Polish	Polski	**1,187,231**	2,512,391	46,977,973	113	775,509	3,732	23
12	Vietnamese	Tiếng Việt	**1,149,098**	3,305,214	25,430,375	23	513,254	1,370	27
13	Japanese	日本語	**1,032,802**	3,008,109	62,418,057	49	1,137,005	12,218	76

Notes: *The 'Depth' column (defined as [Edits/Articles] × [Non-Articles/Articles] × [1 − Stub-ratio]) is a rough indicator of a Wikipedia's quality, showing how frequently its articles are updated. It does not refer to *academic* quality.

Source: https://meta.wikimedia.org/wiki/List_of_Wikipedias.

9.5 Curse or blessing for minority languages?

Wikipedias in languages such as Alemannic (rank 105), Bavarian (106), Walloon (116), Limburgish (125), Venetian (129), Emilian-Romagnol (140), Zeelandic (172), Upper Sorbian (130), Lower Sorbian (193), Extremaduran (196), Palatinate (212), and Franco-Provençal (206) belong to the category of online encyclopaedias sponsored and generated by language enthusiasts promoting varieties that are generally considered dialects of a national language, whereas the Wikipedias in North Frisian, Saterland Frisian, and West Frisian suggest a set of diverse dialects for which no compromise variety as a base for a standard has yet been found or agreed upon. A similar story underlies the competition of Punjabi and Western Punjabi Wikis. For Fiji Hindi, a variety of emigrant Hindi that has absorbed many elements of other Indian languages, including Dravidian languages, the Wikipedia is an opportune means of augmenting the sparse literature that exists in this language whose site is administered by a single individual.

If a Wikipedia is administered by a small number of individuals, it is likely to be someone's leisure pursuit or political project. The Gothic Wikipedia (𐌰𐌽𐌰𐍃𐍄𐍉𐌳𐌴𐌹𐌽𐌹𐌻𐌰𐌽𐌴𐍃) is a case in point. It has one administrator and fifteen active users who (presumably) delight in the 487 content pages, while Wiki editors have suggested its removal because the usefulness of an encyclopaedia in a language that has been idle for more than thousand years seems doubtful. Other Wikis with a single administrator include Englisc (Ænglisc or Old English), Bikol, another Philippine language, Neapolitan, Corsican, as well as some Creole languages such as Papiamentu and Patois (Jamaican Creole English), while Sranan, a creole spoken in Suriname, has a Wiki site, but no administrator at all.

Wikipedias in Gothic, Franco-Provençal, and Sranan represent attempts to use the internet as a tool for preserving a linguistic heritage or supporting endangered languages. The idea is to carry languages that have been bypassed by history and are therefore not easily adapted to modern life into the age of the network society. The internet offers both status enhancement by making these languages fit for electronic display, and the opportunity for members of their small and dispersed speech communities to continue using them, or so members of the National Geographic's *Enduring Voices* Project[14] and other optimists believe.

---

[14] http://www.nationalgeographic.com/mission/enduringvoices/about-the-project.html.

In the first phase when the new technology was seen as opening up a borderless world for everyone, rather than a profit-generating machine, the idea was that instant communication over any distance would be the solution for languages on the brink of extinction: the internet as a lifeline. Members of small speech communities would not have to forsake speaking their native tongue when they emigrated, and digital tools could be employed to help preserve these languages. They could be given a written form, dictionaries and grammars would be supplied and made available online for free. These were encouraging perspectives, indeed. However, given the force of the technological typhoon sweeping around the globe, it is not so clear whether the internet will be instrumental in saving languages from extinction or much rather speed up their demise. The languages at issue, mainly in Africa, Asia, and Oceania, as documented in the UNESCO Atlas of the World's Languages in Danger, have survived into the present day because their speakers lived in relative isolation, protected from the upheavals of modernization and industrialization. Their continued existence is threatened not because they are small, but because their isolation has been punctured by a world economy that leaves no zone on the globe untouched. And the internet has greatly accelerated this process.

Languages are tools, and not just tools; but they *are* indispensable tools of social intercourse and are as such adjusted to the conditions of their speakers' life habitat. As we know from historical linguistics and from crosslinguistic comparisons, languages are flexible systems that their speakers shape to meet their particular communication needs. No language is incapable of adjustment; however, it is not the language that adjusts to changing circumstances, but its speakers who may or may not consider their language a tool they want to preserve. Given the breakneck speed of material, social, and mental innovation in the ever-changing digital landscape, shifting to a language that is well-adapted to the communication needs of life in the twenty-first century is for many a more viable option. The internet facilitates this process by offering free access to information in languages with richer sources of knowledge and higher economic utility as well as online tools for learning and practising these languages.

In an early study of possible effects of the internet on language endangerment, Sperlich (2005) addressed the question whether cyberforums could be instrumental in saving threatened languages. His initial approach was as an activist who set up such a forum to help speakers of Niuean, living in various countries, to form a virtual community in their native language. Niuean is a Malayo-Polynesian language spoken by some 1500 Niueans on a Pacific island that belongs to New Zealand and many more speakers who live abroad. It can be found on the UNESCO map of endangered languages updated 2016 (Moseley 2010). Niuean is used as the language of instruction in the primary school on the island, but instruction in the secondary school is in English, and pupils increasingly switch to English before entering secondary school. Overseas Niueans rarely use Niuean in daily life. While many speakers are emotionally attached to their language, they lack the time to cultivate it in 'Net meetings'. Unlike a traditional dress taken out of the closet once a year, a language cannot be preserved for special occasions only, and if it is used like that its functional domains will be reduced and it will be a language of the past, with or without a presence on the internet. Sperlich realistically points out that 'after all, the way people communicate is their choice, and yet another medium will not necessarily influence their choice of language', and he concludes that 'the cybermedium promises much and delivers little' (Sperlich 2005: 76). The major reason for this is that the global medium not only makes it easier for dispersed speakers of small languages to rally around a heritage forum, but also to switch to English or another 'big' language with economic utility. Cyberspace thus turns out to be both a chance and a risk for endangered languages.

Sperlich's study was carried out one and a half decades ago, an eternity in the age of global communication tools. In the meantime, supporters of the Niuean language have established a presence on the internet for it in the form of online courses and games for learning the language.[15] Dozens of endangered and minority languages have seen similar developments. There is a heightened level of awareness of the precarity of these languages, and many online initiatives have been undertaken to halt their decline, be it in order to provide information,[16] in the name of fairness and 'building inclusive knowledge societies',[17] or, most realistically, for the purpose of language documentation.[18]

---

[15] http://www.digitaldialects.com/Niuean.htm, http://learnniue.co.nz/learnniueanlanguage/.

[16] Omniglot, 'Links: Endangered and minority languages': http://www.omniglot.com/links/endangered.htm; The Endangered Languages Project: http://www.endangeredlanguages.com/.

[17] UNESCO, Digital Content for Building Inclusive Knowledge Societies: http://www.itu.int/net/wsis/implementation/2014/forum/agenda/session_docs/253/UNESCO%20multilingualism%20MoW%20sh.pdf.

[18] VolkswagenStiftung, Documentation of Endangered Languages: https://www.volkswagenstiftung.de/en/funding/completed-initiatives/documentation-of-endangered-languages/.

In another study about language diversity on the internet carried out with the support of UNESCO that, among others, examined the impact of multimedia technology on minority languages, Paolillo (2007) discusses the potentially helpful effects of online translation, which has been made available for many languages. While under certain circumstances, such as labour migration, it can be quite useful, Paolillo also cautions: 'Text translation is not a guarantee that heretofore unwritten languages, of which there are many, will be able to be used on the internet' (Paolillo 2007: 427). He furthermore refers to the admonition frequently voiced by language conservationists that translation through the introduction of foreign concepts will change these languages beyond recognition, thus pinpointing the dilemma facing many small languages that as the result of the rapid diffusion of technological innovation are suddenly propelled into modern life: turn away from tradition by radically adjusting vocabulary and structure to contemporary needs, or fall out of use altogether.

Will digital tools, then, turn the supposedly borderless internet into a safe haven for endangered languages or minority languages that have a hard time surviving in the modern nation state? There are at present no data that would support a definite answer to this question one way or the other. But tools are at hand, and they are—'awesome'.

9.6 Online tools of multilingualism

After all, the world is multilingual, which not only gives us reason to marvel at the flexibility and creativeness of the human mind, but also makes us run into communication problems. Diversity also means fragmentation. And online tools have added a new dimension to dealing with the resultant difficulties. To return to the beginning of this chapter, who would have imagined a quarter of a century ago that people ask their mobile phone what tonsillitis or hay fever mean in language X? Nowadays, this is exactly what migrants and tourists do when they need to consult a doctor who may not speak a language they understand. Refugees often use the help of online translation on first contact with the authorities.

Without the internet automatic translation would not be what it is today. Professional translators insist, and rightly so, that they cannot be replaced by machines, but there are few translators left who do not make use of the available tools. 'Post-editing', the work of correcting and pol-ishing machine-generated translations, has become routine for many. Their work has changed.

The most significant improvement of machine translation this past decade has come about with the transition from rule-based machine translation to statistical machine translation (SMT) which works with huge bilingual databases looking for phrases that have been translated before (Pym et al. 2016). In clearly defined contexts where the same expressions are used over and over again, such as, for example, EU legislation, this approach works very well. Because of the massive trans-lation needs of its various institutions, the European Union maintains very powerful machine translation programs (European Commission 2015) that are equalled only by programs of the internet giants Google and Microsoft. SMT depends on large text corpora and is, therefore, ill-suited for small languages. Yet, machine translation software has been developed for many languages, including minority languages. Microsoft maintains a service that allows a speech community to build its own translation system (Translator Hub). So manifold are the opportunities for recording, learning, and developing new translation programs that Simonite (2012) feels encouraged to declare: 'Translation tools could save less-used languages.' But will they?

The actual use of these and other digital tools is, of course, at the dis-cretion of the speech communities in question, and is hard to predict. For instance, there are no fewer than eleven machine translation sys-tems that work with Catalan (Pym et al. 2016: 12), a language that with some eight million L1 speakers is not endangered, but is strongly pro-moted as a symbol of Catalan identity by many politicians and activists who feel unduly dominated by Spanish. The response to these appeals by the speech community at large is, however, rather restrained. In a study of language choice among young Catalan speakers on social net-works, Sorolla Vidal (2016) found that as many as 25 per cent of them 'tend to use Spanish with their classmates, displacing the use of Catalan even in intra-group interactions'. Why this should be so is a question to which an analysis of the technology does not hold the answer, for digital tools support Catalan as well as Spanish.

While almost the only unproblematic generalization about questions of language choice is that generalizations are problematic, there is little evidence that for other lesser-used languages digital tools have had more beneficial effects than for Catalan. A language with a long literary tradition, contemporary writers and institutional backing, Catalan is still at risk of being crowded out by Spanish, which many Catalans view as more inclusive, metropolitan, and suitable for out-group contacts. And this is not for lack of digital tools. There are online dictionaries, grammars, self-study programs, speech recognition resources, a *Viquipèdia en català*, of course, all available for free. And yet, many Catalans feel that their language is under threat, a threat though not posed by the international 'killer language' English, but by Spanish. Clearly, in the event the internet spells neither rescue nor ruin.

The internet makes writing hitherto unwritten languages easier, but in and of itself it does nothing for the online presence of minority languages. Central to the future of these languages and thus to linguistic diversity on the planet is not just the linguistic diversity of the internet but the online and offline behaviour in the networked society. In the past, the unequal distribution of literacy brought about diglossia ('with and without bilingualism' (Fishman 1967)), a relatively stable division of communicative labour between two varieties that obtained for centuries. Already we can see a similar situation with regard to communication online and offline. Do Niueans search the internet in Niuean? Will they ever? Greek in roman letters was a stopgap at first, but continued to be used by some who felt that it was more suitable for the new technology than the autochthonous script. Many young Catalans prefer to use Spanish in cyberspace. Speakers of 'big' languages such as Italian, French, and German regularly visit websites and seek information in English. Is this the first step towards language shift? This would be a rash conclusion. Instead, new communication patterns are evolving in many societies where, on one hand, national language standards are undermined by putting dialects and sub-standard varieties in writing online and, on the other, dominant languages are becoming even more dominant as the preferred languages of access to knowledge.

In sum, there are two visions regarding the role of the internet for the future of minority languages. One is that technology empowers minorities and gives their endangered languages a new lease on life by offering the opportunity of using them in writing and, since it neutralizes geographical distance, enabling the speakers to keep in touch by individual as well as many-to-many communications. The other is that technology overpowers minorities, that it is invasive and forces small language groups to part with their way of life to which their languages are adapted, bringing well-adapted languages into easy reach and thus promoting language shift. While the latter one of these visions is, perhaps, more realistic than the former, there is at present little evidence to show the isolated impact of the internet. It has made global communication a reality, but it is part of and shaped by the societies that use it.

9.7 Conclusions

New technologies bring change. Just as printing with moveable type changed the way and dimension of linguistic communication, the mode of mediation and the relative cost, Digital brought about deep-reaching changes in the republic of letters. When we trace the short history of personal computing and the successive waves of innovation from PCs to mobile phones and on to smartphones; when we see that since 1993 mobile phone penetration rose continuously around the globe to surpass 100 per cent in many countries by 2013,[19] then winning an argument against techno-determinism seems to be a tall order. However, we must not forget that technology is not god-given but man-made and that, as a matter of principle, you have a choice. Yet, strangely, people all make the same choice. Thus, what we see at present, the ubiquitous real-time communication by means of portable devices that characterizes the network society, is best understood as resulting from a combination of technological advance and social pressure that was planned by no one.

In this chapter we have explored some of the consequences of the digital revolution for multilingual communication management. Some of them have greatly enhanced communication across geographic, social, and linguistic boundaries, but not all of them are very satisfying. When Tim Berners-Lee invented the World Wide Web in 1989 he surely did not imagine, nor did anyone else, that before long it would turn into the most appalling rubbish dump ever seen, a morass of crime, harassment, and pornography and sheer nonsense that couldn't be further removed from the idea of enlightenment for all, optimistically associated with online surfing in the early days. And those will be excused who remember in this connection Karl Marx's remark in *The Eighteenth Brumaire of Louis Bonaparte*: 'Men

[19] http://www.cartesian.com/the-rise-of-mobile-phones-20-years-of-global-adoption/.

make their own history, but they do not make it as they please.' The internet exemplifies this notion as we watch. How multilingual it is can be estimated at best, and whether it will eventually be helpful or detrimental to sustaining multilingualism offline is quite beyond our capacity to predict. Meanwhile, the 'technology of the intellect'—a concept Social Anthropologist Jack Goody (1977) used to refer to writing—keeps changing our ways with words, as we keep creating new apps for it.

Problems and questions for discussion

1. Will unedited, spontaneous writing online lead to the erosion of language standards. Find arguments pro and contra this view in your own language.
2. Did you ever *decide* to communicate with your friends online?
3. Do you ever codeswitch/mix languages in your online communications? If so, on what occasions and why?
4. What is Verlan? Where did it originate and why? Is there a variety that is comparable in your language?
5. Do you think it possible that an online/offline diglossia emerges, that is, a tacit social agreement as to what forms, styles, and genres are used in linguistic communication online and offline?

Further reading

Crystal, David. 2011. *Internet Linguistics: A Student Guide*. London: Routledge.

Jones, Mari C. (ed.) 2014. *Endangered Languages and New Technologies*. Cambridge: Cambridge University Press.

Tagg, Caroline. 2015. *Exploring Digital Communication*. London: Routledge.

10

Integration and separation

Language

10.1 Clouds

No two clouds are exactly alike, and all clouds are always changing. Because it happens so fast, there is no room for doubt. The shapes of clouds evaporate as we watch, whenever we watch. They evolve, dissolve, split up, form anew, and merge to make bigger clouds. When they are electrically charged, they sometimes send lightning bolts to the ground, and when the electric current immediately (with the speed of light) bounces back, the cloud expands with a big bang. Thunder. And when we send an airplane up there to sprinkle a cloud with silver iodide it will change its shape at our command and release precipitation. Speaking of airplanes, the contrails crisscrossing the skies are artificial clouds that contribute their (by no means insignificant) share to climate change. And not just contrails. The composition of clouds is influenced by every kind of emission that rises from the ground, relegating the notion of pure natural clouds, undisturbed by human intervention, to a distant past. Clouds are ever-changing systems, objects of wonder, poetry, and scientific curiosity.

No two languages are exactly alike, and all languages are always changing; not quite as fast as clouds, but when we are attentive, we can see it. They evolve, dissolve, split up, form anew, and merge to form bigger languages. They are susceptible to various external influences that change their composition and their internal logic. Languages are ever-changing systems, objects of wonder, poetry, and scientific curiosity. How far this analogy carries is one of the questions we will discuss in this chapter. It ponders the challenges that the phenomena described in the previous chapters pose for theory building.

For the purposes of general linguistic theory, languages have been conceptualized as distinct systems of rules. Their investigation is concerned with what most famously Noam Chomsky called the competence of 'an ideal speaker-listener, in a completely homogeneous speech community, who knows its language perfectly and is unaffected by such grammatically irrelevant conditions as memory limitations, distractions, shifts of attention and interest and errors in applying his knowledge of the language in actual performance' (Chomsky 1965: 25). On the basis of this postulate, linguistic theory made spectacular progress. However, insightful and consequential as this abstraction was, it shielded the linguists' view from important aspects of linguistic reality that are common enough to deserve theories in their own right: languages that split up and others that cannot easily be separated one from the other; speakers whose communication abilities are not in doubt, but who cannot answer the question what their native language is in the singular; speakers whose mother tongue and dominant language are not the same; speakers who are fully competent in three or more languages; speakers who switch from one language to another on a regular, that is, rule-governed basis. These and several other phenomena cannot be accounted for by a linguistic theory that models a native speaker in the Chomskyan sense. Discussing several specific examples from different parts of the world, we will examine the theoretical problems of separating languages and integrating language skills.

10.2 Integration: enrichment or contamination?

The notion of a completely homogeneous speech community was meant to lay bare the fundamental principles of grammar, and not just some grammar, but universal grammar. As conceived by Chomsky, it was a very abstract concept, far removed from the social reality of language use, let alone any political instrumentalization. However, a superficially similar, though fundamentally different, notion of what a language is, or ought to be, frequently informs public attitudes, that is, the idea that there is such a thing as the integrity of a language which should be preserved.

Consider as an example the Dutch *Bond Tegen Leenwoorden* (Association against loanwords), which 'dedicates itself to promoting the use of pure Dutch and curbing loanwords'.[1] Established in 1994, it initially focused on stemming the tide of Anglicisms and recommending native alternatives, but then extended its efforts to cleanse the Dutch language of long established words of non-Dutch origin, such as internationalisms in the natural sciences—e.g. *natuurkunde* (lit. 'nature lore') instead of *fysica*, *scheikunde* (lit. 'separation lore') instead of *chemie*—and even the Latin-derived common pan-European names of calendar months. In 'pure' Dutch, 'Oktober' would thus be *wijnmaand* (wine month), 'November' *slachtmaand* (slaughter month), etc. This is going to extremes and, accordingly, taken seriously by hardly anyone in the Dutch-speaking world, but the idea that some lexical items belong to a language and others do not, is quite common. It is supported by a linguistic culture that relies on schooling and reference works: 'If xyz isn't in the dictionary, it's not part of our language.' This logic is easily turned around: 'Since xyz isn't part of our language, it must not be included in the dictionary.'

Linguistic purism is a multifaceted phenomenon affecting language change in complex ways (Thomas 1991). It seems unlikely that there is a language without loanwords, but some languages have, in their history, been more susceptible than others to accepting foreign lexical items. With a vocabulary that is half Romance origin, one third Germanic and for the rest indebted to dozens of other languages, English is a prime example of inclusiveness. Integrating lexical items from other languages is easier in some languages than in others. Take the French word *baguette*, for example. The *OED* lists it as such, defining it as 'a long, narrow French loaf'. The German *Duden* similarly gives the meaning of the word as *französisches Stangenweißbrot*, but alerts the reader that it can be used as a neuter noun or, less frequently, a feminine noun. The French noun

---

[1] De Bond Tegen Leenwoorden: http://bondtegenleenwoorden.nl/index.html (accessed January 2017).

is feminine, *la baguette*. Should the gender be taken along with the noun? In German the preferred usage is with the neuter article *das*, perhaps in analogy to other loanwords such as *Menuett, Duett, Quartett, Korsett, Kabarett*, etc. which are neuter and whose final syllable is homophonous with that of *baguette*, the <e> being mute. However, a paradigm forming analogy on orthographic grounds with feminine *Epaulette, Facette, Stafette, Sufragette, Manschette, Serviette*, etc. would also be conceivable, although the final <e> is pronounced in these cases. In any event, this kind of gender ambiguity cannot occur in languages that do not mark nouns for gender. Put in more general terms, there are structural frame conditions for the integration of extraneous elements, just as there are rules of word formation. Morphological, phonological, and orthographic principles are to be taken into account, but language culture may also interfere. Do you try to preserve the pronunciation a loanword has in the source language, or do you apply to it the phonological and phonetic rules of the receiving language? Both individuals and speech communities vary in their attitudes and flexibility in this regard. And conditions may differ with regard to the overall sociolinguistic situation. With their influential model, Thomason and Kaufman (1988) argue that language contact-induced effects are of two kinds. Those that do not affect the system of the receiving language constitute borrowing, while those that do are indicative of imminent language shift. In other words, speakers who pronounce the phrase *honi soit qui mal y pense* as /ɒnɪ ˌswɑː kiː mal iː ˈpõs/ rather than /oʊni swɑt ki ˌmɑl i ˈpæns/ are about to shift to French, or are they? Of course, pronouncing French words in English *à la française* can have various reasons that have nothing to do with abandoning English to continue the conversation or life in French. As is so often the case in matters of language, a clean-cut division without any overlap—either borrowing or language shift—is a theoretical abstraction that is hard to substantiate in real life.

Many studies of language contact have shown that borrowing is not restricted to lexical items, but that structural patterns, too, can be adopted from other languages, without necessarily leading to language shift. Just think of *no can do*, a direct translation of Chinese 不可以 (bù kě yǐ 'cannot'). In a classic paper, Einar Haugen proposed a scale of adoptability that is still useful. On the basis of a corpus analysis of the influence of English on Norwegian in the United States, he demonstrated that 'the more habitual and subconscious a feature of a language is, the harder it will be to change' (Haugen 1950: 224).[2] Accordingly, nouns are easier to borrow than grammatical morphemes or phonological patterns. The important point Haugen made was that all linguistic features can travel across linguistic borders and that—unlike earlier assumptions and unlike the notion of the fully competent native speaker of one and only one language suggests—phonology, morphology, and syntax are not closed systems impervious to the intrusion of external elements. What is more, the capacity of system adjustment can change over time. 'Adaptation', 'integration', 'assimilation', 'nativization', and even 'naturalization' are terms that have been used to describe the progressing change of words from other languages as they move from the periphery of occasional borrowing to the core of inconspicuous elements of a language's lexicon. Conceptually these terms suggest a one-way process of making loanwords compliant to the structure of the receiving language, although effects of lexical borrowing on the grammar and phonology of the receiving language have also been studied (e.g. King 2000; Mesthrie and Dunne 1990).

How and to what extent the openness of the language system to external elements is utilized depends not just on the structural similarity or distance between source and target language; non-linguistic factors such as zeitgeist, power relations between communities and countries, and social change also come into play. Based on a large-scale study, Poplack et al. (1988) analysed 20,000 loan tokens for degree of integration into Canadian and European French. Their measure of integration is not only structural but also statistical, that is, the more frequently a loanword is used and the greater the number of speakers using it, the more highly integrated it is. Both structural and use conditions have a bearing on adopting and adapting external elements, but the mix of the two is contingent. Generalizations are therefore hard to justify.

In the eighteenth century, when for large parts of the European nobility speaking French was a matter of amour propre, many French words entered languages such as Dutch, German, Polish, Russian, etc. Nowadays, since power and popular culture have made English *cool*, French is out, and there does not seem to be any limit to the influx of Anglicisms in many languages around the globe. Unlike French in

---

[2] Linguistic borrowing is an intensely studied phenomenon, of interest both from a grammatical and sociolinguistic point of view. For an overview, see Haspelmath (2009). However, Haugen's 1950 paper is still a central reference point in any discussion of linguistic borrowing.

eighteenth- and nineteenth-century Europe, there is little social grading. Owing to the rise of English to the status of global lingua franca and the immediacy of communication through digital media, using English, including loanwords, is associated with social class much less than French once was as the elite language of Europe and the international language of diplomacy. The lexical impact of French on Polish, German, etc. (and English, for that matter) did not result in language shift in eighteenth- and nineteenth-century Europe, and English loanwords per se will not have that effect today. Language shift is not *caused* by borrowing, but is conditional on a combination of multiple linguistic and social factors to which speech communities react in various ways; with indifference, in some cases, and with purist defence campaigns, in others.

An example of politically motivated purism is the anti-French movement in Germany before and during the First World War. French loanwords in particular were disparaged as contaminating the purity of the German language like a cancer (Polenz 1967). Similarly, in connection with the formation of Turkey as a nation state and the replacement of the Perso-Arabic alphabet by a Latin alphabet for Turkish in the 1920s, the Turkish Linguistic Society embarked on a campaign to cleanse Turkish of Arabic loanwords promoting 'authentic' Turkic neologisms instead (Perry 1985). France's 1994 language protection act, *Loi Toubon*, mockingly known as 'Loi Allgood',[3] should also not go unnoticed. In response to the manifest advance of English in France, it mandates the use of French in official and other public domains (Hagège 2006).[4] Lest it be thought that initiatives of this sort were limited to Europe, consider Hindi purism. During British rule of India and more so after independence and the partition of India, Hindi purism was above all anti-Urdu

---

[3] The law is named for then French Minister of Culture Jacques Toubon, under whose direction it was drafted. 'Loi Allgood' plays on his name, being a morpheme for morpheme translation of *tout bon*. The full text of the law is available here: https://www.legifrance.gouv.fr/affichTexte.do?cidTexte=LEGITEXT000005616341.

[4] Under *Terminologie et néologie*, the Académie française publishes regularly updated lists of anglicisms and their suggested French alternatives, for instance:

Instead of	one can say
hashtag	mot-dièse
big data	mégadonnées
digital native	enfant de numérique

http://www.academie-francaise.fr/la-langue-francaise/terminologie-et-neologie.

and driven by Hindu nationalism (Rahman 2011). It targeted Persian- and Turkish-origin words that were thought to be shameful reminders of Muslim Mughal rule and should, therefore, be replaced by Sanskrit formations, Sanskrit being the ancient sacred language of Hindus.

In many cases, formations of this kind, be it Sanskrit-based Hindi words or Germanic-based Dutch words, are loanwords in disguise, commonly called loan translations or calques. Rather than the body of the word, the underlying concept is borrowed and represented morpheme for morpheme, such as, for instance, Hindi दिमाग धोना (dimaag dhoma), 'brain-wash' (just like the above-mentioned *no can do*). The proclivity for borrowing or calquing is conditioned in part by the relative structural similarity of the languages involved. The writing system may be an additional factor sometimes acting as a filter. As an example, consider three contemporary loans in Chinese and Japanese in Table 10.1.

Even in the absence of any knowledge of Chinese and Japanese, when you read the romanized words aloud, you realize that only the Japanese words resemble the English models. The individual katakana signs used to reproduce the English words represent meaningless syllables. The borrowed words are thus adapted to the syllable structure of Japanese which is why in the roman transliteration some vowels appear that are not in the English words, but with a little bit of imagination you can easily decipher them, whereas the phonetics of the Chinese calques reveal nothing about the foreign origin of the words. Not that loanwords are unknown in Chinese; on the contrary, they have entered the language from many languages inside and outside China, since the reform period of the 1980s, above all from English (Sun and Jiang 2000).

Table 10.1 Preferred strategies of lexical innovation: calquing in Chinese, borrowing in Japanese.

English	Chinese	Japanese
green food	绿色食品 lǜ sè shí pǐn	グリーンフーズ gurīnfūzu
white collar	白领 báilǐng	ホワイトカラー howaitokarā
passive smoking	被动吸烟 bèi dòng xī yān	パッシブスモーキング passhibusumōkingu

However, owing to the great difference between English and Chinese phonology, their origin is often much harder to guess than that of English loans in other languages, including Japanese. For instance, to realize that hǔlièlā (虎列拉) represents the phonetic form of *cholera* is a bit of a challenge, but proficient readers of Chinese, if they do not know the word anyway, notice that 'tiger-string-pull', the morpheme-for-morpheme rendering of the three characters, does not make much sense and the word is, therefore, to be read as a whole for sound. Since the Chinese reader is used to reading for meaning when encountering unfamiliar words, however, there is a certain preference for calquing. Ideally, the two strategies can be combined, as in 隔都 gédō < *ghetto*, where the pronunciations of the two characters are reasonably close to the two syllables of the borrowed word and together mean 'separate-city'.

Are some writing systems therefore more amenable to linguistic purism than others? In light of the available evidence, that would be a hard case to argue. However, since language contact and borrowing occur in writing as well as in speech, a common writing system facilitates borrowing, as discussed with regard to social media in Chapter 9. Thus French words such as *amuse, banquette, critique, dossier, entrepreneur, forte,* etc. escape even the English spell checker's attention, and vice versa, while самова́р, агитпро́п, сове́т (samovar, agitprop, Soviet, respectively) make the untrained reader stumble (and the spell checker). In like fashion, Chinese, Japanese, and Korean share hundreds of words that are graphically identical, although pronounced differently. No matter whether they were first coined in China, Korea, or Japan, they are inconspicuous in all three languages, and many of their users are not aware of their origin, much like the common Greco-Latin lexical stratum in European languages. On the other hand, in the same way as Cyrillic words in Western Europe, katakana words are not typically integrated into Chinese or Korean writing. In this regard, Japanese is exceptional, being very receptive not only to loanwords, but integrating non-native scripts as well. Figure 10.1 illustrates.

In medieval manuscript culture, quotes and loanwords were reproduced in *ipsissimae litterae*, 'their proper letters'—e.g. Greek phrases in Latin texts—but in modern times, it is rare that language contact in the written medium finds expression in graphic code-switching or borrowing. One of the reasons is the culture of books, including the notion that

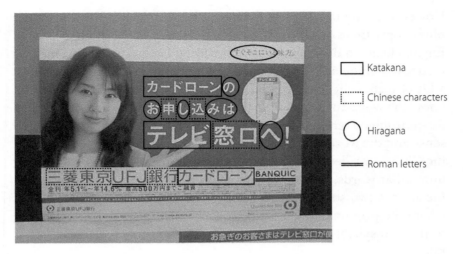

Figure 10.1 Loanwords and loan graphs in Japanese. Katakana: kādo rōn 'card loan', terebi 'TV'; hiragana: native grammatical morphemes; Chinese characters: content words like madoguchi 'teller' and the here underlined parts of the name of the bank, Mitsubishi Tokyo UFG ginkō; roman letters: the other part of the bank's name, acronym UFG, and BANQUIC.
© Florian Coulmas.

a language can be stored between the two covers, which reinforces the idea of a closed system. Dictionaries are typically organized according to an ordering principle derived of the writing system. The question then arises what to do with lexical items that do not fit the ordering principle. One obvious solution is to make them fit. The instruments for doing this are transliteration schemes that map different writing systems onto each other.[5] Thus самовáр becomes *samovar* in English, except for the acute accent on the stressed <a>, a one-to-one match. However, because in German the normal pronunciation of the letter <v>, which corresponds to Cyrillic <в>, is /f/, the German spelling is <Samowar>, for the sake of approximating the Russian pronunciation. Adaptation and incorporation of loanwords through the written medium is a multilevel process involving writing system, script, and spelling conventions.

As we have seen in the case of the Chinese rendering of 'cholera' above, the origin of loanwords is not always recognizable. Since European

[5] The International Organization for Standardization (ISO) provides coded character sets for the transliteration of several languages at: http://www.iso.org/iso/products/standards/catalogue_ics_browse.htm?ICS1=01&ICS2=140&ICS3=10.

orthographic conventions usually do not tolerate the incorporation of different writing systems, loanwords are romanized (or cyrillicized), no matter where they come from. Outside Japan, すし or 寿司 is acceptable on shop signs, but not in running text, although *sushi* has become a loanword in English and, most probably from there, in several other languages, for example, German. Because in German, word-initial <s> is pronounced as a voiced alveolar sibilant, Germans tend to pronounce *sushi* as /zúʃɪ/ rather than /súʃɪ/. Spelling it <zushi> instead would not solve the problem because word-initial <z> is pronounced /ts/ in German. Since German morpho-phonology does not provide for word-initial /z/, there is no system-conforming solution. However, breaching the rules of German phonology is not a crime, and hence some speakers do say /súʃɪ / rather than /zúʃɪ /, which again is not necessarily a sign of imminent language shift or a break-up of the phonological system of German.

To stay with the example, is *sushi* an English word, a German one, an Italian one? If so, it belongs in the dictionary. *OED*: noun; *Duden*: noun, n.; *Dizionario Italiano*: noun, m. Which leads us to the question of how loanwords are dealt with lexicographically. In the *OED sushi* is listed, since 1986, between *suscitation*, *suscite*, and *Susian*, *suslik*, *suspect*, etc., as the alphabetic order requires, without distinguishing entries for origin (although the *OED* also issues a 'Dictionary of Difficult Words'). In other lexicographic traditions, a distinction is made between native words, (integrated) loanwords, and (not yet integrated) foreignisms. Thus, in Dutch you can consult the *Groot Leenwoordenboek* by Nicoline van der Sijs, in German the *Duden Fremdwörterbuch*, in Italian the *Dizionario delle parole straniere nella lingua italiana* by Tullio De Mauro and Marco Mancini, in French the Larousse *Dictionnaire des mots d'origine étrangère*, and in Japanese Sanseido's *Katakanago jiten*, for example. With Digital, however, the ghettoization of parts of the vocabulary in separate dictionaries becomes obsolete. At our disposal are increasingly huge databases in which all entries are indexed for spelling, meaning, pronunciation, etymology, usage, first listing, frequency of occurrence, and other features that might be of interest. At the stroke of a key, lists of words with all sorts of common features can be generated—words that rhyme, farraginous words, five-letter words beginning with <t>, words of Arabic origin, words having to do with horologiographia, politics, or floromancy, anything. It is, of course, possible that foreign word dictionaries will continue to be published, online

215

or in print; but the function of sequestering such lexical items for ideological reasons rather than taking lexical interchange as a routine procedure will then be hard to ignore. Giorgos Seferis considered it a routine procedure: 'Multilingualism means that many languages influence each other...as established in Koraïs's "middle way".'[6]

If a common writing system facilitates borrowing, other parts of the linguistic system are, to varying degrees, also susceptible to external influence and favour different strategies of dealing with it. Whereas many Indian languages are, like English, prone to borrowing (Khubchandani 1983: 37), other languages, such as Chinese, German, and Hebrew tend to prefer loan translations over loanwords. German and Hebrew have a relatively complex morphology, and as a tone language Chinese has a phonological dimension lacking in many other languages with which it is in contact. In order to incorporate loanwords, these system-internal conditions necessitate composite formal alterations that may make loan translations seem the simpler solution.

To sum up, let us return to the meteorological image. We can conceive the lexicon as a huge cloud, constantly changing, absorbing anything that comes its way, industrial emissions as well as the scent of flowering fields, contaminations and enrichments, driven by trade winds that are quite unpredictable, if we look only at words. Is the sphere of the lexicon more susceptible to control than the weather? Soldiers of purism, language academies, and conservationists of endangered languages think so, but from a scientific point of view, one must approach this question with circumspection and careful consideration of available data. Whether lexical borrowing amounts to enrichment or contamination is in the eye of the beholder. Can it be effectively promoted—for example, for the purposes of language development—or curbed, in the interest of protecting the authenticity of a language? These are empirical questions concerning languages *and* their speakers. For it is the interaction of the structural constraints of the language and normative constraints of the society that determines the flow of words across borders. This cannot be anything but a dynamic piecemeal process. Capturing its essence by means of theoretical models that consist of fixed categories—

[6] Πολυγλωσσία σημαίνει πολλές γλώσσες που επηρεάζουν η μια την άλλη ... όπως την καθιερώνει η «μέση οδός», Giorgos Seferis, Δοκιμές Α΄, Ερωτόκριτος, (Essays I, Erotokritos). Athens 1974, p. 298. The second part of the quotation refers to Adamantios Koraïs, an early nineteenth-century modernizer of the Greek language.

bounded languages, closed subsystems, a sharp line separating the authentic from the alien, native from foreign words and patterns—is like trying to pack clouds into cartons, for category assignments and shifts are a matter of degree and of time.

10.3 Separation: isolation or break-up?

In the public mind, words embody the language, and the codification of languages in dictionaries is manifest proof of their distinctness: two dictionaries, two languages. The fewer languages you know, the more credible is this principle. In Europe in particular, dictionaries came to be 'regarded with veneration and respect for authority amounting in certain cases almost to superstition' (Harris 1980: 78). Dictionaries represent languages and stand for what is known as 'reification', that is, the materialization of a process or human praxis. In the context of foreign language education where you want to know what is and what is not part of the language you are studying, this vision is strongly reinforced. Likewise, when we look at clear cases it is tempting to conceive of languages as isolated objects; for example, Frisian and Tetum. Friesian (Frysk) is a West Germanic language spoken in the Dutch province of Noord-Holland, while Tetum (Tetun) is a Malayo-Polynesian language spoken in Timor-Leste. Separated by some 12,000 kilometres, Frisian and Tetum look like good candidates for near-complete disconnectedness. Both languages are very local and have small speech communities, approximately 350,000 speakers of Frisian and 800,000 speakers of Tetum, that have never been in contact with each other. But no leaping to conclusions!

East Timor was, until 1975, a Portuguese colony, and Portuguese is still one of the official languages of present-day independent Timor-Leste. Commenting on widespread bilingualism, Luís Filipe Thomaz observed that 'the parallel use of Portuguese and Tetum...facilitates the contamination of Tetum by Portuguese vocabulary' (quoted in Hull 1994: 355). What is more, Dutch colonial rule of the Malay Archipelago has left thousands of loanwords behind in Indonesian, a language well-known for borrowing from languages as different as Arabic, English, Hindi, Japanese, and Tamil (Lowenberg 1983), which in turn exercised an influence on Tetum. At the same time, many Dutch words, while often resisted by purists, infiltrated the Frisian language. And then there are Dutch words of Portuguese origin, such as *bamboe* < *bambu* and *kaste* < *casta* as well as words of a third origin shared by both languages, such as *banana/banana, caramel/caramel, creole/creool, marmalade/ marmelade*, among many others. There is hence a good chance that even though Frisian and Tetum are spoken in worlds apart, their vocabularies will exhibit some overlap (Table 10.2).

The specimens listed in Table 10.2 are taken from a common stock consisting of thousands of words. Make the ending *-tie* and it is Dutch, *-ção* for Portuguese, *-si* for Indonesian, *-sje* for Frisian, and *-saun* for Tetum. There is, as these few examples show, a linguistic dimension to globalization which has two sides; first, that all languages are expressions of one and the same system, and second, that they are all different. Of course, this is not a by-product of today's globalization; rather, the circulation and exchange of words between languages is as old as trade, migration, conquest, colonization, and other forms of population contact. The lexicon is just one part of it, but the very fact of borrowing, that is, the possibility of transplanting elements of one language into any other is proof of their underlying commonality. In the example at hand, the lexical flow is mediated through Dutch and Portuguese, languages that were carried to many places around the globe centuries ago. The endings are markers of grammatical integration, which is quite regular in each case. The connection between the words listed in Table 10.2 is evident; yet, *ymmigraasje* is Frisian and *imigrasaun* Tetum. The orthography highlights the dissimilarity and, together with morphology and syntax, leaves no doubt that, notwithstanding the lexical overlap, Frisian and Tetum are clear cases of distinct languages, as are the other three languages in Table 10.2.

Table 10.2 Shared words in Dutch, Portuguese, Indonesian, Frisian, and Tetum.

Dutch	Portuguese	Indonesian	Frisian	Tetum
imigratie	imigração	imigrasi	ymmigraasje	imigrasaun
informatie	informação	informasi	ynformaasje	informasaun
democratie	democracia	demokrasi	demokrasy	demokrasia
exploitatie	exlporação	eksploitasi	eksploitaasje	esplorasaun
elektrificatie	eletrificação	elektrifikasi	elektrifikaasje	eletrifikasaun

If, by contrast, we put comparable dictionaries of two less distant languages side by side and go through them, we may arrive at a different conclusion. Croatian and Serbian, for example, or Czech and Slovak, Danish and Norwegian, Bengali and Sylheti, Hindi and Urdu, or Dutch and Afrikaans (Table 10.3). In these cases, the lexical overlap of content words is in excess of 90 per cent, and the shared stock of function words and grammatical elements is equally high. From a descriptive linguistic point of view, it makes just as much sense to conceive of one dictionary with an appendix of localisms for each of these language pairs.

As exemplified in Table 10.3, over 90 per cent of the Afrikaans lexicon is of Dutch origin. Orthographic distinctions are minimal, consisting in most cases of simplifications on the part of Afrikaans which, however do not obscure the identity and homophony of the words, for example *lidmaatskap* vs. *lidmaatschap*. Language separation is not decided by lexical statistics alone, but grammatical differences between Afrikaans and Dutch are also quite moderate. As compared to Dutch, the inflectional morphology of Afrikaans is reduced. There is no grammatical gender, and the stem form of verbs is widely used where Dutch requires inflections. Further, unlike Dutch, Afrikaans uses double negation. Dutch: *Ik praat geen Xhosa* vs. Afrikaans: *Ek praat geen Xhosa nie*, lit. 'I speak no Xhosa not'. None of these differences stand in the way of mutual intelligibility. Yet, rather than speaking forever a derided pidginized dialect of Dutch, the speakers of Kaaps Hollands ('Cape Dutch'), as it was known at the time, decided in 1917 to set up the *Suid-Afrikaanse Akademie vir Wetenskap en kuns* (South African Academy for Science and Art) charged with codifying the Dutch vernacular to become a language in its own right. They were successful in that Afrikaans is today generally accepted as a language, one of South Africa's official languages, and a recognized minority language in Namibia (Deumert 2004; Van Rooy and van den Doel 2011). The goal was linguistic independence, but the conditions under which it was achieved were informed by European normative postulations about what languages are. As if to prove the existence of Afrikaans in distinction to Dutch for everyone to see, a huge monument dedicated to the Afrikaans language was erected in 1975 to commemorate its being afforded official status fifty years earlier (Figure 10.2). If one was needed, this is a monument for language reification, celebrating as it does one language's independence from another. It also stands, if unwittingly, for the transfer from Europe to Africa of the concept that identifies language with nation and/or ethnicity.

Table 10.3   Afrikaans and Dutch words (English for reference).

Afrikaans	Dutch	English
aandeel	aandeel	share
aanbel	aanbellen	to ring
betaal	betalen	to pay
belangrijkheid	belangrijkheid	concern
beurs	beurs	stock exchange
blad	blad	leaf
blank	blank	white
bliksemen	bliksem	lightning
blom	bloem	flower
blom	bloeien	to flourish
boer	boer	farmer
boete	boete	fine
chirurg	chirurg	surgeon
chroom	chroom	chromium
daad	daad	act
daarom	daarom	therefore
dag	dag	day
dal	dal	valley
dankbaar	dankbaar	grateful
eensaam	eenzaam	lonely
ernstig	ernstig	serious
fase	fase	phase
fout	fout	mistake
gedagte	gedachte	thought
leenwoord	leenwoord	loanword
leeu	leeuw	lion
lemon	sinaasappel	orange
lewe	leven	life
lyf	lijf	body
maanjaar	maanjaar	lunar year
maklik	makkelijk	easy
merkwaardig	merkwaardig	remarkable
veeltalig	meertalig	multilingual

Figure 10.2 *Afrikaanse Taalmonument* (language monument) dedicated to Afrikaans, located in Paarl, Western Cape, South Africa.

Afrikaans is geographically separated from its close cognate in the Netherlands, as well as linguistically, although the split on this plane is not very wide, especially in the written language. In other cases of forced separation, such as Croatian/Serbian (Bugarski 2001), Rumanian/Moldovan (Ciscel 2006), Hindi/Urdu (King 2001), and Bengali/Sylheti (Nabila 2012) there is little in terms of geographic division, as the varieties in question are spoken in contiguous territories. In all of these pairs, however, the script is employed to compensate for lack of geographic detachment and marking the difference, Roman vs. Cyrillic, in the first two cases, and Devanagari vs. Perso-Arabic and Bangla vs. Syloti-Nagri, respectively. One language, two scripts—many linguists hold that this is just another expression of the complexity of the multilingual world and call it 'digraphia' (Grivelet 2001), but it is also an expression of the determination to deepen the ditches that run through otherwise unbroken expanses of dialect-continua. Their emblematic nature makes scripts and writing systems suitable to function as catalysts of community separation and often strife, hence the title of King's (2001) account of the separation of Hindi and Urdu, 'the poisonous potency of script'. This potential serves as a midwife for 'children of linguistic nationalism', as Bugarski (2001: 83) put it with regard to post-Yugoslavian Serbian and Croatian, to which Bosnian and Montenegrin were since added, as mentioned above in Chapter 1. On the subject of Bosnian, Croatian, and Serbian Magner (2001: 23) observes: 'comparing the three renditions of the approximately 1,000-word Codex [regulations issued by the Independent Media Commission on 5 June 1998, F.C.] and noting only about a dozen word variants, one realizes how arbitrary and essentially political the definition of language is.'

In the case of Afrikaans and Dutch, the geographic distance between South Africa and the Netherlands seemed to provide a rationale for linguistic separation; but in other similar cases distance was not decisive. Surinamese Dutch, although different from European Dutch, is still Dutch, Macanese Portuguese is still Portuguese, Québécois French is still French, and American Spanish is still Spanish. On the other hand, the speech communities of Serbian and Croatian, Czech and Slovak, and Bengali and Sylheti live in close proximity, even overlapping territories. Hence, in a world fragmented and united by political, ethnic, and religious distinctions and the all-encompassing complexity of networks, geographic distance is not a good predictor of linguistic distinction, as perceived by the speakers of languages.

10.4 Fluidity and distinction

The discussion about borrowing, lexical overlap, and graphical differentiation has shown two things about the reality of multilingualism on the ground:

fluidity as a matter of fact, and
distinction as a matter of design.

The cloudy nature of speech is real, and speakers have a say in determining where one cloud ends and another begins. In the course of the past several decades, the language sciences, notably sociolinguistics, have reacted to the realization that, if they take this insight to heart, the object of their investigation will slip through their fingers, by turning away from the structuralist project of describing and analysing languages as objects of and by themselves. This process continues, and discussions about new concepts and terminologies (which do not necessarily refer to new phenomena) must be understood against this backdrop.

The general trend has been to move away from the 'language monument' in order to describe instead language practices that are hard to reconcile with the notions of a closed language system and the fully competent monoglot native speaker. The most salient phenomena that have attracted scholarly attention are (i) pidginization and creolization (Kouwenberg and Singler 2009)—a reduction in the complexity of languages and formation of new ones resulting from language contact; (ii) diglossia (Fernández 1993)—the function-specific division of labour between two grossly distinct varieties and (iii) code-switching (Gardner-Chloros 2009)—the alternating use of resources of different languages by the same speaker in one conversation. However, it has proved difficult to break out of the conceptual framework underlying a structuralist paradigm that takes the existence of what are now called 'named languages' as its point of departure.

For instance, the notion of code-switching is predicated on the assumption that there are two independent, non-overlapping 'codes' between which, under certain circumstances, speakers alternate. Recognizing in this practice a kind of rule-governed speech behaviour rather than defective proficiency in the (locally) dominant language meant progress, certainly for communities that regularly engage in this kind of practice.

However, the insight that code-switching may actually blur the distinction between native and foreign and puncture the idea of distinct languages was slow in coming. To cite but one influential theory, the model proposed by Myers-Scotton (1993) stipulates that irrespective of the extent of mixing and switching back and forth, code-switching is characterized by structural relationships between a superordinate (matrix) language and a subordinate (embedded) language. The parallel with the conceptual distinction between the (more prestigious) superstrate language and the (less prestigious) substrate language in pidgin and creole studies is hard to overlook. In both cases, theoretical suppositions establish structural order where chaos seems to hold sway. While recognizing code-switching and pidginization as expressions of the general human faculty of language and thus worthy objects of study was an important step towards liberating linguistic investigation from normative assumptions, the conceptual heritage of structuralism lingers on. Code-switching is in some cases better described as a code in its own right rather than an alternation between two codes, but this insight took a long time to gain ground. The fact that it is not always possible to decide on structural grounds which is substrate and which superstrate in a pidgin–creole situation has likewise been acknowledged only recently (Michaelis 2008). Pointing this out is not meant as a criticism but is done to show that, in the language sciences, theoretical tools and unquestioned preconceptions have an impact on how the object of investigation is constituted. Sociolinguists in particular, because they ventured beyond investigating normatively established languages, continue to broaden their scope to deal with ostensibly 'new' border-crossing language practices, which, however, may not be so new to the communities engaging in them. No science can do without abstractions, but making the right abstractions requires perpetual effort. Creating new technical terms and discussing their proper meaning is part of this endeavour, one which still continues.

The term 'dialect' was once mainly used to distinguish different regional varieties of a language, especially those spoken in outlying rural areas. Sociolinguistics came into its own when linguistic variation in compact metropolitan areas turned out to be as differentiated as across wide geographic expanses. The terms 'city dialect' and 'sociolect' were thus added to linguistic terminology to account for the social dimension of variation. In Europe, the distribution of urban varieties was analysed successfully by linking them to social class (Bernstein

1971); however in American inner cities race turned out to be a more salient fault line distinguishing varieties, African American Vernacular English being the paradigm case (Labov 1973). Mapping population divisions along racial/ethnic lines onto linguistic variation gave rise to the 'ethnolect', a new term used to mark a variety as being associated with a certain ethnic group, typically spoken in multilingual urban settings, such as New York City and London (while hardly anyone asked whether people also spoke ethnolects in Ibadan or Manila).

Of course, cities have always been places of encounter where people of different nations, races, and creeds mingled, where multiple migrant and domestic minority languages were heard, exercising an influence on the majority language. Language fashions and language contact-induced changes have always been more fast-paced in cities than in the countryside, a tendency that shows no sign of abating in the network society. On the contrary, many observers have identified linguistic practices they think are even more susceptible to influences from an ever wider range of languages and varieties and, therefore, once again require new descriptive and/or explanatory terms. On closer inspection, 'ethnolect', too, turned out to be too rigid a concept that could not capture certain aspects of the social reality of urban speech. Careful empirical observation revealed that speakers do not necessarily respect the boundaries the terminology is intended to reflect. For instance, London's ethnic and social mix produced unexpected varieties, notably among younger speakers. Not only were there Blacks with a cockney accent, white youths also exhibited features in their speech formerly associated with Jamaican or Punjabi ethnolects, crossing lines that were thought to be solid. To account for these new forms of urban dialect, Rampton (1995) introduced the term 'crossing'. Similar phenomena were observed in other European cities such as Copenhagen (Møller and Jørgensen 2009) and Berlin (Wiese 2012), among others.

The allegedly new urban varieties have in common that they are more clearly indexed to age—youth—than to race, ethnicity, and social class. In societies where race, although not openly acknowledged as such, plays a major role as a determiner of social stratification, this came as a surprise and provoked discussions in the media (Kerswill 2014). Hitchings describes what came to be known as Multicultural London English as 'intriguingly free from institutional influence.... Its distinctive features include Afro-Caribbean cadences, vocabulary absorbed from a wide range of sources (Jamaican Creole, certainly, but also Bengali, Hindi, Urdu, Romani and various African Englishes) and a relentless use of question tags, of which *innit?* is one of the less confrontational examples' (Hitchings 2011: 213). Describing analogous language practices in Denmark, Gregersen remarks, 'since these linguistic items do not belong to any one system of national languages, the term polylingual languaging has been coined in referring to the urban youth practice of using mainly Turkish, Danish and English linguistic items and structures' (Gregersen 2011: 52). And Vermeij characterizes *straattaal* ('street language') in the Netherlands as a multiethnic register consisting of 'words, pronunciations and grammar derived from languages of immigrant groups mixed with Dutch' which is also marked by 'deliberately made language mistakes' (Vermeij 2002: 260). Of theoretical interest is that yet another category, the 'ethnolect', proved deficient, as emergent new urban varieties are indicative of more integration and less intentional mutual separation of ethnically diverse groups than had been widely assumed. The term 'multi-ethnolect' (briefly referred to in Chapter 7 above), first used by Michael Clyne (2000), is intended to capture this particular aspect of changing linguistic divisions in urban environments. Notice, however, that it carries a testimony to its own theoretical gestation with it. If a quasi-natural association of language/ variety and ethnicity was not taken for granted, the term 'multi-ethnolect' would be meaningless. Whether these new urban registers will bring about deep reaching change in the local majority languages remains to be seen; for the time being they constitute a marked register that can be distinguished from, and is often criticized as a corruption of, the integrity of national languages, which continues to dominate common sense ideas about what a language is.

At the same time, the migration-induced plurality of languages in the classroom has become more audible and visible in recent decades, posing new challenges to pedagogues who have to deal with the hybrid registers of multilingual speakers using various language resources without much regard to their origin or 'proper belonging'. In the same sense that code-switching is no longer necessarily regarded as deficient competence, these forms of language mix have motivated researchers to emphasize the richness of children's varied linguistic repertoires and its potential for helping them to learn. Rather than insisting on describing an individual's linguistic competence as competence or proficiency in one language and marking the inclusion of other elements as unwelcome 'interference', a 'multicompetence that functions symbiotically for the different languages in one's repertoire' (Canagarajah 2011: 1) is posited. 'Translanguaging' is a new term that seeks to account for multilingual practices as a fluid process without presupposing clearly separated codes between which speakers switch, more or less consciously, back and forth. While the constituent languages of speakers practising translanguaging remain identifiable to the observer, as for instance in Li Wei's (2011) study of young Chinese men in London who make use of English, Mandarin, and Cantonese in various combinations, the heterogeneity and range of resources across languages is wielded together for these speakers into a multilingual practice that defies established normative assumptions of separate languages and separate competencies.

In sum, coupled with heightened attention to the educational needs of 'atypical' pupils, the conspicuous presence of multiple languages in schools, on the street, and in many other translocal and transnational settings that traditionally operated on monolingual assumptions has given rise to several new analytic terms, notably 'crossing', 'polilingual languaging', 'multi-ethnolect' (Cheshire et al. 2015), and 'translanguaging'. On the one hand, these terms are indicative of and embody a plea for more tolerance and less rigidity, and on the other, they cannot, and are not designed to, deny the existence of named languages. Rather, they should be seen as part of an evolving scientific discourse that attempts conceptually to reconcile and rearrange the existence of languages (without undue reification), on one hand, and speakers' varied linguistic resources, on the other. Intriguing as the varied forms of speech behaviour in multilingual settings are, they must not blind us to the fact that languages continue to exist, if only because speakers want them to. Flores and Lewis argue that in order to avoid any ideologically tinted essentialism, language 'should be understood as an inherently local practice that emerges through social interactions that are a product of the complex interrelationship between historical and contemporary processes and multiple scales of social life' (Flores and Lewis 2016: 110). That point is well taken, but the conclusion that the focus of research should, therefore, no longer be on the static subject of language, but on 'emergent linguistic practices' goes over the target. For while there is in multilingual situations integration, fusion, and crossing, there is also separation, division, and redrawing of boundaries.

Finally, since no scientific discourse takes place in a vacuum or outside a tradition, with regard to theory building about linguistic pluralism and the integration and separation of languages, a note of caution is in order. Coetzee-Van Rooy (2016: 240) points out a distinction in theorizing multilingualism between a monolingual-oriented Western concept of language, on the one hand, and multilingual-oriented African and Asian views, on the other. This is in keeping with what Khubchandani said about India where 'the interlanguage boundaries have remained fluid in many regions' and 'the phenomenon of plurality in mother tongues is much more widespread than has been recorded in linguistic studies of the subcontinent' (Khubchandani 1983: 8, 9). It is certainly true that in Western countries the notion of the mother tongue is typically conceptualized in the singular, and it would, therefore, be only prudent to reckon with the possibility that such a preconception may impregnate scholarly views, even where the plurality of languages and their influence on each other are at issue.

10.5 Conclusions

Like clouds, languages are ever-changing systems. In this chapter we have discussed some of the implications of this view with respect to integrating foreign elements into a language and separating languages one from the other. For the better part of the last half-century, the language sciences have tried to come to grips with various practices observed in multilingual settings that a theory that conceptualizes language as an autonomous, clearly delimited system must abstract from or treat as abnormalities. Sociolinguists have increasingly directed their attention, at the level of individual speakers, to the complexity of linguistic repertoires and various degrees of bilingual competence that defy traditional classifications. At the level of languages, sociolinguists have studied contact-induced language change, new forms of mixing, borrowing, and transfer. As a result, the fact that languages and their speakers are not just locally rooted entities, but also elements of a global system, has come into the foreground. The example of two very distant languages, Tetum and Frisian, has shown that words can travel around the world on intricate and sometimes unexpected routes, changing as they do so. Their speakers, likewise, cross borders. How they change along the way, separate and integrate into new social systems is the subject of the next chapter.

Problems and questions for discussion

1. How do news broadcasters in your language/country pronounce names of foreign dignitaries? Do they make an effort to approximate the original pronunciation, or do they use spelling pronunciation? Is there a general tendency?

2. Can you think of a universal language resource dictionary that encompasses the words of all languages of the world? In the networked world, is this an achievable project? Make an educated guess about the order of magnitude of such a universal dictionary.

3. **'Džíny, hamburgry, and komputry: is Czech under threat from English?** 'English is attacking Czech from all sides', one newspaper columnist recently despaired, while others talk of Czech's 'battle for survival' in a world in which ever more English is spoken. From terms like 'setobox', 'vygooglovat', and 'mobil' on the one hand to words like 'sorry', 'byzy', and 'lůzr' on the other, English does seem to be making an impact on today's Czech. But are these English borrowings really a threat to the Czech language, or do they enrich it instead? (Radio Praha 9 July 2009). Discuss this question.

4. An excerpt from the plaque inscription at the entrance of the language monument dedicated to Afrikaans reads as follows:

Afrikaans is the language that connects Western Europe and Africa....But what we must never forget is that this change of country and landscape sharpened, kneaded and knitted this newly-becoming language....Our task lies in the use that we make and will make of this gleaming vehicle.

   What does this tell you about the development of a language and the idea of a language as the result of deliberate work?

5. What is the etymology of English 'sine', and what does it tell us about language contact?

Further reading

Haspelmath, Martin and Uri Tadmor (eds). 2009. *Loanwords in the World's Languages: A Comparative Handbook*. Berlin: De Gruyter.

Nortier, Jacomine and Bente A. Svendsen (eds). 2015. *Language, Youth and Identity in the 21st Century. Linguistic Practices across Urban Spaces*. Cambridge: Cambridge University Press.

Palmer, Deborah K. et al. 2014. Reframing the debate on language separation: Toward a vision for translanguaging pedagogies in the dual language classroom. *The Modern Language Journal* 98: 757–72.

11

Integration and separation

Society

11.1 The world today

Two countervailing tendencies characterize our time, the emergence of a unified global information space fuelled by fluid communication flows across national borders and increasing heterogeneity and fractures inside each nation. Driven by trade, information exchange and disparities of wealth and resources, population dynamics change the demographic composition of many countries and with it the meaning of the egalitarian ethos grounded in the French and American Revolutions of the eighteenth century, which for a long time seemed so indisputable, even though it has not led to an egalitarian world order. Inequality between nations and within many nations is more pronounced than ever, and as a consequence the international order is coming under pressure. The 'end of history' has not arrived yet (Fukuyama 1992), nor have national boundaries become meaningless with the onset of the global information society, as French diplomat Jean-Marie Guéhenno (1993) predicted; but great changes are sweeping around the world, affecting societies and their languages. Some of the parallels that are discernible already are summarized in Table 11.1 which will guide us through this chapter.

Table 11.1 Common aspects of society and language in the world today.

	Society	Language
Territoriality	Nation state	National language
Code of conduct	Law	Grammar
Essentialism	A race, a people Ethnic group	A language Ethnic language
Ideology	Ethnic cleansing, xenophobia	Purism, identity
Migration	Population flows	Lexical flows
Contact	Crossbreed	Loanwords
Segregation	Ghetto, separate registration	Loanword dictionary
Fusion	Mixed community	Multi-ethnolect
Minority protection	Political representation	'Mother tongue' education
Stratification	Social class, ethnic hierarchy	Sociolects, ethnolects
Integration	Degrees of ethnic incorporation	Scale of adoptability
Globalization	Liberal capitalism	Lingua franca English

11.2 Territoriality

You cannot come and go as you like. Nomads are not supposed to exist anymore.[1] You need a passport and a permit to stay. This is so patently obvious that it rarely warrants discussion, although it is the cornerstone of the contemporary international system. Territoriality is its foundation. There is no state without a territory and (almost) no territory that is not under the sovereignty of a state, or claimed by a state. Where anarchy rules, we have become accustomed to speak of 'failed states', 'a situation where the structure, authority (legitimate power), law, and political order have fallen apart and must be reconstituted in some form' (Zartman 1995: 1), a situation where the state is incapable of sustaining itself and no authority is able to provide minimal functions for

---

[1] In marginal territories like the steppes of Kazakhstan and Mongolia, the Amazonian rainforest, the Sahara, and the Canadian Arctic, among others, nomads still live. Because there is very little research, exact numbers are hard to obtain. Estimates range between 10 million and 30 million people worldwide. As part of its long-standing literacy campaign, UNESCO maintains a 'Use of Radio in a Nomadic Education Programme' (http://www.unesco.org/uil/litbase/?menu=4&programme=18).

the wellbeing and security of the population. Because the territoriality of the political order is commonly taken for granted and hardly ever called into question, it makes us forget that human history is the history of migration (Cohen 1995). In the course of the twentieth century on the back of two world wars, the European idea of nationhood became the universal model of political organization. Initially the language-based nation was largely fictitious, since there were virtually no mono-lingual/monoethnic states in Europe, but the political elites successfully imposed their language on ever wider parts of the population, and many minorities assimilated through institutional coercion or more or less voluntarily, 'pleased to see their children educated in the language of modernity' (Mann 2005: 59). Mann refers here to France where the state was particularly successful in framing the 'patois'—all languages of France other than French—as languages of backwardness, but in his lengthy study of ethnic conflicts he shows that 'linguistic cleansing' was a constitutive part of nation state-building almost everywhere.

The territory-bound state with its dominant language was exported to non-Western countries (Badie 2000), and it is only against the back-drop of the universalization of this political model that the concept of societal multilingualism unfolds its full meaning as a counterpoint to state monolingualism. Language is part of the political order and, from a social point of view, cannot be dissociated from the institutional structures and political jurisdictions that determine the identity and order within their confines.

Thus, every person belongs to a state (has a citizenship), is obliged to abide by its law and entitled to lay claim to the services it provides. Those who do not fit this pattern are highly marked exceptions. The Convention relating to the Status of Stateless Persons[2] that the UN adopted in the wake of the Second World War, only reconfirms the exceptionality of the status of these persons, currently estimated at some 10 million. Not being fully integrated, like migrants, and many of them are migrants, they are considered a challenge to state authority. The UN High Commission for Refugees has established a regime for the protection of stateless persons and sponsored a Convention for the Reduction of Statelessness (1961), testifying to the fact that deprivation of citizenship is considered a disadvantage rather than a privilege

---

[2] UN High Commissioner for Refugees (UNHCR), *Handbook on Protection of Stateless Persons*, 30 June 2014, available at: http://www.refworld.org/docid/53b676aa4.html (accessed January 2017).

(which, if not in theory, in reality of course it is (Sawyer and Blitz 2011)). And while statelessness may be a plight, the situation of the literally countless people who are not supposed to be where they are is just as precarious. Called 'clandestine', 'irregular', 'illegal', 'unauthorized', or 'undocumented', the number of these immigrants is very hard to estimate, precisely because they are not supposed to exist.[3] Their existence, however, is living proof of the contradictions between the global powers of liberal capitalism to which we are all exposed and the institutions of political action which remain by and large tied to the nation state.

11.3 Code of conduct

The law as a constitutive part of the state is inevitably framed in a literary language, which in many cases is sufficient without any explicit provision to bestow official status on that language. The nation state has a national language, and although, as discussed in Chapter 8 above, the correlation is far from a one-to-one match, it is widely seen as a matter of course. Hence the correspondence between law and grammar.[4] While human beings are equipped with a natural sense of fairness and justice as well as the inborn faculty to acquire language, they are not born with a civil code and a reference grammar hard-wired in their brain; rather they need to be instructed that casting more than one ballot constitutes punishable voter fraud and that they should ask, 'whom (not who!) should I vote for?' For the statutes and regulations of the law governing the conduct of individuals in a society in order to secure order and justice, as well as the rules of grammar and spelling governing proper linguistic usage are embedded in historically contingent cultural traditions. Both kinds of rules are enshrined in codes and enforced through various institutions. Societal investment in these institutions—the legal system and the educational system—can be very substantial, which partly explains why these codes tend to be conservative rather than adjust quickly to changing circumstances. It also explains the variable effectiveness of these institutions in different environments.

---

[3] See CLANDESTINO, a database on irregular migration at: http://irregular-migration. net/(accessed January 2017).
[4] The association of law and grammar is very old indeed. One of the oldest known law codes, the Babylonian Code of Hammurabi, dates from 1754 BCE, at which time grammatical terminology for Babylonian was likewise firmly established (Jacobsen 1974).

The (often enough) forced importation of Western institutions in non-Western countries has frequently engendered conflict and continues to do so, as Western laws, property rights and taxation systems cannot always be reconciled with traditional values and customs. In postcolonial situations where both codes were borrowed, the conjunction of the normative instruments of law and grammar creates systems of meanings that differ from their models. The rule of imported law and the dominance of the imported language are among the most durable legacies of colonialism, but detached from their source both codes take on forms of their own. Just as people speaking English, Spanish, and Portuguese throughout the world when indigenized increasingly speak different Englishes, Spanishes, Portugueses, Western penal and civil codes are selectively adopted, modified, and implemented differently in non-Western countries. Ideally, indigenized institutions by way of modifications and adaptations to local conditions contribute to social order, peace, and the welfare of the people, but there is also a dark side to it. New hierarchies of groups and languages evolve and with them new risks of discrimination and conflict.

11.4 Essentialism and ideology

The crux of a code of conduct is to *set* rules rather than just *describe* regularities. Essentializing the population (citizenry, ethnic nation) and the language in question in terms of fixed identities is a predictable corollary. That 'our law' and 'our language' must be defended against infiltration, exploitation, and abuse is, perhaps, not a necessary consequence but certainly a possible one. Purism with regards to language, as discussed in the previous chapter, corresponds to xenophobia, ethnic cleansing, and other forms of exclusion and discrimination, on the social level. Accommodating outsiders thus becomes a challenge which cannot be ignored in the modern state.

Citizenship tied to a nation state is a consequence of today's international order which carries with it the need to establish categories, for people as well as for languages, that allow unequivocal allocations. In order to have an existence for state authorities, an ethnic group must be recognized as such and its language, too, rather than as a dialect of another. There are, for example, only so many languages in which passports are issued, and wherever they are issued in more than one language, it is for symbolic or ideological reasons, as in Bosnia and Herzegovina where passports are in Bosnian, Croatian, Serbian, and English, in New Zealand (English and Māori), the Special Administrative Region of Macau (Chinese, Portuguese, English), among others. Passports of EU member states bear all of the official languages of the EU, another token of the commitment to the privileged status of national languages (cf. Chapter 6).

The hierarchies brought about by the reification and essentialization of the European national languages and their communities of speakers are difficult to reconcile with the mandated equality of all citizens, the cornerstone of democratic government. The 'natural' (organic) as opposed to the republican conception of the State and people is particularly prone to fuelling ethnic strife, witness many recent conflicts in post-Soviet republics and the successor states of Yugoslavia. No sooner had they been established, than controversies about language privileges broke out (Bremmer and Taras 1997; Pupavac 2006; Kamusella 2016). Both the Soviet Union and Yugoslavia disintegrated into multiple new ethnonational states. However, attempts to reduce conflict potential by secession and creating smaller states has proved illusory time and again, both inside and outside Europe, because populations are no more immutable systems than languages. As Habermas put it, 'the diversity of cultural lifestyles, ethnic groups, faiths and worldviews is increasing. There is no alternative to it, except at the normatively insufferable price of ethnic cleansing' (Habermas 1996: 142). This is widely accepted by intellectual and political elites, although not necessarily heeded in practice.

In postcolonial countries, the importation of the European ideology of the national language, which came along with that of European institutions, often had disruptive effects, as for instance in Myanmar. During military rule from 1962 to 2011, Burmese, the L1 of some 60 per cent of the population (South and Lall 2016:), was made the sole language of the state. This policy, especially the assimilationist education system it legitimized, was contested by many of Myanmar's minorities and became a core element of prolonged armed ethnic conflicts. Summarizing the effects of the education policy, in a 2011 report UNESCO characterized the school system in Myanmar as 'a vehicle for social division' through imposing a dominant language on all pupils, regardless of their mother tongue (South and Lall 2016: 135). In other words, the system replicated the educational policies of European countries a century earlier—except that in the meantime UNESCO had adopted the (again European) idea that mother tongue education is good for children (UNESCO 1953, 2003).

Whether or to what extent the demand for mother tongue education is a genuine concern of the groups in question or a catalyst and rallying point for conflicts springing from other sources is difficult to sort out, because of the way ideologies work. Once implanted, they make you see the world differently. Under colonial rule, language became an issue only in the early decades of the twentieth century when Burmese nationalists posited a rivalry between English and Burmese, as Buddhist monastic education lost ground to English-medium schools. Other languages were not part of this confrontation. But once Burma/Myanmar had become an independent nation state with a national language, the pleas for Burmese not to be sidelined by English were turned around in favour of other vernaculars and directed against Burmese. The Rohingya people, whose Indo-Aryan language is unrelated to Sino-Tibetan Burmese, have for many years been embroiled in this conflict. Oppressed and marginalized as Muslims in a Buddhist society, many of them live in camps and are denied the right to a proper education in their language. After the end of military rule in 2014, even democracy champion and Nobel Laureate Daw Aung San Suu Kyi favoured a Burmese and English language-oriented education policy for the whole country. Since this policy can easily be portrayed as disadvantaging ethno-linguistic minorities, the conflict continues. In sum, the national language ideology was brought to Myanmar from Europe, but the notion that ethnolinguistic minorities are deserving of protection did not come with it. In Europe, too, it must not be forgotten, this idea took root and became politically effective only after a long period of coercive and/or voluntary assimilation when the ideological winds had shifted and indigenous minorities were no longer perceived as posing a threat to national integration. It was only after the Second World War that the ideology of a homogeneous populace in combination with the principle that in a democracy the *whole* people must rule began to be translated into operative measures of minority protection and representation (see section 11.8 below). This was a logical consequence of the national language ideology which, among other things, includes the idea that vernacular (mother tongue) education as opposed to education in an imperial or religious language, is expedient to the intellectual development of the child.

11.5 Migration

If in most developed countries autochthonous minorities are no longer seen as challenging the State, immigrant minorities are, notably with regard to the question of mother tongue education. As population flows across and within national borders have soared, this is a pressing question. Over the past quarter of a century, the number of international migrants almost doubled (Table 11.2). The total of about 250 million (2016) or 3.5 per cent of the world population does not seem immense, but considering that this amounts to the populations of France, UK, Italy, Spain, and Portugal put together it should be clear that it is not a minor problem. In addition, there are an estimated 38 million internally displaced persons forced to flee their homes by conflict and violence (iDMC 2015). Two thirds of all international migrants in 2015 resided in Europe (76 million) and Asia (75 million) (UN 2016).

While the bulk of migration is from south to north, migration flows and migratory patterns have diversified greatly in recent decades. As a result of increasing international trade, economic expansion, widening economic disparities, and the greater availability of information, migratory movements are becoming more complex, posing new challenges for countries of destination, their institutions, and societies. World system theorists, critical economists, and transnationalists argue that the world, its population as a whole, and the global division of labour should be the units of social analysis, rather than the society and the state (Blitz 2014: 14). In view of the ongoing population shifts, the idea that a state should be built on a homogeneous nation is being called into question by scholars as well as by advocates of cosmopolitanism who reject as anachronistic, and actively undermine, national borders, emphasizing freedom of movement as the most basic of human rights (Bauböck 2009). The argument for open borders and free international migration has to contend with claims to the protection of national interest, com-

Table 11.2   International migrant stock (millions).

1990	2000	2010	2015
154.2	174.5	220.7	244.5

Source: https://www.oecd.org/els/mig/World-Migration-in-Figures.pdf.

munity rights, and community identity which because rather than in spite of increasing international migration are growing stronger rather than weaker. Mother tongue education for migrants is, therefore, often a contentious political issue, and where it has a place in the school system it is usually considered a concession rather than a matter of course.

The structures that regulate population flows and lexical flows, enforcing normative categories, legitimate membership and exclusion are deeply entrenched, especially in the countries of the North that receive the majority of international migrants. Attachment to parochial culture, the local state, and fellow citizens, which is mediated through nothing more than through the shared language, has gained political traction in many liberal democracies, expelling the Enlightenment project of a *république du genre humain*[5] that recognizes only a global citizenship to the realm of fantasy, much more so in fact than that of a world dictionary and a global republic of letters.

The analogy of migratory patterns of words and people should not be overstretched; words still move across borders more easily than people. Yet certain parallels cannot be overlooked. Both kinds of flows are, if not entirely determined, heavily influenced by economic factors. Both flows meet with resistance and various measures 'to stem the tide', whether that be on the part of the authorities, in the form of building fences, detention centres, more rigid immigration regimes and language protection laws, or whether it be on the part of civil society, by hostile initiatives directed against foreigners and foreign words. Both foreign people and words are subject to assimilation pressure, while not all 'foreigners' are treated alike. Rather there is selective acceptance and much discrimination between those who are welcome and those who are not. In many countries, language tests in the national or dominant language are part of the immigration regime (Extramiana and van Avermaet 2010; Barni 2012). You can greatly improve your chances of being granted permission to settle in Québec if you demonstrate 'an advanced intermediate level of oral French',[6] to mention but one example. In the age of increasingly pluralistic societies, national borders and national

---

[5] The title of a 1793 book by Jean-Baptiste du Val-de-Grâce, baron de Cloots, *Bases constitutionelles de la république du genre humain*, which was one of the first treatises to promote the idea of global citizenship and discuss its legal implications.

[6] Immigration, Diversité et Inclusion Québec: https://www.immigration-quebec.gouv. qc.ca/en/immigrate-settle/temporary-workers/stay-quebec/application-csq/workers-peq/ language-requirements.html (accessed January 2017).

citizenships may seem outdated, but language, the key marker of the nation state continues to be utilized for the political purposes of defining membership and channelling migration flows, in Québec as in many other places.

11.6 Contact

In response to swelling migration flows, language requirements for citizenship have been institutionalized or toughened in many countries (see Chapter 8),[7] but proficiency in the language of the target country does not imply that immigrants abandon their L1 any more than that they renounce their religion. Migration, therefore, implies contact, of people and of languages, again with variable consequences, such as hybridization, loanwords, permanent residents, and return migrants. Whether and how quickly these interlopers will be transformed into unmarked words and naturalized citizens, respectively, depends on cultural traditions, on relative distance, as well as on the immigration regime and the language regime locally in force. For administrative and scientific purposes classifications come to bear on the basis of which people and words are separated and ranked, for instance with regards to immigration or visa status, whether a person is a speaker of language X or Y, and whether a lexical item should be included in the general dictionary or segregated into a loanword dictionary. In this way it is possible to assess the contact situation by counting migrants and lexical items, or this is what administrators would like to believe. However, as Busch (2016) has demonstrated, there are good reasons to distrust census data and statistics about languages and speakers because the categories that are applied are often inaccurate or ad hoc. One example Busch cites of a language to which Austrian authorities allocate speakers is 'Indic', which presumably refers to anything spoken by people originating from the Indian subcontinent. It is not just ignorance that upsets reasoned allocations to languages and ethnicities, but also the association of languages with territories and the administrative need to draw sharp lines where there are none. The case of Slovenian in Austria illustrates. Recognized as one of six ethnic languages by the Austrian constitution, Slovenian is also a language of former Yugoslavia and in Austria, there-

---

[7] See this chapter's internet companion page for examples.

fore, belongs to two different categories. To complicate matters further, some Austrian-Slovenians self-identify as speakers of *Windish* and as such fall into a residual category, not being counted as Slovenian speakers. In addition to the confusion created by different names there is the problem of various degrees of proficiency and bilinguality which are statistically non-existent. Unambiguous classifications of languages and affiliations of speakers to languages are created for the sake of statistical uniformity and clarity. Busch goes a step further arguing that 'the process of naming and counting led to the creation of ethnic identities and categories, but reduced or prevented social permeability and mobility' (Busch 2016: 15).

Regardless of their proficiency in German, statistically Slovenian speakers in Austria fall into three categories as former Yugoslav citizens (Slovenian nationals), recognized minority language speakers, and none of the above, Windish not being an official category. Clearly, such a classification is little more than a rather arbitrary administrative exercise that does not reflect the reality of Slovenian speakers in Austria most of whom use both Slovenian and German proficiently in their daily lives. On the linguistic level, the contact between Austrian German and Slovenian is marked by similar difficulties, as many words such as *ro:batn* 'drudge' (>*robot*), *schapm* 'beat', and *tscherfln* 'shuffle', have been borrowed and borrowed back, sometimes repeatedly, making any attempt at classifying them as German or Slovenian look arbitrary (Pohl 2007).

While the Slovenian–Austrian contact situation creates classificatory problems for Austrian authorities and lexicographers, the situation is no less complex across Austria's southern border in Slovenia. Declaring independence from Yugoslavia, the state of Slovenia constituted itself as an ethno-political construct in 1991. As one of the Socialist Republics of Yugoslavia, Slovenia had pursued a policy of ethnic homogenization strengthening the Slovene majority. In the newly independent state which was founded with the aim of EU membership and therefore accompanied by vocal commitments to pluralistic democracy, these tendencies degenerated into outright xenophobia and ethno-nationalism directed in particular against 'Southerners' from other former Yugoslav republics. Slovenian, the sole official language, and the Roman Catholic heritage were the central elements enlisted to define the new nation. For the autochthonous minorities of speakers of Hungarian and Italian as well as migrants from the south, this made conditions to participate 'in Slovenian society...considerably harder' (Blitz 2014: 149). Slovenia is a mini-state with a population smaller than cities such as Lisbon, Manchester, or Tel Aviv, but not too small to indulge in the exclusion of others.

11.7 Segregation and fusion

The national language is a code that permits citizens to understand each other and is therefore regarded as a prerequisite for social integration and an egalitarian politics of solidarity, but it does not eliminate heterogeneity and hence the pretext for discrimination in society. Most Austrian Slovenes live in the border province of Carinthia. Regionally segregated to some extent, they are bilingual, speaking both Slovene and German. While their bilingualism does not cause any practical problems and never has, its public display has often met with resistance by right-wing political parties and individuals. As mentioned in Chapter 7, bilingual signage has been the symbolic battleground of identities and local meanings, inviting vandalism motivated by and giving expression to ethnic politics. This is a common phenomenon in areas and urban districts where indigenous or migrant minorities concentrate (Rubdy and Ben Said 2015). Bilingual signs are viewed by the majority as claims to a space where, in the eyes of nationalists, visual communication should be reserved for national authorities (e.g. Figure 11.1). Invading it is taken as indicating refusal to assimilate to the 'nation', that is, to the majority and, therefore, unacceptable. In a majority–minority situation, language in public places is the most obvious manifestation of hierarchical relations making it a critical site of conflict and resistance.

Many indigenous minorities have a segregated place within a nation state; immigrants often do not, unless they join their own ethnic group that already has established itself locally in the target country. Rather, their very presence constitutes a denial of homogeneity and the hermetic nature of political and geographical barriers. The experience of migration has familiarized them with transnational orders of information and communication that are in stark contrast to the local order of communication centred upon the local language. But the relevant institutions of political action remain tied to the nation state, which at times of great affluence and labour shortage in rich countries was diagnosed

Figure 11.1   A protest against bilingual signage in Carinthia, Austria: Die Ortsschilder i**h**n Unterkärnten werden **D**eutsch geschr**i**ben ('Town signs in Lower Carinthia are written in German'). The author's proficiency in German is limited, as appears from three spelling mistakes (in bold) in the sentence. (Photograph © Christian Berger, with kind permission.)

as moribund many times over. Nowadays the nation state is celebrating a formidable revival wherever you look in the world of rich countries.

Of course, today's migrations to the prosperous countries of the world do not leave their societies untouched. It is migrants who initiate the gestation of new kinds of community by crossing physical and mental boundaries and living the possibility of fusion. Without them there would be no multi-ethnolect (cf. above section 10.4), no mixed neighbourhoods, and no new forms of creolization in the former colonial mother lands. It is migrants like the Turkish-German writer Feridun Zaimoglu who demonstrate the possibility of conceiving of plural and mutable identities:

Still the false idea of two cultural blocks that clash. Either in this one or in that one, or getting thrashed between them. I have never felt like a commuter between two cultures. I never had an identity crisis either. Rather, I knew that there are many realities, not just a German one.[8]

Not that this is universally welcomed. In the age of navigation apps, conflicts about bilingual road signs seem like remnants from another era, but they are not. They embody the simultaneous existence of territorial provincialism and extraterritorial cyberspace that characterizes the present. Out of it perpetual tensions arise between segregation and fusion, for not everyone agrees with Haruki Murakami's claim, directed at the Japanese government, that by excluding outsiders, 'eventually we just hurt ourselves'.[9] The age of global navigation is at the same time the age of 'the clash of civilizations' (Huntington 1996), as war has been renamed.

Contact-induced fusion changes social conduct, habits, and living practices, or what Bourdieu (1984) called 'habitus', that is, historically shaped dispositions that guide current practices. The advantage of Bourdieu's concept is that it is not categorical and permanent, but allows for change over time, or suddenly under unexpected circumstances. Although migrants have personally experienced diversity and interaction across boundaries that does not mean they do not cling to notions of perennial difference. In their new environments they often get reinforced in such attitudes. Second-generation immigrants in particular respond to assimilation pressure and discrimination by reconstructing traditions and identities framed in terms of pristine culture, language, and religion. In the receiving societies they meet with similar attitudes that presuppose a native culture and language that must be shielded against external influence. Unrealistic as these attitudes are, they inform the mutual insistence on difference, reinforcing tendencies of separation and segregation on both sides.

By way of justifying the expectation for immigrants to adjust, discourses about immigration in the West, in addition to practical considerations, tend to refer to the universality of Western values in which Western culture and Western law are grounded. However, Wallerstein has a point when he says that 'there is nothing so ethnocentric, so particularist, as the

---

[8] Immer noch die irrige Idee von zwei Kulturblöcken, die aufeinanderprallen. Entweder da drin oder dort drin oder dazwischen zerrieben. Ich habe mich nie als Pendler zwischen zwei Kulturen gefühlt. Ich hatte auch nie eine Identitätskrise. Ich wusste vielmehr, dass es nicht nur eine deutsche, sondern viele Realitäten gibt. Interview with Feridun Zaimoglu, *Der Spiegel*, 2000, 47: 68.

[9] Haruki Murakami, Acceptance speech at Denmark's Hans Christian Andersen Literature Award for 2016, 31 October 2016.

claim of universalism' (Wallerstein 2006: 40), for it is a delusion to think that the question of values could be dissociated from the question of power. Whatever negates or challenges the present world order, including the legitimacy and efficient functioning of the nation state, will be suppressed, likely with reference to universal values. The multiformity of the human race cannot very well be denied; however, in the political science literature, the question of whether the recognition of difference should be limited to individuals or extend to groups is hotly debated (e.g. Benhabib 2002; Kymlicka and Patten 2003). While the theoretical discussion goes on, a casual walk through almost any sizeable town in the developed world makes it abundantly clear that groups distinguished by culture, language, and religion do exist and that propelled by the dialectic dynamics of fusion and segregation they show no signs of dissolving. Hence the need to produce not just a theory but a practical modus vivendi that reconciles the recognition of difference with a politics of integration and solidarity. So far, the most common answer found in liberal democracies consists in the adoption of minority protection legislation.

11.8 Minority protection

The rediscovery of diversity in Western countries came from the basis of well-established nation states and after a long period of assimilationist policies. The 1948 Universal Declaration of Human Rights in Article 2 expresses the principle of non-discrimination, mandating that:

Everyone is entitled to all rights and freedoms set forth in this Declaration, without distinction of any kind, such as race, colour, sex, language, religion, political or other opinion, national or social origin, property, birth or other status. (Universal Declaration of Human Rights, Article 2)

This is one of the earliest mentions of language in the context of international anti-discrimination provisions and, accordingly, it is regularly referred to in later legal instruments. It is a 'negative right' in that it seeks to protect individuals from discrimination without implying any 'positive rights' which impose obligations on states. Only as recently as the 1990s was it realized that in order to eliminate discrimination the traditional 'difference blind' model of equality—which stresses shared civil rights rather than shared cultural roots—had to be supplemented by a 'difference aware' model of equality which implies affirmative measures of recognition and official support for minorities. While race, religion, and gender played a prominent role in early anti-discrimination discussions, language also became increasingly topical in a substantial literature (e.g. Skutnabb-Kangas and Phillipson 1995; de Varennes 1996; May 2012).

It is now generally accepted that a liberal democratic order should not be built on a crude majority principle which forever condemns minorities to a marginal position. Instead, suitable measures should enable minorities' participation in social life without having to forfeit their language, culture, or religion. However, with regard to language there are many unresolved issues. One legally very complex question, when considering linguistic minorities, is whether the rights and obligations placed on states are in respect of languages or of their speakers. There are two different arguments in support of these positions (Dunbar 2001). The first refers to the dignity of the individual person. The mother tongue is said to be an integral part of the individual's identity and as such is protected by the Universal Declaration of Human Rights. The second argument considers every language and beyond that linguistic and cultural diversity as a value in itself, deserving of protection in the best interest of humankind. Who, then, is the beneficiary of whatever specific rights are based on these principles? In the first case, it is the individual; but if, in the second case, the beneficiary is humankind, the principle is no more than a well-meant declaration of intent. It is hard to imagine how it could become the object of litigation in a national court. Should any state be held responsible for sustaining the world's linguistic diversity? If so, by whom? While there are various international legal instruments pertaining to language[10] they remain toothless without national legislation derived thereof.

As for the beneficiaries of positive rights, a third position (between the individual and humanity) is that minority groups should be entitled to rights. However, this requires dealing with the vexing problem that the concept of 'minority'[11] is not well-defined in international law

[10] See companion internet page.

[11] Discussing problems of comparing countries by ethnic fractionalization and cultural diversity, Fearon (2003: 200) argues that 'no plausible definition of "ethnic group" will by itself imply a unique list of groups for a country.' In other words, there is an inevitable element of arbitrary demarcation and classification. Notwithstanding this caveat, Fearon (2003) constructs a useful index of cultural fractionalization using distance between languages as a proxy for the cultural distance between groups in a country.

(Thornberry 1997). Moreover, there is no agreement among legal scholars whether group rights exist (Wellman 1995: 157–77). States have found a way around this problem by enumerating the minorities on their territory, rather than laying down a definition of 'minority'.

Academic discussions have moved in the same direction. For example, in her theory of language regimes which is designed to balance collective equality and communicative efficiency, Liu defines 'a system of communication as a "language" if and only if it is considered as one by the relevant state' (Liu 2015: 7). This abstraction enables her to develop a model for weighing the costs and benefits of empowerment versus disenfranchisement of language groups within the framework of a nation state. However, for practical purposes this model is not satisfactory, since the principles on which 'the relevant state' recognizes a language not only vary from one state to another, but in many instances are exactly what is being contested. As an example, consider the controversial status of Sylheti in the Indian state of Assam before and after the Bangladesh War of 1971 which brought many refugees to Assam. The state authorities of Assam categorize Sylheti as a variety of Bengali, while many Sylheti speakers emphasize the differences with Bengali pressing the case to have it recognized as a language in its own right (Bhattacharjee 2013). A similar example is the development of written Cantonese as documented by Snow (2004) and its status in Hong Kong and Guangzhou where many want it accepted as a language, while the Chinese government considers it as a dialect that must not interfere with the nationwide spread of Putonghua (Mandarin) (Liang 2015).

A common distinction states make is between 'traditional' or 'autochthonous' minorities and 'immigrant' minorities, granting various privileges to the former, but not to the latter. Such a distinction is hard to justify theoretically, yet it is very common for practical reasons and as a measure to defend the supremacy of the national language. Equally problematic is the distinction between 'regional minority languages'—for example Frisian in the Netherlands—and 'non-territorial languages'—for example Romani.[12] Like stateless people, stateless languages require

---

[12] 'Discrimination against Romani children in education is multifaceted. Romani children are either disproportionately placed in schools designed for pupils with "mild mental disabilities" or relegated to Roma-only classes and schools. Those attending mixed mainstream schools often face unbearable bullying and harassment' (Amnesty International 2015).

special treatment, recognition, and protection which, however, is rarely reflected in legislation.

Part of the problem lies in the fuzzy nature of the concepts mentioned in this discussion: 'minority', 'language', and 'dialect', in particular. The difficulties they pose for the language of law indicate the limitations of a rights-based approach to the protection of linguistic minorities. Social negotiation may be more promising, although the nation state is institutionally as firmly established as it is ideologically rooted. Nation states are obviously the principal agents of creating minorities, 'traditional' and 'immigrant' alike. No minority without a majority. And, as Eriksen (1993: 125) has remarked, 'the agenda of cultural rights is a recent one in world politics'. In the context of a world system composed of nation states, minority protection inevitably regulates the relationship between a dominating group and dominated groups within the framework of national law. It must not compromise national cohesion or appear to threaten civil loyalty to the state. Because this keeps minorities in a situation of relative powerlessness, transnational networks have become increasingly important in their struggle for survival.[13] Yet, binding international laws remain few, affording minorities little leverage to improve their position in the social stratification order.

11.9 Stratification

While it is sometimes debated whether social class in the sense of inherited distinctions and advantage is still a relevant social structuring principle, there is no doubt that ethnicity has become a dimension of stratification in developed countries. The question is how it affects the social system. Each country blends social class, ethnicity, language, and religion in distinctive ways to build a stratified order. Colonial regimes put one ethnic group at the top of the social hierarchy which was characterized by strict divisions and the absence of a common language, culture, or shared values. In the former colonial mother lands which in one form or another embrace both recognition of plurality *and* equality as a political idea, social relationships have become more complex. The dominant status of European natives and their languages remains, but

---

[13] See this chapter's internet companion page for international organizations and platforms dedicated to minority issues.

the egalitarian ethos that grants the same civil rights to all citizens and residents and outlaws many forms of discrimination leaves little room for ideological justifications of unequal treatment. Yet, the ethnification of social class is a form of inequality observed in many Western countries (Beck and Sznaider 2006). It is reflected, albeit often in contorted ways, in a hierarchy of languages (cf. Chapter 7). As Sen (1992: 23, 24) has shown, equality can be interpreted in many different ways. However, in the modern nation state it has never been interpreted as referring to languages.[14] Instead, the expanding linguistic diversity brought about by immigration is seen as undercutting the basis of the homogeneous nation state because not all immigrants meet the expectation that they would swiftly switch to the dominant language or at least become proficient in it. Studies suggest that if immigrants have low proficiency in the dominant language this has negative effects on their employability and earnings (Chiswick and Miller 1995; Dustmann and van Soest 2002). There should, therefore, be strong incentives for immigrants to learn the dominant language. However, opportunities to do so may be limited. Moreover, the negative effects of low language proficiency are moderated for immigrants in markets with large numbers of highly educated speakers of the immigrants' first language, such as Spanish in Miami (Lewis 2013).

The relationship between immigration, language proficiency, and economic opportunity is therefore a complex one, giving rise to new ethnic and linguistic hierarchies whose particulars must be established for every country separately. To the extent that these new hierarchies become entrenched over generations, they are seen as endangering social harmony. As one social demographer put it, 'when democratic societies acquire multiple cultures [through immigration, F.C.], new wedges may be driven into the social structure' (Coleman 2006: 426). This assessment betrays a concern about rising levels of diversity suggesting that democracy is possible only in a relatively homogeneous society. To be sure, as a result of the capitalist mode of production, in the developed countries there is a strong correlation between economic inequality, social stratification, and linguistic hierarchies. The unresolved question with regards to language is whether the 'new wedges in

---

[14] Canada may come to mind as an exception; however, the Anglophone majority granted nationwide recognition of equality of status to French, but not to autochthonous minority languages.

the social structure' can be eliminated by improving the educational opportunities of migrants, supporting more multilingualism and bilingual education, or by insisting on linguistic assimilation. As discussed in section 11.8, current conceptualizations of democracy do not favour the suppression of indigenous minorities by the majority, while at the same time, continuing immigration makes it more difficult to justify different policies for indigenous and migrant minorities. The tensions between immigration-induced diversity and stratification and the cherished principle of equality thus become a major challenge for social integration.

11.10 Integration

When the incorporation of words from other languages into the dictionary is called 'naturalization', as quoted in section 10.2, we may take this as an indication that the analogy of language and society relative to the foreign is not ill-conceived. Since language is the quintessential expression of the social, this is not surprising. If words are to be incorporated into another language, they must be adapted to its grammatical structure. Similarly, if foreigners are to be incorporated into a social body, they must adapt to its habitus. This is a gradual process rather than an abrupt shift, as transpires from the fact that it is a reasonable question to ask *how* foreign a person or a word is, which calls for an answer of gradual intensity rather than categoricity, depending on relative distance (of cultures and languages) and length of time.

Handelman's typology of ethnic incorporation summarized in Table 11.3 offers a model for applying the language/society analogy to integration. It can be read, from right to left, as a developmental scale. A community identified by an ethnic ascription whose members interact along ethnic lines in goal-oriented ways and have a territorial base is more closely-knit than one whose members are recognized solely by ascription. Think of Chinatown as an example of the first kind and former French President Nicolas Sarkozy, the son of Hungarian immigrants, as an example of the second kind. Associating with their ethnic group may have a practical function for migrants who thus keep their ethnicity alive, while others decide or take advantage of the opportunity to assimilate quickly, being recognizable by name only, or not even that, witness many immigrants who change their name to be less conspicuous or more easily integrated.

Table 11.3 Don Handelman's (1977) typology of ethnic incorporation.

	Category	Network	Association	Community
Standardized ethnic ascriptions	X	X	X	X
Interaction along ethnic lines		X	X	X
Goal-oriented corporate organization			X	X
Territorial base				X

Source: Adapted after Eriksen (1993: 44).

In Handelman's typology, individuals who belong to a community that demonstrates all four of the listed criteria (the rightmost column) are thought to be least integrated in the receiving society, and those identified as foreign origin only by an ascription are the most integrated. The simplest model is that of a container into which an external element must be fitted in such a way as to become structurally and behaviourally indistinguishable from the elements already contained within it. (The habitus in the container does not change.) A more sophisticated approach, sometimes associated with the concept of inclusion as opposed to integration, allows for the possibility of mutual influence. While the element to be integrated must be modified in one way or another, it also has an effect on its environment, such that we may reasonably ask what lexical borrowing does to a language and what immigration does to a society. The emergence of 'multi-ethnolects' discussed in Chapter 10 is an illustrative example. In like fashion, the ethnic composition of many urban environments has changed significantly in a short period of time with various consequences for social stratification, the labour market, and demographic behaviour, for example. The two sides of the process and its bi-directionality thus come into sharper profile. There is, on one side, a society and a language and, on the other, an individual and a word, calling for a twofold comparison. Societies and languages are more or less hermetic, and individual people and linguistic patterns may be more or less malleable.

In the previous chapter, we have seen that integration into another language is easier for some linguistic patterns than for others (e.g. lexical items vs. phonemes). Haugen (1950: 225) furthermore discusses a 'scale of receptivity' of languages. Based on the relative homogeneity of their vocabularies, he makes a threefold distinction between homogeneous, amalgamate, and heterogeneous languages. In the light of the Max Planck Institute's World Loanword Database (Haspelmath and Tadmor 2009), this distinction still holds up. For example, with a level of only 2 per cent, Mandarin has the lowest ratio of loanwords of all forty-one languages studied, while English is at the other end of the scale with 42 per cent. How loanwords are identified and classified may be debatable, but the general principle of the variable receptivity of languages is quite persuasive.

Can we compare this model with the typology of ethnic incorporation? According to the Global Migration Database of the United Nations Population Division,[15] the ratio of the foreign-born population in 2015 was 0.1 per cent in China, at the bottom of the list of most populous countries, and 13 per cent in the UK, number 6 on the same list (Figure 11.2). These numbers suggest at least a parallel worth exploring. What social integration means in practice differs from one society to another, and any correspondence between social and linguistic incorporation of foreign elements will be subject to historical distortion, because the movements of words and people cannot be assumed to be in synchrony, nor are other variables, such as GDP, likely to have the same effect on lexical and population flows. Yet, intuitively some countries are more receptive towards migrants than others. 'Classic' immigrant countries such as Australia and the USA used to be more hospitable to immigrants than states based on ethno-nationalism, but there is no guarantee that this will be so forever. Relative wealth, politics, public sentiment, demographic change, and the international environment can all affect a country's immigration regime. An important question then is how to explain why the relative receptivity of migrants/loanwords differs between countries and why it changes within countries/languages.

The various factors that potentially influence an immigration regime rule out any monocausal explanation. The same can be said of the relative receptivity of a language in Haugen's model. The outcome is always shaped by multiple factors. In our analogy, the point of departure is a

---

[15] http://www.un.org/en/development/desa/population/migration/data/empirical2/index.shtml (accessed September 2017).

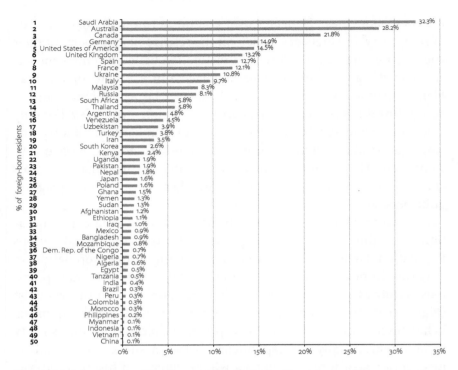

% of foreign-born residents

1 Saudi Arabia	32.3%
2 Australia	28.2%
3 Canada	21.8%
4 Germany	14.9%
5 United States of America	14.5%
6 United Kingdom	13.2%
7 Spain	12.7%
8 France	12.1%
9 Ukraine	10.8%
10 Italy	9.7%
11 Malaysia	8.3%
12 Russia	8.1%
13 South Africa	5.8%
14 Thailand	5.8%
15 Argentina	4.8%
16 Venezuela	4.5%
17 Uzbekistan	3.9%
18 Turkey	3.8%
19 Iran	3.5%
20 South Korea	2.6%
21 Kenya	2.4%
22 Uganda	1.9%
23 Pakistan	1.9%
24 Nepal	1.8%
25 Japan	1.6%
26 Poland	1.6%
27 Ghana	1.5%
28 Yemen	1.3%
29 Sudan	1.3%
30 Afghanistan	1.2%
31 Ethiopia	1.1%
32 Iraq	1.0%
33 Mexico	0.9%
34 Bangladesh	0.9%
35 Mozambique	0.8%
36 Dem. Rep. of the Congo	0.7%
37 Nigeria	0.7%
38 Algeria	0.6%
39 Egypt	0.5%
40 Tanzania	0.5%
41 India	0.4%
42 Brazil	0.3%
43 Peru	0.3%
44 Colombia	0.3%
45 Morocco	0.3%
46 Philippines	0.2%
47 Myanmar	0.1%
48 Indonesia	0.1%
49 Vietnam	0.1%
50 China	0.1%

0%   5%   10%   15%   20%   25%   30%   35%

Figure 11.2   Percentage of immigrant population in the fifty most populous countries, 2015. *Source*: Data from United Nations Population Division.

society and a language, both understood as structured systems. How do they change, or, more pointedly, who makes them change? In the social sciences, this is the question of 'structure or agency', as mentioned in Chapter 1. The two concepts are sometimes seen in opposition to each other. The view that puts structure at centre stage emphasizes the fact that individuals are what they are because society has made them that. This is what having been socialized means. The other view, however, argues that whatever structures there are can be changed, and that change inevitably involves the agency of individuals. Analogously, historical linguistics tried to explain language change as entirely determined by structural forces conceived as natural laws, whereas sociolinguistics reintroduced the individual speaker as an agent of change. Considering externally induced change by migrating populations and linguistic elements, it is, however, particularly clear that in both cases the process is not determined by structure *or* agency, but by the constant interplay of the two.

Relative to the individual, society and language pre-exist, constraining his or her behaviour by limiting, but not eliminating, choices.

In this way, integration is best understood as a dynamic interaction of advancing agency and restraining structure unfolding within the framework of a state and a language both of which, however, are nowadays increasingly subject to external influences.

11.11 Globalization

The ensemble of external influences on societies is summarily referred to as globalization, a development which, strongly reinforced by current communications technology, is beginning to integrate people around the world into a common space of production, division of labour, and information. The great importance of communication in this connection brings one dimension of differentiating languages into sharp focus, their range. It has nothing to do with the relative structural complexity or expressive power of different languages, but very much with what you can do with them. In terms of global migration flows and integration, only very few languages play a role at all, the elephant in the room of any discussion about transnationalism, globalization, and multilingualism being, of course, English. As early as 1993, the editor of the *Wall Street Journal* put it bluntly: 'The world's language is English' (quoted from Huntington 1996: 59). The nature of this source highlights a main reason why this should be so and why it should be important: 'Global business speaks English', to quote another, more recent source (Neeley 2012). Most people do not work for multinational companies, but big business is a major force advancing global integration. Airbus, Daimler-Chrysler, Renault, Samsung, SAP, Technicolor, and of late Volkswagen[16] have adopted an English corporate language strategy, among many others including British and American firms that need not be mentioned in this context.

At the same time, English is also the preferred language of those at the lower end of the global production chain, that is, international labour migrants. Since English is the most widely used foreign lan-

---

[16] Volkswagen decided in 2016 to make English its corporate language, whereupon the *Stiftung Deutsche Sprache* (Foundation German Language) sold its Volkswagen shares in protest, announcing that the words 'Volkswagen' and 'deutsche Sprache' no longer fit together (AFP 23 December 2016).

guage[17] by a large measure, the probability for migrants to speak English is much higher than any other foreign language, regardless of where they come from and where they settle. In his analysis of the world language system, De Swaan sums it up: 'All societies in the contemporary world are being transformed by the spectacular increase in trade, transport and electronic communication. This "globalization" proceeds in English' (De Swaan 2001: 186). Until recently, only high-ranking executives could do their job without regards to the local language, but the number of deterritorialized occupations is growing. Civil society organizations, too, operate more and more in international networks relying on English. Universities in many countries compete in the world market of educational services by offering more courses in English ('International education in XYZ, meet us online!'), while marketing and the infotainment industry drive Americanization forward. These dynamics contribute to the weakening of the nation state as the principal focus of social integration and, by introducing English into the language mix, change the linguistic part of acculturation and integration dynamics.

A global lingua franca clearly facilitates many activities, but even though the alleged 'de-ethnification' of English was considered a major reason why English came to occupy this position (Fishman 1977: 118), English continues to be associated with and criticized because of US domination. Yet, much of the criticism voiced in 'confronting the hydra' of English (Bunce et al. 2016) is articulated in English, which in itself indicates that we are witnessing a mega-shift in the multilingual world that is more easily diagnosed than halted or reversed. In the present context, it alerts us to the fact that the world map of nation states and national languages keeps changing.

11.12 Conclusions

In this chapter, we have explored the conceptual parallel of society and language as ever-changing integrative systems, always subject to the

---

[17] Secondary speakers of English outnumber native speakers by a factor of four, a ratio matched only by French, but on a much smaller scale (according to *The Statistics Portal*, 1,500 million speakers of English compared to 370 million speakers of French (2016 data)) (https://www.statista.com/statistics/266808/the-most-spoken-languages-worldwide/ (accessed September 2017)).

tension between structure and agency. The global reach of commodity, financial, and labour markets has led to intensifying pluralism in many contemporary societies. Some of the causes and consequences of this development have been explored, special attention being paid to the opposing forces of social integration and segregation. Driven by flagrant economic inequality that no longer remains hidden anywhere in the world, migration is beginning to change the demographic composition of prosperous countries on the ground, while ever more economic activity migrates to non-territory-bound spaces. The nation state is caught in the middle, prompting its representatives to re-assert its indispensability, while the supremacy of the (majority) nation is challenged from below, by new minorities, and from above, by global business. The complex social process through which individuals integrate into a society is affected by these developments which are reflected, however indirectly, in changing language use patterns, notably the concurrent rise of ethno-nationalism and the unchecked advance of English. Since language is part of the global, national, and local power structure, social change will affect linguistic change in one way or another, while changing patterns of language use also have a bearing on social constellations.

Integrating external elements into existing structures has been discussed as processes and political programmes whose investigation is beset by conceptual difficulties on both the social and the linguistic plane. Migratory movements of people and words are taking place at different levels of reality; however, the classificatory problems of separating ethnic groups and languages exhibit a certain parallelism in the fuzziness of the relevant concepts. Contact between migrants and natives affect both linguistic and social systems provoking defensive reactions from those who insist that they are entitled to demand assimilation to 'their' culture, language, and way of life, while the forces of globalization continue to bring about change beyond their control.

Problems and questions for discussion

1. In how many languages are passports issued worldwide, and how is this relevant to the study of multilingualism?
2. What is the difference between a 'difference blind' model of equality and a 'difference aware' model of equality?

3. Where is the analogy of integrating migrants into a society and loanwords into a language valid, and where does it come to its limits? Discuss the question with specific examples.
4. What differences are there between autochthonous minorities and immigrant minorities and their languages, and how are these differences dealt with politically in your country?

Further reading

Beck, Ulrich and Natan Sznaider. 2006. Unpacking cosmopolitanism for the social sciences: a research agenda. *The British Journal of Sociology* 57: 1–23.

Eriksen, Thomas Hylland. 1993. *Ethnicity and Nationalism. Anthropological Perspectives*. London: Pluto Press.

Jordan, B. and F Düvell. 2003. *Migration: The Boundaries of Equality and Justice*. Cambridge: Polity Press.

12

Research methods for investigating multilingualism

Multilingualism has many faces: the child growing up with two languages, the polyglot migrant, the diglossia-practising community, the ethnically diverse market place, the international organization, the multinational company, the cosmopolitan city, the country with more than one official language, the World Wide Web as an evolving extraterritorial space in which a multiplicity of languages are used, competing with each other. In view of the diversity of these phenomena, one may ask with some justification whether they constitute a proper research field with its own theories and methods. To be sure, a unified theory of multilingualism does not exist, nor do we have a standardized methodology or a generally agreed upon canon of methods. But the literature on methodological questions with regard to multilingualism research is vast, too extensive indeed to even attempt a review. This short chapter is therefore limited to pointing out some general principles about how to do research on multilingualism and a few select references, in addition to those mentioned in previous chapters.

The most fundamental point is that virtually everything about multilingualism is a matter of degree. Individuals, communities, cities, and nations are *relatively* multilingual, and it is with gradations of multilinguality that many studies in the field are concerned. Language contact and linguistic change likewise take place gradually, involving relative frequencies of lexical items and grammatical constructions in a community. Accordingly, the research tools have to be suitable for measuring, calculating, and depicting gradual shifts and differences of degree. This makes statistical treatment of data indispensable (Brezina and Meyerhoff 2014). A related but conceptually different aspect of multilingualism research is that much of it is comparative in nature: a bilingual child's proficiency at ages 2 and 5; the frequency of use in a given setting of language α versus language β; the probability of the members of a given community in the course of one day interacting with a speaker of another language; the relative similarity/difference of language pairs; the linguistic diversity of two neighbourhoods; the comparative economic returns to minority language knowledge in countries A and B. Keeping these two features—gradualness and comparatism—in mind and without going into detail, the following pages summarize some of the recurrent methodological issues in multilingualism research, proceeding from individual to social studies.

12.1 Individual language behaviour: naturalistic data

On the level of individual language behaviour, psycholinguistic research focuses on acquisition, speech processing, production, and attrition. The many methods that have been developed for these topical subfields can be divided into two types, naturalistic observation and experiments.

The former emphasizes the importance of naturally occurring unsolicited speech that must form the data of any linguistic analysis, regardless of whether they serve the study of grammar, language development, bilingual performance, language impairment, or language attrition. Bilingual speech production can be recorded in many different ways that should be weighed up in the planning phase, since data collection procedures have to be attuned to the questions and claims of the study at hand. What kind of speech—conversation, classroom interaction, interview, campaign speech, etc.; number of participants; the researcher among them or not; face-to-face or telephone; the length of the recording(s)—all of these features have to be considered in advance. Audio- and video-recordings are standard procedures for data gathering used to study the course of development, for instance of children growing up bilingual or of bilingual aphasia patients, but the diary method of documenting observations about the research setting, the subjects and external influences may still be a valuable supplement. Portable, unobtrusive recording devices are nowadays readily available. (The smaller and easier to hide these devices have become, the more important it is to abide by the ethical standards of research including human participants.) Since the publication of Hatch and Lazaraton's (1991) useful research manual, electronic information technology has had a huge impact on the development of new methods of data collection and analysis, both online and offline (e.g. Sekerina et al. 2008; McEnery and Hardie 2012).

Once recorded, speech data must be organized in a corpus and administered for further reference. Technology has enabled the creation of many digital spoken corpora, which are beginning to have an influence on how linguistic analysis is carried out and what it can accomplish (Ruhi et al. 2014). For the time being, however, the transcription of speech data remains indispensable for analysing languages. Reliable speech recognition software that automatically produces a correct transcript does not yet exist, not even for the most intensely researched languages. This is so for the same reason why language is such a complex and fascinating object of investigation. In actual use it is continuous, often blurred, inarticulate, tinted by accents, hoarseness, lisps, and other peculiarities; variable in volume, velocity, and many other ways. These chacteristics do not usually hinder people, who can parse and understand utterances correctly, but to machines and algorithms they pose huge difficulties. Transcribing recorded data therefore remains the researchers' painstaking job. They have to resolve early on how fine-grained the transcription should be for the purpose of the investigation and accordingly settle on a [nærəʊ fəʊˈnɛtɪk trænsˈkrɪpʃⁿn], a /brɔːd tranˈskrɪpʃn/, or use standard orthography. Is a transcription for content in a linear format sufficient, or does the project at hand require the representation of turn taking, overlap, hesitation, backchannel signals, laughter, and pauses (measured in milliseconds) in a musical score format? Organizing and archiving transcripts are the subsequent steps for which helpful software packages have been developed and can be found online (MacWhinney 2000).

Concerning recording and transcription, there is no difference in principle between monolingual and multilingual production, but the analytic organization of recorded speech including elements of multiple languages may pose methodological problems, such as those of differentiating languages. Error analysis (Richards 1997; Poulisse 1999) and the study of code-switching (Gardner-Chloros 2009) are two major sources of knowledge about how two or more languages coexist and interact in the mind. It is assumed that both mistakes and switches do not occur randomly, and that the patterns that can be found allow us to draw conclusions about how the linguistic resources of bi-/multilingual speakers differ from those of monolinguals. What can be inferred about the mental lexicon from word substitutes of language Y in a verbal exchange conducted in language X? Is a switch from X to Y indicative of dominance? On the basis of recorded samples, questions of this kind can be posed with some prospect of finding an answer.

A major methodological question concerns the availability of data that are amenable to quantitative processing. Qualitative data gathered through careful observation are of great interest in themselves and can provide the basis for developing a heuristic, but they do not allow for easy generalizations. Quantitative methods help researchers discover tendencies and patterns and test linguistic hypotheses (Johnson 2008).

12.2 Individual language behaviour: experimental data

Naturalistic data are a necessary resource for investigating multilingual communication, but many questions about the acquisition, development, proficiency, and choice of language(s) cannot be answered on the basis of recordings alone. A second line of approach consists of experimental research. In the event, the focus of any project is on a particular linguistic phenomenon, and the experimental design includes techniques of eliciting speech that can be used as data for studying it. While in observational research a theory may emerge from the data, in experimental research a theory-informed hypothesis or at least a theoretically motivated research question precedes data gathering. The collection of articles by Blom and Unsworth (2010) offers a synopsis of recent experimental methods in language acquisition research.

Due to the professionalization of language education, the demand for foreign language skills from companies, and the pressure exerted on schools to optimize their performance, language testing has become a veritable industry prompting the construction of a range of methods in bilingual education and language learning (Nunan 2008). Since experimental research relies on elicited as opposed to spontaneously occurring speech, elicitation techniques are of crucial importance. They should produce suitable data for answering the research question, but should not produce the research question and thus lead to circular results. A general caveat here is that experimental psychometric research often studies problems that do not exist outside the laboratory. For instance, isolating syntactic structures and testing the comprehension of isolated words are unnatural tasks. Similarly, there is nothing in everyday communication that corresponds to naming tests, the recognition of non-words and word skeletons, or forced code-switching at fixed intervals. Many experiments comprise measuring response times in carrying out predefined tasks, such as picture matching, object naming, enumerating cognate words, translating, etc. These measurements show how fast a subject or groups of subjects execute a task, but what else do they show? Can a shorter response time be equated with anything but a shorter response time, for instance, the relative complexity of the underlying mental operation or the relative competency of the subject? If such inferences are intended, they must be well-founded theoretically.

Of course, tests comprising response time measurements are in no way illegitimate, but substantiated theoretical motives for performing them must be given, explaining why the testing of often very unnatural tasks may offer indirect insights into unobservable cognitive skills and should justify conclusions about the reality of mental language processing, speech production, causes of errors, etc. Since different elicitation techniques and tests can lead to different conceptualizations and interpretations of data, reflecting the risks of bias inherent in the experimental design is a crucial part of the research process. Because the majority of all psycholinguistic research about multilingualism is nowadays experimental in nature, this is particularly important.

Research that tries to minimize control over data by relying entirely on observing unsolicited speech bears the risk of failing to perceive interesting phenomena simply because they do not occur in the corpus. By contrast, experimental research that maximizes control over data by making subjects pass judgements and carry out highly specific tasks risks constructing a world that is far removed from reality. Many researchers in the social sciences therefore advocate a multi-method approach. In doing research about a phenomenon such as multilingualism with so many variables that defy abstraction and streamlining, it is advisable to combine information of different sorts: meticulous case studies, large datasets that reveal statistical patterns, and experiments with selected subjects (Berthele 2012).

12.3 Societal multilingualism

While the methodological problems of investigating societal multilingualism differ from those of studying multilingual individuals, the preference for integrating qualitative and quantitative approaches is the same. The qualitative–quantitative opposition is sometimes portrayed as an unbridgeable gap. Qualitative researchers have denigrated quantitative work as pursuing the unobtainable goal of objective knowledge and producing numbers without real meaning instead, whereas quantitative researchers have denied that subjective observation, especially introspection, count as data at all. However, both positions are untenable. Qualitative ethnographic descriptions and quantitative surveys are not incompatible but can supplement each other fruitfully. Case studies can make statistical patterns more meaningful, and quantitative survey data can confirm that a case study captures features that characterize a community and is, therefore, of general interest, rather than being a negligible outlier. Like individual linguistic proficiency, the linguistic repertoire of a community is ever-changing and thus always characterized by fuzzy sets of more or less competent speakers of more or less clearly distinguished varieties. Given such a mutable object of investigation, using data of both kinds can only be helpful. The obvious difference between individual and societal multilingualism research is that the former seeks to understand how languages are arranged in the mind, while the latter is interested in how languages are arranged in a community. There is methodological overlap, for instance with regard to transcription techniques, but there are also characteristic differences.

12.4 Fieldwork

The study of societal multilingualism concentrates on speech behaviour in different social domains, such as family, school, work, market place, and worship. Empirical methods used in sociological and ethnographic field work, such as social surveys and interviews, are widely used (Mallinson et al. (2013)). If the researcher is not a member of the community under study, the first steps are getting access to that community, establishing a relation of trust, identifying interview partners, and selecting informants and research sites. Many of the factors that influence the choice and use of languages in multilingual communities can be established by means of standard instruments of social research. Methodological preparation for fieldwork includes designing interview schedules and questionnaires for relevant communities, such as, indigenous minority communities, immigrant communities, mixed communities, endangered language communities, etc.

Inter communal relationships constitute a major subfield, research on language attitudes forming an important approach (Garrett 2010). In terms of values, social stereotypes, ideologies, and prejudices, language attitudes influence the way people use language and relate to each other. Methodologically language attitudes are challenging, as they are not always directly accessible and cannot, therefore, be ascertained by means of direct questions in interviews with individual speakers or large-scale surveys. Although learned through socialization, they operate subconsciously. Various techniques are designed to unveil the structures of prejudice and discrimination, some of which raise issues of research ethics, as they deceive subjects or keep them in the dark about the true purpose of the questions they are asked to answer (Tileagă 2016). There are, of course, also overt attitudes that are of interest for societal multilingualism research, such as attitudes towards bilingual education held by teachers, parents, and other relevant groups. For example, that parents from different ethnic and socioeconomic backgrounds favour or reject bilingual education programmes to greater or lesser degrees can be assessed by means of standard polling techniques.

How multilingualism evolves in a community is another important question researchers address, paying much attention to minority languages (see Chapter 8 for different types of minorities). Methods for assessing the linguistic vitality of languages, dialects, and other varieties play an important role. Fishman's (1991) 'Graded Intergeneration Disruption Scale' is a widely used methodological tool that puts observable changes of the language use of different age cohorts and/or generations at the centre. Along similar lines, target groups of speakers are questioned, for instance, about which language they 'like best', 'use most', and 'find beautiful'. Divergent results, such that a majority of speakers find their heritage language most beautiful, but use the dominant language most frequently and in most domains, are indicative of ongoing changes in language choice patterns. Marked differences in the language preferences of old and young cohorts of respondents may point to imminent language shift, although that is not necessarily so, as individual language use patterns may change without reflecting community change over time. As is true of social research in general, such changes are hard to predict and ascertain in the absence of quantitative data, which, however, does not mean that qualitative methods cannot contribute valuable information. Rather, in-depth expert interviews, group discussions, and participant observation are often decisive prerequisites for determining relevant research questions and developing suitable interview schedules and questionnaires, and help to interpret survey results. Participant observation is a method that strives to integrate the researcher into the researched community. For instance, researchers may work part-time as teachers in a bilingual school and in this way become more natural/less conspicuous members of the institution they want to study and thus reduce the risk of influencing the object of investigation, that is, the 'observer paradox'.

12.5 Secondary data

Not every research project works with original data. Fieldwork and surveys are expensive and time-consuming, while many datasets are available for studying questions not anticipated when the data were first collected as well as for probing earlier findings. When used for such purposes by researchers who did not collect the data, it is called 'secondary data'. A common source of secondary data is census records. Many national censuses contain questions relating to language. If conducted at regular intervals, the demographic strength of ethnolinguistic groups and other features of multilingual societies can be traced over time. Secondary data of this kind is not just convenient, but offers information that may not otherwise be available. Yet, census and other datasets must be used with circumspection, as they may be based on assumptions not shared by the researcher. Census data of different countries are notoriously difficult to compare because questionnaires are prepared differently; because individual questions are phrased differently; or because of different national/cultural traditions of opinion polling. As we have seen repeatedly, 'language' is defined variously by different people and for different purposes, and these differences may inadvertently or deliberately inform the treatment of linguistic issues in census questionnaires. If, for example, a questionnaire includes a question about the respondent's mother tongue which allows for an answer in the singular only, little can be learnt about the reality of societal multilingualism. Generally speaking, when using secondary data, one has to make sure that the purpose for which it was originally collected is compatible with one's research design, which cannot be taken for granted.

12.6 Written language data

Long shunned by many sociolinguists, language in its written form has of late become an object of multilingualism research prompting the development of suitable methods. Three subfields of investigation stick out, linguistic landscape, social media, and corpus linguistics.

Linguistic landscape. Initially, research on the display of multiple languages in public spaces was largely descriptive and limited to notable case studies, but it quickly became clear that if the linguistic landscape is to be studied as a reflection of a society's multilingualism qualitative accounts must be backed up by quantitative data (Backhaus 2007; Shohamy and Gorter 2009). A single memo in language X in a shop window says nothing about the incidence of X as a minority language in the community, while just counting occurrences of X may also be insufficient for explaining the function and social significance of X in that community. Hence, once again a multimethod approach is favoured. Since collecting data for linguistic landscape research is very different from collecting speech data, methodological questions revolve around the classification (what to collect), recording (how to record), limitation of the field (where to collect), and systematization (how to organize) of data. The temporal difference between ephemeral speech and durable writing poses additional methodological questions because the individual items that together constitute a linguistic landscape are indexed to different periods of time.

Social media. The relative permanence of writing also has a bearing on the study of CMC which, thanks to the technology-induced expansion of communication in social media has become a new field of multilingualism research. Social media data are easily accessible and used as a valuable source of insight about language use and social behaviour. However, while various techniques of systematizing and analysing them have been proposed (e.g. Kim et al. (2014) and Jurgens et al. (2014) for Twitter), not least by social media providers, a comprehensive methodology for examining the multilingualism of social media is still missing (Bolander and Locher 2014). This is so because of the great variety of language use online (one-way or two-way transmission; received in real time or with delay;

265

accessible to third parties; restriction on length, to mention just the most obvious aspects of diversity). The multimodality of CMC raises the problem of suitable transcription/visualization schemes for the analysis and presentation of data. Yet another aspect of uncertainty with respect to methods has to do with research ethics. While there is intense awareness of the new challenges posed by the blurring and redefinition of the public–private distinction CMC has brought about, ethical norms for doing research in this field are still evolving.

Corpus linguistics. Digital technologies have changed the way we use writing and how to investigate written language. The digitization of literature and other written material has produced huge text corpora that are computer-searchable. Methods summarily referred to as corpus linguistics are a response to these innovations which are beginning to have repercussions for language enquiry in various sub-disciplines including the study of multilingualism (Baker 2010; Schmidt and Wörner 2012). For instance, by screening corpora for changing frequencies of occurrence of words and syntactic structures over time, the process of incorporating loanwords and the influence on grammatical patterns by other languages can be studied in ways that were much more laborious or outright impossible for researchers whose data were limited to concordances and the texts they could process by reading them. Some corpus linguists argue that the changes brought about by corpora consisting of many millions of words are not just quantitative in nature, but that quantity here translates into quality in as much as the corpus perspective may push our understanding of language further in the direction of a statistical as opposed to a categorical conception. In any event, corpus linguistics puts research about the evolution, differentiation, and relative proximity of languages on a new footing. And while modern linguistics in general and sociolinguistics in particular used to prioritize spoken language, corpus linguistics puts written language centre stage.

The potential applications of corpus-based approaches to the study of multilingualism are many. One is in political science where Average Distance of Language (ADOL) has recently been used as a proxy for the relative ethnic fractionalization of countries (Ginsburgh and Weber 2011), the conflict potential within countries, and the Human Development Index of countries (Laitin and Ramachandran 2016). ADOL is a notion proposed in the 1950s by linguist Joseph Greenberg (1956) to determine the linguistic diversity of a given population (cf. Chapter 1). He realized that localizing languages in genealogical family trees and measuring linguistic diversity depend on how different varieties/languages within a society were coded. Since corpus linguistic tools were not available at the time, using these tools to further develop Greenberg's diversity index would be a promising application. It is now generally understood that for distinguishing languages from each other social factors, notably public opinions and speaker attitudes, weigh heavier than 'purely linguistic' factors such as the number of nodes between languages on a genealogical family tree. Research on digital corpora could advance our knowledge of how linguistic and social factors interact over time to reduce or increase the distance between languages/varieties.

12.7 Concluding remarks

Research methods are an important part of the scientific process, yet the attention methodology receives is very uneven. At one time, many scholars engage in debates about *how to do* research. Defending or debunking a method therefore seems more important than whatever findings researchers produce. At other times, methodological questions recede into the background, as most researchers in a field concur on the most significant insights that have been achieved, are committed to a shared set of assumptions and agree on the models to further improve on these insights. They find themselves in a phase of what Kuhn (1970) called 'normal science', working to resolve problems defined by the model, solvable by known rules and techniques. However, discoveries, inventions, and extraordinary new ideas may call received beliefs into question and produce problems the proven model cannot handle or that its conceptual apparatus cannot even begin to tackle. (For example, if the model is predicated on the idea that language change follows natural laws, there is no place for studying the potential impact of writing on language, because writing is an artefact.)

Technological innovation can also lead to paradigm shifts. With the advance of big data into ever more research fields, we are witnessing such a shift at the present time, but we are so close to it that the consequences are still hard to assess. Digital tools bring change to all spheres of life, including the scientific enterprise of analysing them. As a result, methods once again appear on the scientific agenda. In this chapter, I have just hinted at some of the changes affecting our conception of language, how languages are acquired and used, and how they affect each other, in individual minds and in communities.

What lies ahead in terms of new models for investigating multilingualism it is still too early to say. Causal relationships between technology, social circumstances, and methodology are not always direct or obvious, but that massive amounts of data and vast statistical computations change the way we look at things is undeniable. To what extent the market-oriented approach that has driven the development of digital technology and algorithms these past two decades will dominate everyday life and scientific enquiry is a question which, at this point, divides optimists—who prefer to believe that we still have a say in this—and pessimists—who see this possibility fading away fast. Things are very much in flux, with regard both to how speakers make language choices and to how researchers investigate these choices. Research methods are inevitably subject to influences of the societies in which they are developed and to which they are applied. Reflecting on this contingent interaction, rather than accepting it as given, is indispensable for carrying the quest for knowledge further. Today, it seems crucial to try to be masters rather than slaves of big data, that is, not to allow the methods we use to be determined entirely by the enormous possibilities offered by digital tools. What we want to know about language in a world in motion and how we conduct research should be a matter of our decision rather than one of following paths outlined by algorithms.

Multilingual corpora

Canada Multilingual Spoken Corpus http://www.coelang.tufs.ac.jp/multilingual_corpus/ca/index.html?contents_xml=top&menulang=en

Center scientific da cumpetenza per la plurilinguitad, Database for the European Charter for Regional and Minority Languages: http://www.centre-plurilinguisme.ch/centre-de-documentation/webguide/documents/database-for-the-european-charter-for-regional-or-minority-languages.html#.WGEjo1wfRxc

Corpora of the Research Centre on Multilingualism (University of Hamburg) https://www.corpora.uni-hamburg.de/sfb538/en_overview.html

Corpus.byu.edu http://corpus.byu.edu/

National Institute for Japanese Language and Linguistics Corpora and Databases https://www.ninjal.ac.jp/english/database/

National Research Centre for Foreign Language Education, Beijing Foreign Studies University http://www.bfsu-corpus.org/channels/corpus

Linguistic Data Consortium for Indian Languages: http://www.ldcil.org/

Open source statistics software 'R': https://www.r-project.org/

Online Resources

The online resources listed below include references and links to websites of various institutions and research organizations dealing with languages, from various points of view and for various purposes. They are listed here by chapter, although many of them are pertinent to more than one chapter.

Chapter 1, The polyphonic world

World maps of languages and language families:

http://www.geocurrents.info/cultural-geography/linguistic-geography/
    world-maps-of-language-families
http://www.mapsofworld.com/world-language-map.htm
http://www.unesco.org/new/en/culture/themes/endangered-languages/
    atlas-of-languages-in-danger/
http://wals.info/
http://www.omniglot.com/

Countries and languages

http://www.infoplease.com/ipa/A0855611.html

Languages by number of speakers

http://research.omicsgroup.org/index.php/List_of_languages_by_total_
    number_of_speakers

Chapter 3, Descriptive and theoretical concepts

Office of Management and Budget, US Government, about Standards for the Classification of Federal Data on Race and Ethnicity: https://www.whitehouse.gov/omb/fedreg_race-ethnicity/

The Italian office of statistics, **Istituto nazionale di statistica**, gathers data about non-Italian nationals' mother tongue (madrelingua) http://www.istat.it/it/archivio/129285

The UK Office for National Statistics does not use the term 'mother tongue', but surveys that look at language in England and Wales provide data on the population's 'main language'.

http://www.ons.gov.uk/peoplepopulationandcommunity/culturalidentity/
    language/articles/languageinenglandandwales/2013-03-04

The German office of statistics, **Statistisches Bundesamt**, uses the term Muttersprache ('mother tongue') for some statistics, but also refers to Sprache des Herkunftslandes ('language of country of origin').
https://www.destatis.de/DE/Publikationen/Thematisch/Bevoelkerung/
MigrationIntegration/Migrationshintergrund2010220147004.pdf?__
blob=publicationFile

Chapter 4, Power, inequality, and language

Maps of the World: World Gross National Income per Capita Map

http://www.mapsofworld.com/thematic-maps/gni-per-capita-map.html

One World Nations Online: Most widely spoken languages in the world

http://www.nationsonline.org/oneworld/most_spoken_languages.htm

The Modern Language Association Language Map of the United States

https://apps.mla.org/map_main

India Languages Map

http://www.mapsofindia.com/culture/indian-languages.html

LanguageHelpers.com: Chinese language facts

https://www.languagehelpers.com/languagefacts/chinese.html

Minority Map and Time Line of Europe

http://mmte.eu/

Power Language Index

http://www.kailchan.ca/wp-content/uploads/2016/06/KC_Power-Language-
Index_May-2016.pdf

Language Conflict and Violence, David D. Laitin

https://www.nap.edu/read/9897/chapter/14

Chapter 5, The polyglot individual

ERIC Digests on Bilingual Education

http://www.cal.org/ericcll/digest/subject.html#bilingual

Centre for Research on Bilingualism, Stockholm University

http://www.biling.su.se/

International Journal of Bilingualism

http://www.ncl.ac.uk/speech/research/ijb.htm

Bilinguisme Conseil

https://www.bilinguisme-conseil.com/

Bilingue per gioco

http://bilinguepergioco.com/2009/10/27/9-passi-per-scegliere-il-proprio-
metodo-per-crescere-un-bambino-bilingue/

Resources for teachers:

http://www.mansioningles.com/

Center for Teaching for Biliteracy

http://www.teachingforbiliteracy.com/

Bilingual and Multilingual Children

http://www.linguistlist.org/~ask-ling/bilingual-multilingual-children.html

Growing up bilingual, online resources for parents and children

http://growingupbilingual.com/resources/

*The Bilingual Pages, a website designed for 'parents and others who are
interested in bringing up children'*

http://www.angelfire.com/ut/henrikholm/bilingual/bilingual01.html

Study.com: Bilingual Education Programmes for Teachers

http://study.com/articles/Bilingual_Education_Programs_for_
Teachers.html

Chapter 6, Multilingual (international) institutions

United Nations, Official Languages

http://www.un.org/en/sections/about-un/official-languages/

Consolidated Version of the Treaty on European Union

http://eur-lex.europa.eu/legal-content/EN/TXT/PDF/?uri=CELEX:12012M/
TXT&from=en

EUR-Lex, Glossary of summaries

http://eur-lex.europa.eu/summary/glossary/glossary.html?locale=en

Europass Language Passport

http://europass.cedefop.europa.eu/it/documents/european-skills-passport/
   language-passport/examples

European Language Equality Network

http://elen.ngo/

Special Eurobarometer 386, Europeans and their Languages

http://ec.europa.eu/public_opinion/archives/ebs/ebs_386_en.pdf

UNESCO: The Mother Tongue Dilemma

http://www.unesco.org/education/education_today/ed_today6.pdf

Chapter 7, Talk of the town: Language in super-diverse cities

Urban population of the world (% of total), World Bank

http://data.worldbank.org/indicator/SP.URB.TOTL.IN.ZS?end=2015&
   start=1960

Victoria Line: London's underground languages as depicted by BBC:

'Central London's linguistic diversity is brought into relief by the map below.
   Along many stretches of the Victoria Line more than 11 different languages
   are listed as a main language by at least 1% of residents.'
http://www.bbc.co.uk/news/resources/idt-1e4fbcb9-5bd6-4e14-adf5-
   bf3ab1ba79bb

How to separate rubbish correctly in twelve languages:

https://www.awista-duesseldorf.de/de/content/Downloads/Downloads.htm
Scroll down to 'Für Privathaushalte', 'Was gehört wohin?'

Kawaski city, multilingual information

http://www.city.kawasaki.jp/shisei/category/60-7-3-0-0-0-0-0-0-0.html

Chapter 8, Multilingual (multiethnic) countries

Department of Statistics Singapore: Population and Population Structure

http://www.singstat.gov.sg/statistics/browse-by-theme/population-and-
   population-structure

The Macro Data Guide—An International Social Science Resource

The Fractionalization dataset was compiled by Alberto Alesina and
associates, and measures the degree of ethnic, linguistic, and religious
heterogeneity in various countries.
http://www.nsd.uib.no/macrodataguide/set.html?id=16&sub=1

Ethnicity and Race by Countries

http://www.infoplease.com/ipa/A0855617.html

The Linguistic Survey of India is part of the Census of India which includes
language data collected and published at the successive decennial
censuses for more than a century.
http://lsi.gov.in/MTSI_APP/(S(cememibrivtsdc455csi5a45))/default.aspx

Australian Bureau of Statistics. Languages spoken at home

http://search.abs.gov.au/s/search.html?query=language&collection=abs&form=
simple&profile=_default_preview

Office for National Statistics: Language in England and Wales: 2011

http://www.ons.gov.uk/peoplepopulationandcommunity/culturalidentity/
language/articles/languageinenglandandwales/2013-03-04

United States Census Bureau: Language Use Census

http://www.census.gov/search-results.html?q=home+language&search.
x=0&search.y=0&page=1&stateGeo=none&searchtype=web&cssp=SERP

Programme for International Student Assessment (PISA)

https://www.oecd.org/pisa/aboutpisa/

World Map of Countries by Age

http://www.targetmap.com/viewer.aspx?reportId=26659

Chapter 9, Diversity in cyberspace: The multilingual internet

International Telecommunication Union

http://www.itu.int/en/ITU-D/Statistics/Documents/facts/
ICTFactsFigures2016.pdf

Internet World Stats, usage and population statistics

www.internetworldstats.com/stats7.htm

Internet Society, Global Internet Report

http://www.internetsociety.org/globalinternetreport/?gclid=
CKOL2Nmqh9ACFakKowodV3ADIw

China Internet Network Information Center

http://cnnic.com.cn

China Academic Journals full-text database

http://oversea.cnki.net.eresources.shef.ac.uk/kns55/brief/result.
  aspx?dbPrefix=CJFD

Learn the Niuean language!

http://learnniue.co.nz/learnniueanlanguage/

Learn Esperanto online

https://www.duolingo.com/course/eo/en/Learn-Esperanto-Online

E@I, a politically neutral organization for intercultural learning

http://www.ikso.net/en/pri_ecxei/index.php

Online dictionaries and thesauri

http://www.refseek.com/directory/dictioaries.html

The polyglot game

https://www.babbel.com/en/magazine/polyglot-game

Chapter 10, Integration and separation: Language

Transliteration schemes

Romanization of Indian languages:
http://www.acharya.gen.in:8080/multi_sys/transli/schemes.php

International Organization for Standardization (ISO)

http://www.iso.org/iso/products/standards/catalogue_ics_browse.htm?
  ICS1=01&ICS2=140&ICS3=10

Bibliography of internationalisms

http://referenceworks.brillonline.com/entries/brill-s-new-pauly/
  internationalisms-ct-e1406440

Chapter 11, Integration and separation: Society

Language requirements for immigration

UK: Prove your knowledge of English for citizenship and settling:
https://www.gov.uk/english-language/overview

Canada: Gouvernement du Canada, Évaluation des compétences linguistiques—Immigrants qualifiés:
http://www.cic.gc.ca/francais/immigrer/qualifie/langues-test.asp
Netherlands: Rijksoverheid (Dutch Authorities): Taal- en inburgeringscursussen in de buurt (language and citizenship courses in the neighbourhood):
https://www.rijksoverheid.nl/onderwerpen/nieuw-in-nederland/vraag-en-antwoord/hoe-kan-ik-de-nederlandse-taal-leren
Federal Republic of Germany: Bundesamt für Migration und Flüchtlinge (Federal agency for migration and refugees): Zertifikat Integrationskurs:
http://www.bamf.de/DE/Willkommen/DeutschLernen/Integrationskurse/Abschlusspruefung/ZertifikatIntegrationsKurs/zertifikatintegrationskurs-node.html
Italy: Ministero dell'Interno, test di conoscenza della lingua italiana (for foreigners living in Italy leagally for five years or more who intend to apply for permanent residency):
http://www.interno.gov.it/it/temi/immigrazione-e-asilo/modalita-dingresso/test-conoscenza-lingua-italiana
France: Citoyenneté française et test TFI pour les immigrants:
http://www.testdenationalite.fr/
Spain: Obtener la nacionalidad española: exámenes CCSE y DELE A2:
http://tlcdenia.es/examenes-nacionalidad-espanola-ccse-dele/

International legal instruments pertaining to language

The Universal Declaration of Human Rights
http://www.un.org/en/universal-declaration-human-rights/
United Nations Declaration on the Rights of Persons Belonging to National or Ethnic, Religious and Linguistic Minorities
http://www.un.org/documents/ga/res/47/a47r135.htm
The European Charter for Regional or Minority Language
https://www.coe.int/en/web/conventions/full-list/-/conventions/treaty/148
Council of Europe: European Convention on Human Rights
http://www.echr.coe.int/Documents/Convention_ENG.pdf
Council of Europe: Convention for the Protection of Human Rights and Fundamental Freedoms
https://rm.coe.int/CoERMPublicCommonSearchServices/DisplayDCTMContent?documentId=0900001680063765
Universal Declaration of Linguistic Rights (Barcelona Declaration)
http://www.linguistic-declaration.org/decl-gb.htm

Minority support initiatives

Minority Rights Group International

http://minorityrights.org/
World Directory of Minorities and Indigenous Peoples
http://minorityrights.org/directory/
Organization for Security and Co-operation in Europe (OSCE)
http://www.osce.org/minority-rights
UN Division for Social Policy and Development. Indigenous Peoples
https://www.un.org/development/desa/indigenouspeoples/
Center for World Indigenous Studies
http://cwis.org/GML/TribalAndInter-TribalResolutionsAndPapers/WCIP.php
Connexions
http://www.connexions.org/Groups/Subscribers/CxG6684.htm

Chapter 12, Research methods for investigating multilingualism

Links to research institutes devoted to or concerned with multilingualism research:

SO 639-1 Codes for the representation of names of languages—Part 1:
    Alpha-2 code
http://www.iso.org/iso/home/store/catalogue_tc/catalogue_detail.
    htm?csnumber=22109
ISO 639-2 Codes for the representation of names of languages—Part 2:
    Alpha-3 code
http://www.iso.org/iso/home/store/catalogue_tc/catalogue_detail.
    htm?csnumber=4767
ISO 639-3 Codes for the representation of names of languages—Part 3:
    Alpha-3 code for comprehensive coverage of languages
http://www.iso.org/iso/home/store/catalogue_tc/catalogue_detail.
    htm?csnumber=39534
ISO 639-4 Codes for the representation of names of languages—Part 4:
    General principles of coding of the representation of names of languages
    and related entities, and application guidelines
http://www.iso.org/iso/home/store/catalogue_tc/catalogue_detail.
    htm?csnumber=39535
The Mosaic Centre for Research on Multilingualism at the University of
    Birmingham,
http://www.birmingham.ac.uk/research/activity/education/mosaic/index.
    aspx
The Babylon Center for the Study of Superdiversity at Tilburg University,
https://www.tilburguniversity.edu/research/institutes-and-research-groups/
    babylon/
The European Bureau of Lesser-Used Languages,

http://eblul.eurolang.net/

The Centro di Competenza Lingue of Libera Università di Bolzano, https://www.unibz.it/it/public/research/languagestudies/default.html

The National Institute for Japanese Language and Linguistics, http://www.ninjal.ac.jp/english/

The Dutch Language Union, http://taalunie.org/dutch-language-union.

Institutions more practically involved in multilingualism are also of interest, e.g. the Tokyo Metro Guide in five languages, http://www.tokyometro.jp/en/tips/guide/index.html

Bildungsportal of German federal state North Rhine Westphalia on bilingual education, https://www.schulministerium.nrw.de/docs/Schulsystem/Unterricht/ Lernbereiche-und-Faecher/Fremdsprachen/Bilingualer-Unterricht/index. html

The Minzu University of China (for ethnic minorities), http://baike.baidu.com/view/8874.htm

The Directorate-General for Translation of the European Commission, http://ec.europa.eu/dgs/translation/index_en.htm,

The Multilingual Counselling Service of the awareness centre, http://theawarenesscentre.com/counselling-and-therapy-services/ multilingual-counselling

European Observatory for Plurilingualism, http://www.observatoireplurilinguisme.eu/index.php?lang=en-us

The Canadian Census Program, http://www12.statcan.gc.ca/census-recensement/index-eng.cfm

The Directorate-General for Translation of the European Commission, http://ec.europa.eu/dgs/translation/index_en.htm,

The Central Institute of Indian Languages (CIIL), http://www.ciil.org/

The Tokyo Metro Guide in five languages, http://www.tokyometro.jp/en/tips/guide/index.html

Bildungsportal of German federal state North Rhine Westphalia on bilingual education, https://www.schulministerium.nrw.de/docs/Schulsystem/Unterricht/ Lernbereiche-und-Faecher/Fremdsprachen/Bilingualer-Unterricht/index. html

The Minzu University of China (for ethnic minorities), http://baike.baidu.com/view/8874.htm

Bibliography

Abutalebi, Jubin, Stefano F. Cappa, and Daniela Perani. 2001. The bilingual brain as revealed by functional neuroimaging. *Bilingualism, Language and Cognition* 4/2: 179–90.

Agirdag, Orhan. 2014. The long-term effects of bilingualism on children of immigration: Student bilingualism and future earnings. *International Journal of Bilingual Education and Bilingualism* 17: 449–64.

Aiden, Erez and Jean-Baptiste Michel. 2013. *Unchartered. Big Data as a Lens on Human Culture.* New York: Riverhead.

Akerlof, George A. and Rachel E. Kranton 2010. *Identity Economics.* Princeton, NJ: Princeton University Press.

Albirini, Abdulkafi. 2011. The sociolinguistic functions of codeswitching between Standard Arabic and Dialectal Arabic. *Language in Society*, 40: 537–62.

Alesina, Alberto et al. 2003. Fractionalization. *Journal of Economic Growth* 8: 155–94.

Alladi, Suvarna et al. 2013. Bilingualism delays age at onset of dementia, independent of education and immigrant status. *Neurology*, 82: 1936.

Alsagoff, Lubna. 2010. English in Singapore: Culture, capital and linguistic variation. *World Englishes* 29: 336–48.

Amaro, Vanessa. 2015. 'We'. 'They' and the spaces in-between: Hybridity in intercultural interactions between Portuguese and Chinese residents in Macau. *Multilingua* 34: 293–318.

Ammon, Ulrich. 2014. *Die Stellung der deutschen Sprache in der Welt.* Berlin: DeGruyter Mouton.

Amnesty International. 2015. Segregation, bullying and fear: The stunted education of Romani children in Europe. https://www.amnesty.org/en/latest/news/2015/04/the-stunted-education-of-romani-children-in-europe/ (accessed January 2017).

Androutsopoulos, Jannis. 2006. Introduction: Sociolinguistics and computer-mediated communication. *Journal of Sociolinguistics* 10/4: 419–38.

Androutsopoulos, Jannis. 2009 'Greeklish': Transliteration practice and discourse in a setting of computer-mediated digraphia. In: Alexandra Georgakopoulou and Michael Silk (eds), *Standard Languages and Language Standards: Greek, Past and Present.* Farnam: Ashgate, 221–49.

Androutsopoulos, J. 2013. Networked multilingualism: Some language practices on Facebook and their implications. *International Journal of Bilingualism*: 19/2: 185–205.

Androutsopoulos, Jannis and Kasper Juffermans (eds) 2014. Digital language practices in superdiversity. Special issue, *Discourse, Context & Media* 4–5: 1–6.

Annamalai, E. 1998. Nativity of language. In: Rajendra Singh (ed.), *The Native Speaker: Multilingual Perspectives*. New Delhi: Sage, 149–50.

Arinze, Cardinal Francis. 2006. *Latin and Vernacular: Language in the Roman Liturgy*. https://www.ewtn.com/library/Liturgy/latinvernac.htm (accessed January 2017).

Athanassiou, Phoebus. 2006. The application of multilingualism in the European Union context. Legal Working Paper Series No. 2. European Central Bank. https://www.ecb.europa.eu/pub/pdf/scplps/ecblwp2.pdf (accessed August 2017).

Auer, Peter. 1999. From codeswitching via language mixing to fused lects. Toward a dynamic typology of bilingual speech. *International Journal of Bilingualism* 3, 309–32.

Aurizi, Federica (ed.). 2011. La Communita Cinese in Italia. http://docplayer. it/11773736-La-comunita-cinese-in-italia-a-cura-di-federica-aurizi.html (accessed August 2017).

Australian Bureau of Statistics. 2009. *A Picture of the Nation: The statistician's report on the 2006 census, 2006*. http://www.abs.gov.au/ausstats/abs@.nsf/mf/2070.0/.

Backhaus, Peter. 2007. *Linguistic Landscapes. A Comparative Study of Urban Multilingualism in Tokyo*. Clevedon: Multilingual Matters.

Backus, Ad. 1999. The intergenerational codeswitching continuum in an immigrant community. In: Guus Extra and Ludo Verhoeven (eds), *Bilingualism and Migration*. Berlin, New York: Mouton de Gruyter, 261–79.

Badie, Bertrand. 2000. *The Imported State: The Westernization of the Political Order*. Palo Alto: Stanford University Press.

Baker, Colin. 2006. Becoming bilingual through bilingual education. In: Peter Auer and Li Wei (eds), *Handbook of Multilingualism and Multilingual Communication*. Berlin, New York: Mouton de Gruyter, 131–52.

Baker, Colin. 2008. Postlude. In: Jasone Cenoz and Durk Gorter (eds), Multilingualism and Minority Languages. *AILA Review* 21: 104–10.

Baker, Colin. 2011. *Foundations of Bilingual Education and Bilingualism*. Bristol: Multilingual Matters.

Baker, Paul. 2010. *Sociolinguistics and Corpus Linguistics*. Edinburgh: Edinburgh University Press.

Bakhtin, Mikhail M. 1935. Discourse in the novel. In: M. Holquist (ed.), *The Dialogic Imagination*. Austin TX: University of Texas Press, 1981, 259–422.

Bamgboṣe, Ayọ. 1998. *Language and Exclusion: The Consequences of Language Policies in Africa*. Münster: LIT Verlag.

Barasa, Sandra N. 2015. *Ala! Kumbe?* 'Oh my! Is it so?' Multilingualism controversies in East Africa. In: Dick Smakman and Patrick Heinrich (eds), *Globalising Sociolinguistics. Challenging and Expanding Theory.* London and New York: Routledge, 39–53.

Barnes, Susan B. 2001. *Online Connections: Internet Interpersonal Relationships.* New York: Hampton Press.

Barni, Monica. 2012. *Diritti linguistici. Diritti di cittadinanza: L'educazione linguistica come strumento contro le barriere linguistiche.* In: Silvana Ferreri (ed.), *Linguistica educativa,* Atti del 55 Congresso della Società di Linguistica Italiana. Rome: Bulzoni, 213–23.

Barni, Monica and Guus Extra (eds) 2008. *Mapping Linguistic Diversity in Multicultural Contexts.* Berlin, New York: Mouton de Gruyter.

Baron, Naomi S. 2008. *Always On. Language in an Online and Mobile World.* Oxford: Oxford University Press.

Bassiouney, Reem. 2009. *Arabic Sociolinguistics.* Washington, DC: Georgetown University Press.

Bastardas-Boda, Albert. 2013. Sociolinguistics: Towards a complex ecological view. In: A. Massip-Bonet and A. Bastardas-Boda (eds), *Complexity Perspectives on Language, Communication and Society.* Berlin: Springer, 15–34.

Bauböck, Rainer. 2009. Global justice, freedom of movement and democratic citizenship. *European Journal of Sociology/Archives Européennes de Sociologie* 50: 1–31.

Baur, Arthur. 1983. *Was ist eigentlich Schweizerdeutsch?* Winterthur: Gemsberg.

Beck, Ulrich and Natan Sznaider. 2006. Unpacking cosmopolitanism for the social sciences: A research agenda. *The British Journal of Sociology* 57: 1–23.

Bekerman, Zvi. 2005. Complex contexts and ideologies: Bilingual education in conflict-ridden areas. *Journal of Language, Identity, and Education* 4: 1–20.

Bel, Germà. 2013. Strangers in our own land. In: Liz Castro (ed.), *What's up with Catalonia? The Causes Which Impel Them to the Separation.* Ashfield, MA: Catalonia Press, 129–33.

Benhabib, Seyla. 2002. *The Claims of Culture: Equality and Diversity in the Global Era.* Princeton, NJ: Princeton University Press.

Bernstein, Basil. 1971. *Class, Codes and Control: Volume 1—Theoretical Studies Towards a Sociology of Language.* London, New York: Routledge.

Berthele, Raphael. 2012. Multiple languages and multiple methods: Qualitative and quantitative ways of tapping into the multilingual repertoire. In: Andrea Ender, Adrian Lehmann, and Bernhard Wälchli (eds), *Methods in Contemporary Linguistics.* Berlin: De Gruyter, 195–218.

Bhatia, Tej K. and William C. Ritchie (eds) 2013. *The Handbook of Bilingualism and Multilingualism.* Second edition. Oxford: Wiley-Blackwell.

Bhattacharjee, Nabanipa. 2013. 'We are with culture but without geography': Locating Sylheti identity in contemporary India. In: Tanweer Fazal (ed.), *Minority Nationalisms in South Asia*. Abingdon: Routledge, 53–73.

Bialystok, Ellen. 2001. *Bilingualism in Development: Language, Literacy and Cognition*. New York: Cambridge University Press.

Bialystok, Ellen, Fergus I. M. Craik, and Morris Freedman. 2007. Bilingualism as a protection against the onset of dementia. *Neuropsychologia* 45: 459–64.

Birdsong, David (ed.) 1999. *Second Language Acquisition and the Critical Period Hypothesis*. Mahwah, NJ: Lawrence Erlbaum.

Birdsong, David. 2005. Nativelikeness and non-nativelikeness in L2A research. *International Review of Applied Linguistics and Language Teaching* 43: 319–28.

Blitz, Brad K. 2014. *Migration and Freedom. Mobility, Citizenship and Exclusion*. Cheltenham: Edward Elgar.

Blom, Elma and Sharon Unsworth (eds) 2010. *Experimental Methods in Language Acquisition Research*. Amsterdam: John Benjamins.

Blommaert, Jan. 2010. *The Sociolinguistics of Globalization*. Cambridge: Cambridge University Press.

Bokhorst-Heng, Wendy D. and Rita E. Silver. 2017. Reconsidering 'pragmatic' choices: Language shift within Singapore's Chinese community. *International Journal of the Sociology of Language* 248: 73–95.

Bolander, Brook and Miriam A. Locher. 2014. Doing sociolinguistic research on computer-mediated data: A review of four methodological issues. *Discourse, Context and Media* 3: 14–26.

Bolt, Gideon. 2009. Combating residential segregation of ethnic minorities in European cities. *Journal of Housing and the Built Environment: HBE*, 24: 397–405.

Bonfiglio, Thomas Paul. 2010. *Mother Tongues and Nations. The Invention of the Native Speaker*. Berlin, New York: DeGruyter.

Bourdieu, Pierre. 1982. *Ce que parler veut dire. L'économie des échanges linguistiques*. Paris: Fayard [English translation: *Language and Symbolic Power*. Oxford: Polity Press, 1991].

Bourdieu, Pierre. 1984. *Distinction: A Social Critique of the Judgement of Taste*. London: Routledge.

Boyd, Danah and Nicole Ellison. 2008. Social network sites: definition, history and scholarship. *Journal of Computer-Mediated Communication* 13: 210–30.

Bremmer, Ian and Ray Taras (eds) 1997. *New States, New Politics: Building the Post-Soviet Nations*. Cambridge: Cambridge University Press.

Brenzinger, Matthias (ed.) 2008. *Language Diversity Endangered*. Berlin, New York: Mouton de Gruyter.

Breton, Roland J.-L. 1991. *Geolinguistics: Language Dynamics and Ethnolinguistic Geography*. Ottawa: University of Ottawa Press.

Brezina, Vaclav and Miriam Meyerhoff. 2014. Significant or random? A critical review of sociolinguistic generalisations based on large corpora. *International Journal of Corpus Linguistics* 19: 1–28.

Brohy, Claudine, Theodorus du Plessis, Joseph-G. Turi, and José Woehrling (eds) 2012. *Law, Language and the Multilingual State. Conference Proceedings of the 12th International Conference of the International Academy for Linguistic Law.* Bloemfontein: University of the Free State.

Browner, Stephanie, Stephen Pulsford, and Richard Sears. 2000. *Literature and the Internet. A Guide for Students, Teachers and Scholars.* New York: Garland Publishing.

Bugarski, Ranko. 2001. Language, nationalism and war in Yugoslavia. *International Journal of the Sociology of Language* 151, 69–87.

Bunce, Pauline, Robert Phillipson, Vaughan Rapatahana, and Ruanni Tupas. 2016. *Why English? Confronting the Hydra.* Bristol: Multilingual Matters.

Bunčić, Daniel. 2016. A heuristic model for typology. In: Daniel Bunčić, Sandra L. Lippert, and Achim Rabus (eds), *Biscriptality. A Sociolinguistic Typology.* Heidelberg: Universitätsverlag Winter, 51–71.

Busch, Brigitta. 2016. Categorizing languages and speakers: Why linguists should mistrust census data and statistics. *Working Papers in Urban Language & Literacies* #189.

Calvet, Louis Jean. 1974. *Linguistique et colonialisme.* Paris: Payot.

Calvet, Louis Jean. 1987. *La guerre des langues et les politiques linguistiques.* Paris: Payot [English translation: *Language Wars and Linguistic Politics.* Oxford: Oxford University Press, 1998].

Calvino, Italo. 1993. *Le città invisibili.* Milan: Oscar Mondadori.

Canagarajah, Suresh. 2011. Translanguaging in the classroom: Emerging issues for research and pedagogy. *Applied Linguistics Review* 2: 1–28.

Canetti, Elias. 1993. *Gesammelte Werke*, vol. 4. Munich: Hanser

Carson, Lorna. 2005. *Multilingualism in Europe. A case study.* Bruxelles: P.I.E.-Peter Lang.

Cartier, Carolyn. 2002. Transnational urbanism in the reform era Chinese city: Landscapes from Shenzhen. *Urban Studies*, 39: 1513–32.

Casebourne, Imogen, Chris Davies, Michelle Fernandes, and Naomi Norman. 2012. *Assessing the accuracy and quality of Wikipedia entries compared to popular online encyclopaedias: A comparative preliminary study across disciplines in English, Spanish and Arabic.* Epic, Brighton, UK. http://commons.wikimedia.org/wiki/File:EPIC_Oxford_report.pdf (accessed August 2017).

Castells, Manuel. 2002. *The Internet Galaxy: Reflections on the Internet, Business and Society.* Oxford: Oxford University Press.

Castells, Manuel. 2010. *The Rise of the Network Society.* Second edition. Chichester: Wiley-Blackwell.

Caubet, Dominique. 2008. Immigrant languages and languages of France. In: Monica Barni, and Guus Extra (eds), 2008. *Mapping Linguistic Diversity in Multicultural Contexts*. Berlin, New York: Mouton de Gruyter, 163–93.

Cenoz, Jasone (ed.) 2008. *Teaching through Basque. Achievements and Challenges*. Clevedon: Multilingual Matters.

Ceramella, Nick. 2012. Is English a killer language or an international auxiliary? Its use and function in a globalized world. *International Journal of Language, Translation and Intercultural Communication*. DOI: http://dx. doi.org/10.12681/ijltic.7

Chaudhary, Shreesh. 2001. Language education, language modernization and globalization. In: C. J. Daswani (ed.), *Language Education in Multilingual India*. New Delhi: UNESCO, 141–85.

Cheshire, Jenny, Jacomine Nortier, and David Adger. 2015. Emerging multiethnolects in Europe. *Occasional Papers Advancing Linguistics* # 33. http://linguistics.sllf.qmul.ac.uk/linguistics/media/sllf-migration/department -of-linguistics/33-QMOPAL-Cheshire-Nortier-Adger-.pdf (accessed July 2017).

Chiswick, Barry R. and Paul W. Miller. 1995. The endogeneity between language and earnings: International analyses. *Journal of Labor Economics* 13: 246–88.

Chomsky, Noam. 1965. *Aspects of the Theory of Syntax*. Cambridge, MA: MIT Press.

Chomsky, Noam. 2012. *The Science of Language: Interviews with James McGilvray*. New York: Cambridge University Press.

Chríost, Diarmait Mac Giolla. 2007. *Language and the City*. London: Palgrave Macmillan Ltd.

Ciscel, Matthew. 2006. A separate Moldovan language? The Sociolinguistics of Moldova's *Limba de Stat. Nationalities Papers. The Journal of Nationalism and Ethnicity* 34: 575–97.

Clyne, Michael. 1991. *Community Languages. The Australian Experience*. Cambridge: Cambridge University Press.

Clyne, Michael. 2000. Lingua franca and ethnolects in Europe and beyond. *Sociolinguistica* 14: 83–9.

Clyne, Michael. 2008. The monolingual mindset as an impediment to the development of plurilingual potential in Australia. *Sociolinguistic Studies* 2: 347–66.

CNNIC. 2016. Statistical Report on Internet Development in China (January 2016). China Internet Information Center http://cnnic.com.cn/IDR/Report Downloads/201604/P020160419390562421055.pdf (accessed September 2017).

Codrea-Rado, Anna. 2014. European Parliament has 24 official languages, but MEPs prefer English. *The Guardian*, 24 May.

Coetzee-Van Rooy, Susan. 2016. Multilingualism and national unity or social cohesion: Insights from South African students. *International Journal of the Sociology of Language* 242: 239–65.

Cohen, Marcel. 1956. *Pour une sociologie du langage*. Paris: Albin Michel.

Cohen, Robin. 1995. *The Cambridge Survey of World Migration*. Cambridge: Cambridge University Press.

Coleman, David. 2006. Immigration and ethnic change in low-fertility countries: A third demographic transition. *Population and Development Review* 32: 401–46.

Cook, Vivian. 2001. Linguistics and second language acquisition: One person with two languages. In: Mark Aronoff and Janie Rees-Miller (eds), *The Handbook of Linguistics*. Oxford: Blackwell, 488–511.

Coulmas, Florian (ed.) 1981. *A Festschrift for Native Speaker*. The Hague: Mouton.

Coulmas, Florian. 2009. Linguistic landscaping and the seed of the public sphere. In: Elana Shohamy and Durk Gorter (eds), *Linguistic Landscape. Expanding the Scenery*. New York and London: Routledge, 13–24.

Coulmas, Florian. 2013. *Writing and Society. An Introduction*. Cambridge: Cambridge University Press.

Coulmas, Florian. 2016. *Guardians of Language. Twenty Voices through History*. Oxford: Oxford University Press.

Crystal, David. 2006. *Language and the Internet*, Second edition. Cambridge: Cambridge University Press.

Crystal, David. 2011. *Internet Linguistics: A Student Guide*. Abingdon: Routledge.

Danesi, Marcel. 2016. *Language, Society, and New Media*. London: Routledge.

Danet, Brenda and Susan C. Herring (eds) 2007. *The Multilingual Internet. Language, Culture, and Communication Online*. Oxford: Oxford University Press.

D'Anieri, Paul J. 1999. *Economic Interdependence in Ukrainian–Russian Relations*. Albany, NY: State University of New York Press.

Darwin, Charles. 1859. *On the Origin of Species by Means of Natural Selection, or the Preservation of Favoured Races in the Struggle for Life*. London: John Murray.

Dasgupta, Probal. 1998. The native speaker: A short history. In: Rajendra Singh (ed.), *The Native Speaker. Multilingual Perspectives*. New Delhi, London: Sage Publications, 182–92.

Daswani, C. J. (ed.) 2001. *Language Education in Multilingual India*. New Delhi: UNESCO.

Davies, Alan. 1991. *The Native Speaker in Applied Linguistics*. Edinburgh: Edinburgh University Press.

Davies, Janet. 2014. *The Welsh Language: A History*. Cardiff: University of Wales Press.

Deboosere, P., T. Eggerickx, E. Van Hecke, and B. Wayens. 2009. The population of Brussels: A demographic overview. *Brussels Studies*. http://brussels. revues.org/891(accessed July 2017).

De Groot, Annette M. B. 2011. *Bilingual Cognition: An Introduction*. New York and Hove: Psychology Press.

De Mauro, Tullio. 2014. *In Europa son già 103. Troppe lingue per una democrazia?* Rome: Editori Laterza.

De Mejía, Anne-Marie. 2002. *Power, Prestige, and Bilingualism: International Perspectives on Elite Bilingual Education*. Clevedon: Multilingual Matters Ltd.

Den Besten, Hans. 2012. *Roots of Afrikaans: Selected Writings of Hans Den Besten*. Amsterdam: John Benjamins.

De Swaan, Abram. 2001. *Words of the World*. Cambridge: Polity Press.

Deumert, Ana. 2004. *Language Standardization and Language Change: The Dynamics of Cape Dutch*. Amsterdam: John Benjamins.

De Varennes, Fernand. 1996. *Language, Minorities and Human Rights*. Leiden: Brill.

De Varennes, Fernand. 2012. Language policy at the supranational level. In: Bernard Spolsky (ed.), *The Cambridge Handbook of Language Policy*. Cambridge: Cambridge University Press, 151–73.

DeVotta, Neil. 2004. *Blowback: Linguistic Nationalism, Institutional Decay, and Ethnic Conflict in Sri Lanka*. Stanford: Stanford University Press.

Dijkstra, Lewis and Hugo Poelman. 2012. Cities in Europe. The new OECD-EC Definition. http://ec.europa.eu/regional_policy/sources/docgener/focus/ 2012_01_city.pdf (accessed January 2017).

Djité, Paulin G. 2008. *The Sociolinguistics of Development in Africa*. Clevedon: Multilingual Matters.

Doğruöz, A. Seza and Ad Backus. 2010. Turkish in the Netherlands: Development of a new variety? In: M. Norde, B. de Jonge, and C. Hasselblatt (eds), *Language Contact. New Perspectives*. Amsterdam: John Benjamins, 87–102.

Dorian, Nancy C. 1980. Language Shift in Community and Individual: The Phenomenon of the Laggard Semi-Speaker. *International Journal of the Sociology of Language* 25: 85–94.

Duchêne, Alexandre and Monica Heller. 2012. *Language and Late Capitalism: Pride and Profit*. London: Routledge.

Dunbar, Robert. 2001. Minority language rights in international law. *The International and Comparative Law Quarterly* 50: 90–120.

Dustmann, Christian and Arthur van Soest. 2002. Language and the earnings of immigrants. *Industrial and Labor Relations Review* 55: 473–92.

Dutton, William H. 2013. *Politics and the Internet*. London: Routledge.

Edwards, John. 1994. *Multilingualism*. London: Penguin Books.

Eisenstein, Elizabeth. 1980. *The Printing Press as an Agent of Change*. Cambridge: Cambridge University Press.

Ellis, Anthony. 2005. Minority rights and the preservation of languages. *Philosophy* 2: 199–217.

Enstedt, Daniel and Enzo Pace (eds) 2015. Religion and Internet. *Annual Review of the Sociology of Religion* vol. 6.

Eriksen, Thomas Hylland. 1993. *Ethnicity and Nationalism. Anthropological Perspectives*. London: Pluto Press.

Ethnologue. *https://www.ethnologue.com/*.

EurActiv.com. 2013. English should be Brussels' official language, Flemish minister says. http://www.euractiv.com/section/languages-culture/news/english-should-be-brussels-official-language-flemish-minister-says/ (accessed January 2017).

European Commission. 2015. Machine Translation Service. http://ec.europa.eu/isa/actions/02-interoperability-architecture/2-8action_en.htm (accessed January 2017).

European Council. N.d. Common European Framework of Reference for Languages: Learning, Teaching, Assessment. Language Policy Unit, Strasbourg. http://www.coe.int/t/dg4/linguistic/source/framework_en.pdf (accessed January 2017).

European Parliament. N.d. *Fact Sheets on the European Union*. Language Policy. http://www.europarl.europa.eu/atyourservice/en/displayFtu.html?ftuId=FTU_5.13.6.html (accessed January 2017).

European Parliament. 2014. Rules of Procedure. 8th parliamentary term. Brussels, July 2014, http://www.europarl.europa.eu/sipade/rulesleg8/Rulesleg8.EN.pdf (accessed January 2017).

Extra, Guus and Durk Gorter (eds) 2008. *Multilingual Europe: Facts and Policies*. Berlin: De Gruyter.

Extra, Guus and Ludo Verhoeven. 1999. Processes of language change in a migration context: The case of the Netherlands. In: Guus Extra and Ludo Verhoeven (eds), *Bilingualism and Migration*. Berlin, New York: Mouton de Gruyter, 29–57.

Extra, Guus and Kutlay Yağmur. 2004. Introduction. In: Guus Extra and Kutlay Yağmur (eds), *Urban Multilingualism in Europe. Immigrant Minority Languages at Home and School*. Clevedon: Multilingual Matters, 1–132.

Extramiana, Claire and Piet van Avermaet. 2010. *Language Requirements for Adult Migrants in Council of Europe Member States: Report on a Survey*. Brussels: Council of Europe. https://ec.europa.eu/migrant-integration/librarydoc/language-requirements-for-adult-migrants-in-council-of-europe-member-states-report-on-a-survey (accessed January 2017).

Fabricius, Anne H., Janus Mortensen, and Hartmut Haberland. 2017. The lure of internationalization: Paradoxical discourses of transnational student mobility, linguistic diversity and cross-cultural exchange. *Higher Education* 4: 577–95.

Fearon, James. 2003. Ethnic and cultural diversity by country. *Journal of Economic Growth* 8: 195–222.

Ferguson, Charles A. 1959. Diglossia. *Word* 15: 325–40.

Fernández, Mauro A. 1993. *Diglossia: A Comprehensive Bibliography, 1960–1990 and Supplements*. Amsterdam, Philadelphia: John Benjamins.

Fidrmuc, Jan and Victor Ginsburgh. 2007. Languages in the European Union: The quest for equality and its cost. *European Economic Review* 51: 1351–69.

Field, Fredric W. 2011. *Key Concepts in Bilingualism*. New York: Palgrave Macmillan.

Filipović, Luna and Martin Pütz (eds) 2014. *Multilingual Cognition and Language Use. Processing and Typological Perspectives*. Amsterdam, Philadelphia: John Benjamins.

Fiorentino, Giuliana. 2006. Dialetti in rete. *Rivista Italiana di Dialettologia* 29: 111–49.

Fishman, Joshua A. 1966. *Language Loyalty in the United States. The Maintenance and Perpetuation of Non-English Mother Tongues by American Ethnic and Religious Groups*. The Hague: Mouton.

Fishman, Joshua A. 1967. Bilingualism with and without diglossia; diglossia with and without bilingualism. *Journal of Social Issues* 23: 29–38.

Fishman, Joshua A. 1968. Some contrasts between linguistically homogeneous and linguistically heterogeneous polities. In: J. A. Fishman, C. A. Ferguson, and J. Das Gupta (eds), *Language Problems of Developing Nations*. New York: Wiley, 53–68.

Fishman, Joshua A. 1977. The spread of English as a new perspective for the study of language maintenance and language shift. In: J. A. Fishman, R. L. Cooper, and A. W. Conrad (eds), *The Spread of English: The Sociology of English as an Additional Language*. Rowley, MA: Newbury House, 109–33.

Fishman, Joshua A. 1983. The rise and fall of the 'ethnic revival' in the USA. *Journal of Intercultural Studies* 4: 5–46.

Fishman, Joshua A. 1991. *Reversing Language Shift*. Clevedon: Multilingual Matters.

Flege, James. 1999. Age of learning and second language speech. In: David Birdsong (ed.), *Second Language Acquisition and the Critical Period Hypothesis*. Mahwah, NJ: Lawrence Erlbaum, 101–32.

Flores, Nelson and Mark Lewis. 2016. From truncated to sociopolitical emergence: A critique of super-diversity in sociolinguistics. *International Journal of the Sociology of Language* 241: 97–124.

Forchtner, Bernhard. 2014. Multilingualism in the European Commission: Combining an observer and a participant perspective. In: Johan W. Unger, Michł Krzyżanowski, and Ruth Wodak (eds), *Multilingual Encounters in Europe's Institutional Spaces*. London: Bloomsbury, 147–69.

Foucher, Pierre. 2007. Legal environment of official languages in Canada. *International Journal of the Sociology of Language* 185: 53–69.

Franceschini, Rita. 2011. Multilingualism and multi-competence. A conceptual view. *Modern Language Journal* 95: 344–55.

Franceschini, Rita. 2013. History of multilingualism. In: Carol A. Chapelle (ed.), *The Encyclopedia of Applied Linguistics*. New York: Wiley-Blackwell, vol. 4, 2526–34.

Franceschini, Rita. 2016. Multilingualism Research. In: Vivian Cook and Li Wei (eds), *The Cambridge Handbook of Linguistic Multi-Competence*. London: Cambridge University Press, 97–123.

Fukuyama, Francis. 1992. *The End of History and the Last Man*. New York: Free Press.

García, Ofelia. 1997. New York's multilingualism: World languages and their role in a U.S. city. In: O. García and J. A. Fishman (eds), *The Multilingual Apple. Languages in New York City*. Berlin, New York: Mouton de Gruyter, 3–50.

García, Ofelia. 2009. *Bilingual Education in the 21st Century: A Global Perspective*. Oxford: Wiley/Blackwell.

García, Ofelia and Li Wei. 2014. *Translanguaging: Language, Bilingualism and Education*. New York: Palgrave Macmillan.

Gardner-Chloros, Penelope. 2009. *Code-Switching*. Cambridge: Cambridge University Press.

Garfield, Leanna. 2016. English is losing its status as the universal languages of the Internet. *Tech Insider*. http://www.techinsider.io/english-is-losing-its-status-as-the-universal-language-of-the-internet-heres-why-thats-a-good-thing-2015-12 (accessed January 2017).

Garrett, Peter. 2010. *Attitudes to Language*. Cambridge: Cambridge University Press.

Gauthier, François, Jacques Leclerc, and Jacques Maurais. 1993. *Langues et Constitutions. Recueil des clauses linguistiques des constitutions du monde*. Québec: Office de la langue française.

Gavrousky, Serge. 1982. Aimé Césaire and the Language of Politics. *The French Review* 56: 272–80.

Gazzola, Michele. 2006. Managing multilingualism in the European Union: Language policy evaluation for the European Parliament. *Language Policy* 5: 393–417.

Ghanem, Renad. 2011. Arabizi is destroying the Arabic language. Arab News 19, 04/20. http://www.arabnews.com/node/374897 (accessed January 2017).

Ginsburgh, Victor and Shlomo Weber. 2011. *How Many Languages Do We Need? The Economics of Linguistic Diversity*. Princeton, NJ: Princeton University Press.

Goody, Jack. 1977. *The Domestication of the Savage Mind*. Cambridge: Cambridge University Press.

Gorham, Michael, Ingunn Lunde, and Martin Paulsen (eds) 2014. *Digital Russia: The Language, Culture and Politics of New Media Communication*. Abingdon: Routledge.

Gorter, Durk (ed.) 2006. *Linguistic Landscape: A New Approach to Multilingualism*. Clevedon: Multilingual Matters.

Green, David W. 1998. Mental control of the bilingual lexico-semantic system. *Bilingualism: Language and Cognition* 1: 67–81.

Greenberg, Joseph. 1956. The measurement of linguistic diversity. *Language* 32: 109–15.

Gregersen, Frans 2011. Language and ideology in Denmark. In: Tore Kristiansen and Nikolas Coupland (eds), *Standard Languages and Language Standards in a Changing Europe*. Oslo: Novus Press, 47–55.

Greschke, Heike Mónika. 2012. *Is there a Home in Cyberspace? The Internet in Migrants' Everyday Life and the Emergence of Global Communities*. New York: Routledge.

Grillo, R. D. 1989. *Dominant Languages. Language and Hierarchy in Britain and France*. Cambridge: Cambridge University Press.

Grin, François. 2003. Language planning and economics. *Current Issues in Language Planning* 4: 1–66.

Grin, François and Britta Korth. 2005. On the reciprocal influence of language policies and language education: The case of English in Switzerland. *Language Policy* 4: 67–85.

Grivelet, Stéphane (ed.). 2001. *Digraphia: Writing Systems and Society. International Journal of the Sociology of Language* 150.

Grosjean, François. 1998. Studying bilinguals: Methodological and conceptual issues. *Bilingualism, Language and Cognition* 1/2: 131–49.

Grosjean, François. 2010. *Bilingual: Life and Reality*. Cambridge, MA: Harvard University Press.

Guéhenno, Jean-Marie. 1993. *La fin de la démocratie*. Paris: Flammarion.

Guerini, Federica. 2006. *Language Alternation Strategies in a Multilingual Setting. A case study: Ghanian Immigrants in Northern Italy*. Bern: Peter Lang.

Gumperz, John. 1982. *Discourse Strategies*. Cambridge: Cambridge University Press (2nd edn, 1991).

Haberland, Hartmut. 2013. Hybridity and complexity: Language choice and language ideologies. In: Hartmut Haberland, Dorte Lønsmann, and and Bent Preisler (eds), *Language Alternation, Language Choice and Language Encounter in International Tertiary Education*. Dordrecht: Springer, xiii–xxiv.

Habermas, Jürgen. 1996. *Die Einbeziehung des Anderen. Studien zur politischen Theorie*. Frankfurt: Suhrkamp.

Hagège, Claude. 2006. *Combat pour le français: au nom de la diversité des langues et des cultures*. Paris: Odile Jacob.

Hamers, Josiane F. and Michel H. A. Blanc. 1989. *Bilinguality and Bilingualism*. Cambridge: Cambridge University Press.

Handelman, Don. 1977. The organization of ethnicity. *Ethnic Groups* 1: 187–200.

Harley, Birgit. and W. Wang. 1997. The Critical Period Hypothesis: Where are we now? In: A. de Groot and Judith F. Kroll (eds), *Tutorials in Bilingualism: Psycholinguistic Perspectives*. Hillsdale: Erlbaum, 19–52.

Harmon, David and Jonathan Loh. 2010. The index of linguistic diversity: A new quantitative measure of trends in the status of the world's languages. *Language Documentation & Conservation* 4: 97–151. http://scholarspace. manoa.hawaii.edu/bitstream/handle/10125/4474/harmonloh.pdf?sequence=1 (accessed 08/2017).

Harris, Roy. 1980. *The Language Makers*. Ithaca, NY: Cornell University Press.

Haspelmath, Martin. 2009. Lexical borrowing: Concepts and issues. In M. Haspelmath and U. Tadmor (eds), *Loanwords in the World's Languages: A Comparative Handbook*. Berlin: de Gruyter, 35–54.

Haspelmath, Martin and Uri Tadmor (eds) 2009. *Loanwords in the World's Languages: A Comparative Handbook*. Berlin: de Gruyter. (Also accessible as a database at: http://wold.clld.org/).

Hatch, Evelyn M. and Anne Lazaraton. 1991. *The Research Manual: Design and Statistics for Applied Linguistics*. Rowley, MA: Newbury House.

Haugen, Einar. 1950. The analysis of linguistic borrowing. *Language* 26: 210–31.

Hechter, Michael. 1975. *Internal Colonialism: The Celtic Fringe in British National Development, 1536–1966*. London: Routledge and Kegan Paul.

Heinrich, Patrick. 2012. *The Making of Monolingual Japan. Language Ideology in Japanese Modernity*. Bristol, Buffalo, Toronto: Multilingual Matters.

Heller, Monica. 2006. *Linguistic Minorities and Modernity*. London: Continuum.

Heller, Monica. 2011. *Paths to Postnationalism: A Critical Ethnography of Language and Identity*. Oxford: Oxford University Press.

Helliwell, John F. 1999. Language and trade. In: A. Breton (ed.), *Exploring the Economics of Language*. Toronto: Department of Economics, University of Toronto (New Canadian Perspectives), 5–30.

Hernandez, Arturo E. 2013. *The Bilingual Brain*. Oxford: Oxford University Press.

Hitchings, Henry. 2011. *A History of Proper English*. London: John Murray.

Hodgkin, Adam. 2017. *Following Searle on Twitter. How Words Create Digital Institutions*. Chicago and London: University of Chicago Press.

Hoffmann, Charlotte. 1991. *An Introduction to Bilingualism*. Essex: Pearson Education Limited.

Holmes, Prue and Fred Dervin (eds) 2016. *The Cultural and Intercultural Dimensions of English as a Lingua Franca*. Bristol: Multilingual Matters.

Hopp, Holger and Monika S. Schmid. 2013. Perceived foreign accent in first language attrition and second language acquisition: The impact of age of acquisition and bilingualism. *Applied Psycholinguistics* 34: 361–94.

Hosking, Geoffrey. 1997. *Russia: People and Empire*. London: HarperCollins.

Hudson, Richard. 2008. Word grammar, cognitive linguistics, and second language learning and teaching. In P. Robinson and N. Ellis (eds), *Handbook of Cognitive Linguistics and Second Language Acquisition*. London: Routledge, 89–113.

Hull, Geoffrey. 1994. A national language for East Timor. In: István Fodor and Claude Hagège (eds), *Language Reform. History and Future*, vol. VI. Hamburg: Helmut Buske Verlag, 347–66.

Hull, Rachel and Jyotsna Vaid. 2005. Clearing the cobwebs from the study of the bilingual brain: Converging evidence from Laterality and electrophysiological research. In: Judith F. Kroll and Annette M. de Groot (eds), *Handbook of Bilingualism. Psycholinguistic Approaches*. New York: Oxford University Press, 480–96.

Huntington, Samuel P. 1996. *The Clash of Civilizations and the Remaking of World Order*. New York: Simon&Schuster.

iDMC (internal displacement centre). 2015. *Global Overview 2015: People internally displaced by conflict and violence, May 2015*. http://www.internal-displacement.org/publications/2015/global-overview-2015-people-internally-displaced-by-conflict-and-violence (accessed July 2017).

Islam, Rafiqul. 1978. The Bengali language movement and the emergence of Bangladesh. In: Clarence Maloney (ed.), *Language and Civilization Change in South Asia*. Leiden: Brill, 142–53.

Jacobsen, Thorkild. 1974. Very ancient linguistics. Babylonian grammatical texts. In: Dell Hymes (ed.), *Studies in the History of Linguistics: Traditions and Paradigms*. Bloomington: University of Indiana Press, 41–62.

Janssens, Rudi. 2007. Van Brussel gesproken. Taalgebruik, taalverschuivingen en taalidentiteit in het Brussels Hoofdstedelijk Gewest [Told from Brussels. Language use, language shift and language identity in the Brussels Capital Region]. Brusselse Thema's 15. Brussels: VUBPRESS.

Jaspers, Jürgen and Jef Verschueren. 2011. Multilingual structures and agencies. *Journal of Pragmatics* 43: 1157–60.

Jespersen, Otto. 1964 [1922]. *Language. Its Nature, Development and Origin.* New York: W.W. Norton.

Johnson, Keith. 2008. *Quantitative Methods in Linguistics.* Hoboken, NJ, Oxford: Wiley-Blackwell.

Jones, Mari C. (ed.) 2014. *Endangered Languages and New Technologies.* Cambridge: Cambridge University Press.

Jones, Peter. 2016. Group Rights. *The Stanford Encyclopedia of Philosophy* (Summer 2016 Edition), Edward N. Zalta (ed.), forthcoming URL = <http://plato.stanford.edu/archives/sum2016/entries/rights-group/>.

Jones, Steven (ed.) 1995. *CyberSociety: Computer-Mediated Communication and Community.* London: Sage.

Jordan, Bill and Frank Düvell. 2003. *Migration: The Boundaries of Equality and Justice.* Cambridge: Polity Press.

Jørgensen, J. Norman (ed.) 2003. *Bilingualism and Social Change. Turkish Speakers in North Western Europe.* Clevedon: Multilingual Matters.

Judt, Tony and Dennis Lacorne (eds) 2004. *Language, Nation, and State. Identity Politics in a Multilingual Age.* New York: Palgrave Macmillan.

Jurgens, David, Stefan Dimitrov, and Derek Ruths. 2014. Twitter users #codeswitching hashtags! #moltoimportante#wow. In: *Proceedings of the First Workshop on Computational Approaches to Codeswitching*, 51–61.

Kamusella, Tomasz. 2012. The global regime of language recognition. *International Journal of the Sociology of Language* 218: 59–86.

Kamusella, Tomasz. 2016. The idea of a Kosovan language in Yugoslavia's language politics. *International Journal of the Sociology of Language* 242: 217–37.

Kaur, Jagroop and Jaswinder Singh. 2015. Toward normalizing romanized Gurumukhi text from social media. *Indian Journal of Science and Technology* 8. DOI: 10.17485/ijst/2015/v8i27/81666.

Kaushanskaya, Margarita and V. Marian. 2009. The bilingual advantage in novel word learning. *Psychonomic Bulletin and Review* 16: 705–10.

Keen, Andrew. 2015. *The Internet is not the Answer.* London: Atlantic Books.

Kern, Friederike and Yazgül Simsek. 2006. Türkendeutsch: Aspekte von Einheitenbildung und Rezeptionsverhalten. In: Dieter Wolff (ed.), *Mehrsprachige Individuen—vielsprachige Gesellschaften.* Frankfurt am Main: Peter Lang, 101–19.

Kerswill, Paul. 2011. *Multicultural London English: The Emergence, Acquisition and Diffusion of a New Variety.* http://www.lancaster.ac.uk/fss/projects/linguistics/multicultural/ (accessed July 2017).

Kerswill, Paul. 2014. The objectification of 'Jafaican': The discoursal embedding of Multicultural London English in the British media. In: Jannis

Androutsopoulos (ed.), *The Media and Sociolinguistic Change*. Berlin: DeGruyter, 428–55.

Kerzer, David and Dominique Arel (eds) 2002. *Census and Identity. The Politics of Race, Ethnicity and Language in National Censuses*. Cambridge: Cambridge University Press.

Khang, Hyoungkoo, Eyun-Jung Ki, and Lan Ye. 2012. Social media research in advertising, communication, marketing, and public relations, 1997–2010. *Journalism & Mass Communication Quarterly*, 89: 279–98.

Khoo, Chian Kim. 1980. *Census of Population, 1980, Singapore*. Release no. 2, Demographic characteristics. Singapore: Department of Statistics.

Khubchandani, Lachman M. 1983. *Plural Languages, Plural Cultures*. Honolulu: University of Hawai'i Press.

Kim, Suin, Ingmar Weber, Li Wei, and Alice Oh. 2014. Sociolinguistic analysis of Twitter in multilingual societies. In: *Proceedings of the 25th ACM Conference on Hypertext and Social Media*, 243–8.

Kimura, Goro Christoph. 2014. Language management as a cyclical process: A case study on prohibiting Sorbian in the workplace. *Slovo a slovesnost* 2014/11.

King, Lid and Lorna Carson (eds) 2016. *The Multilingual City. Vitality, Conflict and Change*. Bristol, Buffalo, Toronto: Multilingual Matters.

King, Robert D. 2001. The poisonous potency of script: Hindi and Urdu. *International Journal of the Sociology of Language* 150: 43–59.

King, Ruth. 2000. *The Lexical Basis of Grammatical Borrowing: A Prince Edward Island French Case Study*. Amsterdam and Philadelphia: John Benjamins.

Koutsogiannis, Dimitris and Bessie Mitsikopoulou. 2003. Greeklish and Greekness: Trends and discourses of 'glocalness'. *Journal of Computer-Mediated Communication* 9, DOI: 10.1111/j.1083-6101.2003.tb00358.x.

Kouwenberg, Silvia and John Victor Singler (eds) 2009. *The Handbook of Pidgin and Creole Studies*. Oxford: Blackwell.

Kuhn, Thomas. 1970. *The Structure of Scientific Revolutions*. Chicago: University of Chicago Press.

Kuzio, Taras and Paul D'Anieri. 2002. *Dilemas of State-led Nation Building in Ukraine*. London: Praeger.

Kymlicka, Will (ed.) 1995. *The Rights of Minority Cultures*. Oxford: Oxford University Press.

Kymlicka, Will and Alan Patten (eds) 2003. *Language Rights and Political Theory*. New York: Oxford University Press.

Labov, William. 1973. *Language in the Inner City. Studies in the Black English Vernacular*. Philadelphia: University of Pennsylvania Press.

Labrie, Normand. 1993. *La construction linguistique de la Communauté européenne*. Paris: Honoré Champion.

Laitin, David D. 1998. Nationalism and language: A post-Soviet perspective. In: John A. Hall (ed.), *The State of the Nation: Ernest Gellner and the Theory of Nationalism*. Cambridge: Cambridge University Press, 135–57.

Laitin, David D. and Rajesh Ramachandran. 2016. Language policy and human development. *American Political Science Review* 110: 457–80.

Landry, Rodrigue, Réal Allard, and Kenneth Deveau. 2007. Bilingual schooling of the Canadian Francophone minority: A cultural autonomy model. *International Journal of the Sociology of Language* 185: 133–62.

Language Policy Unit (Strasbourg). 2004. *The Common European Framework of Reference for Languages*. Cambridge: Cambridge University Press.

Länsisalmi, Riikka. 2012. West is English, East is 'Exotic': Exploring East Asian languages in European language policies. In: N. Tomimori, M. Furihata, K. Haida, N. Kurosawa, and M. Negishi (eds), *International Symposium Report 2011: New Prospects for Foreign Language Teaching in Higher Education— Exploring the Possibilities of Application of CERF*. Tokyo: World Language and Society Education Centre (WoLSEC), Tokyo University of Foreign Studies, Vol. 2012: 65–82.

Lanza, Elizabeth. 2004. *Language Mixing in Infant Bilingualism: A Sociolinguistic Perspective*. Oxford: Oxford University Press.

Lasagabaster, David and Ángel Huguet (eds) 2007. *Multilingualism in European Bilingual Contexts. Language Use and Attitudes*. Clevedon, Buffalo, Toronto: Multilingual Matters.

Lee Kuan Yew. 2011. *Hard Truths. To Keep Singapore Going*. Singapore: Straits Times Press.

Lee Kuan Yew. 2012. *My Lifelong Challenge: Singapore's Bilingual Journey*. Singapore: Straits Times Press.

Leimgruber, Jakob R. 2011. 'Singapore English'. *Language and Linguistics Compass* 5/1: 47–62.

Lévy, Pierre. 2001. *Cyberculture*. Minneapolis: The University of Minneapolis Press.

Lewis, Erthan. 2013. Immigrant Native Substitutability: The Role of Language Ability. In: David Card and Steven Raphael (eds), *Immigration, Poverty, and Socioeconomic Inequality*. New York: Russell Sage Foundation, 60–97.

Li, David C. S. 2009. Multilingualism and commerce. In: Peter Auer and Li Wei (eds), *Handbook of Multilingualism and Multilingual Communication*. Berlin: De Gruyter, 422–43.

Li, David C. S. 2013. Linguistic Hegemony or Linguistic Capital? Internationalization and English-medium Instruction at the Chinese University of Hong Kong (CUHK). In A. Doiz, D. Lasagabaster, and J. M. Sierra (eds), *English-Medium Instruction at Universities. Global Challenges*. Bristol, Buffalo, Toronto: Multilingual Matters, 65–83.

Li Wei. 2011. Moment Analysis and translanguaging space: Discursive construction of identity by multilingual Chinese youth in Britain. *Journal of Pragmatics* 43: 1222–35.

Li Wei. 2014. Researching multilingualism and superdiversity: Grassroots actions and responsibilities. *Multilingua* 33: 475–84.

Liang Sihua. 2015. *Language Attitudes and Identities in Multilingual China. A Linguistic Ethnography*. Heidelberg, New York: Springer.

Lichter, Daniel T., Domenico Parisi, and Michael C. Taquino. 2015. Toward a new macro-segregation? Decomposing segregation within and between metropolitan cities and suburbs. *American Sociological Review* 80: 843–73.

Lim, Lisa and Ee-Ling Low (eds) 2009. Multilingual, Globalizing Asia. Implications for Policy and Education. *AILA Review*, Volume 22.

Liu, Amy H. 2015. *Standardizing Diversity: The Political Economy of Language Regimes*. Philadelphia: University of Pennsylvania Press.

Liu, Jin. 2013. *Signifying the Local. Media Productions Rendered in Local Languages in Mainland China in the New Millennium*. Leiden: Brill.

Lo Bianco, Joseph. 1988. Multiculturalism and the National Policy on Languages. *Journal of Intercultural Studies* 9: 25–37.

Lowenberg, Peter. 1983. Lexical modernization in bahasa Indonesia: Functional allocation and variation in borrowing. *Studies in the Linguistic Sciences* 13: 73–86.

Lüdi, Georges. 2007. Basel: einsprachig und heteroglossisch. *Zeitschrift für Literaturwissenschaft und Linguistik* 148: 132–57.

Mabry, Tristan James. 2011. Language and conflict. *International Political Science Review* 32: 189–207.

McEnery, Tony and Andrew Hardie. 2012. *Corpus Linguistics. Method, Theory and practice*. Cambridge: Cambridge University Press http://corpora.lancs.ac.uk/clmtp/main-1.php (accessed July 2017).

McEntee-Atalianis, Lisa. 2015. Language policy and planning in international organisations. Multilingualism and the United Nations: Diplomatic baggage of passport to success? In: U. Jessner-Schmid and Claire J. Kramsch (eds), *The Multilingual Challenge: Cross-Disciplinary Perspectives*. Berlin: DeGruyter, 295–322.

Mackey, William F. 1962. The description of bilingualism. *Canadian Journal of Linguistics* 7: 51–85.

McRae, Kenneth D. 1989. Linguistic conflict: some theoretical reflections. In: Peter H. Nelde (ed.), *Urban Language Conflict*. Bonn: Dümmler, 1–20.

MacWhinney, Brian. 2000. *The CHILDES Project: Tools for Analyzing Talk*. Third edition. Mahwah, NJ: Lawrence Erlbaum Associates.

Magner, Thomas F. 2001. Digraphia in the territories of the Croats and Serbs. *International Journal of the Sociology of Language* 150: 11–26.

Mahapatra, B. P. 1991. An appraisal of Indian languages. In: R. H. Robins and E. M. Uhlenbeck (eds), *Endangered Languages*. Oxford, New York: Berg, 177–88.

Maher, John. 2010. Metroethnicities and Metrolanguages. In: Nikolas Coupland (ed.), *The Handbook of Language and Globalization*. Oxford: Wiley-Blackwell, 575–91.

Mair, Victor. 2010. Hong Kong Multilingualism and Polyscriptism. Language Log July 26, http://languagelog.ldc.upenn.edu/nll/?p=2488 (accessed July 2017).

Major, J. C. 2013. On the prickly matter of language. In: Liz Castro (ed.), *What's Up with Catalonia? The Causes Which Impel Them to the Separation.* Ashfield, MA: Catalonia Press: 85–8.

Mallinson, Christine, Becky Childs, and Gerard Van Herk (eds) 2013. *Data Collection in Sociolinguistics: Methods and Applications.* London: Routledge.

Mamadouh, Virginie. 2002. Dealing with multilingualism in the European Union: Cultural Theory rationalities and language policies. *Journal of Comparative Policy Analysis* 4: 327–45.

Mann, Michael. 2005. *The Dark Side of Democracy. Explaining Ethnic Cleansing.* Cambridge, New York: Cambridge University Press.

Mansoor, Sabiha. 2009. Regional languages of Pakistan: Issues and concerns for language planning in higher education. In: Sabiha Mansoor, Aliya Sikandar, Nasreen Hussain, and Nasreen M. Ahsan (eds), *Emerging Issues in TEFL: Challenges for Asia.* Karachi: Oxford University Press, 31–58.

Marçais, William. 1930. La diglossie arabe. *L'enseignement public* 97: 401–9; 105: 20–39.

Marfany, Joan-Lluís. 2010. Sociolinguistics and some of its concepts: a historian's view. *International Journal of the Sociology of Language* 206: 1–20.

Martin, James. 2013. *Politics and Rhetoric: A Critical Introduction.* Abingdon: Routledge.

Matras, Yaron. 2009. *Language Contact.* Cambridge: Cambridge University Press.

May, Stephen. 2003. Language, nationalism and democracy in Europe. In: Gabriele Hogan-Brun and Stefan Wolff (eds), *Minority Languages in Europe.* Basingstoke and New York: Palgrave Macmillan, 211–32.

May, Stephen. 2012. *Language and Minority Rights: Ethnicity, Nationalism, and the Politics of Language.* Second edition. New York: Routledge.

Meara, Paul, James Milton, and Nuria Lorenzo-Dus. 2001. *Language Aptitude Tests.* Newbury: Express Publishing.

Mechelli, Andrea., Jenny T. Crinion, Uta Noppeney, John O'Doherty, John Ashburner, Richard S. Frackowiak, and C. J. Price. 2004. Neurolinguistics: Structural plasticity in the bilingual brain. *Nature* 431: 757.

Merritt, Marilyn. 1992. Socialising Multilingualism: Determinants of Code-Switching in Kenyan Primary Classrooms (with A. Cleghorn, J. Abagi and G. Bunyi). *Journal of Multilingual and Multicultural Development* 13/1–2: 103–22.

Messili, Zouhour and Hmaid Ben Aziza. 2004. Langage et exclusion. La langue des cités en France. *Cahiers de la Méditerranée* 69, 23–32.

Mesthrie, Rajend and Timothy T. Dunne. 1990. Syntactic variation in language shift: The relative clause in South African Indian English. *Language Variation and Change* 2: 31–56.

Mettewie, Laurence and Rudi Janssens. 2007. Language use and language attitudes in Brussels. In: David Lasagabaster and Ángel Huguet (eds,) 2007. *Multilingualism in European Bilingual Contexts. Language Use and Attitudes.* Clevedon, Buffalo, Toronto: Multilingual Matters, 117–43.

Michaelis, Susanne. 2008. *Roots of Creole Structures: Weighing the Contributions of Substrates and Superstrates.* Amsterdam and Philadelphia: John Benjamins.

Miola, Emanuele. 2015. Chì pòdom tucc scriv come voeurom. Scrivere in lombardo online. In: S. Dal Negro, F. Guerini, and Gabriele Iannàccaro (eds), *Elaborazione ortografica delle varietà non standard.* Bergamo: Bergamo University Press, 79–96.

Modood, Tariq. 2013. *Multiculturalism.* Second Edition. Cambridge: Polity Press.

Møller, Janus and J. Normann Jørgensen. 2009. From language to languaging: Changing relations between humans and linguistic features. *Acta Linguisticia Hafniensia* 41: 143–66.

Moratinos Johnston, Sofía. 2001. *Multilingualism and EU Enlargement.* Luxembourg: Office des publications officielles des Communautés européennes.

Moseley, Christopher (ed.) 2010. *Atlas of the World's Languages in Danger* Third edition. Paris, UNESCO Publishing. Online version: http://www.unesco.org/culture/en/endangeredlanguages/atlas.

Mouthon, Michaël, Jean-Marie Annoni, Asaid Khateb. 2013. The bilingual brain. *Swiss Archives of Neurology and Psychiatry* 164/8: 266–73.

Mufwene, Salikoko S. 1998. Native speaker, proficient speaker and norms. In: Rajendra Singh (ed.), *The Native Speaker in Multilingual Perspectives.* New Delhi: Sage, 111–23.

Mukud, Smruthi and Rohini K. Srihari. 2012. Analyzing Urdu social media for sentiments using transfer learning with controlled translations. *Proceedings of the 2012 Workshop on Language and Social Media, Montréal, Canada, June 7, 2012,* 1–8.

Musterd, Sako, Wim Ostendorf, and S. De Vos. 1998. *Multi-Ethnic Metropolis: Patterns and Policies.* Dordrecht: Kluwer.

Myers-Scotton, Carol. 1993. *Duelling Languages.* Oxford: Clarendon Press.

Myers-Scotton, Carol. 2006. *Multiple Voices: An Introduction to Bilingualism.* Oxford: Blackwell.

Nabila, Sailo. 2012. Dialects of Brahmanbaria and Sylhet: A Linguistic Analysis. University of Dhaka: MA thesis.

Neeley, Tsedal. 2012. Global business speaks English. Harvard Business Review, https://hbr.org/2012/05/global-business-speaks-english (accessed July 2017).

Nelde, Peter. 1994. Languages in contact and conflict: The Belgian experience and the European Union. *Current Issues in Language and Society* 1: 165–82.

Nettle, Daniel. 1998. Explaining global patterns of language diversity. *Journal of Anthropological Archaeology* 17: 354–74.

Ng, Patrick. 2011. Mandarin language and the cultural identity of Chinese dialect speaking Singaporeans. *Journal of Intercultural Communication.* Society for Intercultural Education, Training, and Research (SIETAR) 14: 1–13.

Nichols, Johanna. 1992. *Linguistic Diversity in Space and Time.* Chicago: Chicago University Press.

Nicoladis, Elena. 2003. Cross-linguistic transfer in deverbal compounds of preschool bilingual children. *Bilingualism: Language and Cognition* 6: 17–31.

Nitobe, Inazō. 1921. Esperanto and the Language Question of the League of Nations. http://www.esperanto.ie/en/PDF_files/Espo_Leag_Nations.pdf (accessed July 2017).

Nortier, Jacomine and Bente A. Svendsen (eds) 2015. *Language, Youth and Identity in the 21st Century. Linguistic Practices across Urban Spaces.* Cambridge: Cambridge University Press.

Nunan, David. 2008. *Research Methods in Language Learning.* Cambridge: Cambridge University Press.

O'Connell, James F. and Jim Allen. 2003. Dating the colonization of Sahul (Pleistocene Australia-New Guinea): A review of recent research. *Journal of Archaeological Science* 31: 835–53.

Paikeday, Thomas M. 1985. *The Native Speaker is Dead!* Toronto and New York: PPI.

Palmer, Deborah K., Ramón Antontio Martínez, Suzanne G. Mateus, and Kathryn Henderson. 2014. Reframing the debate on language separation: Toward a vision for translanguaging pedagogies in the dual language classroom. *The Modern Language Journal* 98: 757–72.

Paolillo, John C. 2007. How much multilingualism? Language diversity on the Internet. In: Brenda Danet and Susan C. Herring (eds), *The Multilingual Internet. Language, Culture, and Communication Online.* Oxford: Oxford University Press, 408–30.

Paradis, Johanne. 2009. Early bilingual and multilingual acquisition. In: Peter Auer and Li Wei (eds), *Handbook of Multilingualism and Multilingual Communication.* Berlin: De Gruyter, 15–44.

Paradis, Michel. 2004. *A Neurolinguistic Theory of Bilingualism*. Amsterdam: John Benjamins.

Paradis, Michel. 2014 [1987]. *The Assessment of Bilingual Aphasia*. New York: Psychology Press.

Pariser, Eli. 2011. *The Filter Bubble. What the Internet is Hiding from You*. London: Penguin.

Pattanayak, D. P. 1998. Mother tongue: An Indian context. In: Rajendra Singh (ed.), *The Native Speaker: Multilingual Perspectives*. New Delhi: Sage, 124–47.

Pavlenko, Aneta. 2014. *The Bilingual Mind. And What it Tells us about Language and Thought*. Cambridge: Cambridge University Press.

Pennycook, Alastair. 1994. *The Cultural Politics of English as an International Language*. London: Longman.

Peou, Sorpong. 2016. How solid are ASEAN's democracies? *East Asia Forum*, 16 March.

Perry, John R. 1985. Language reform in Turkey and Iran. *International Journal of Middle Eastern Studies* 17: 295–311.

Pháidín, Caoilfhionn Nic and Seán Ó Cearnaigh (eds) 2008. *A New View of the Irish Language*. Syracuse, NY: Syracuse University Press.

Phillipson, Robert. 1992. *Linguistic Imperialism*. Oxford: Oxford University Press.

Pietikäinen, Sari and Helen Kelly-Holmes (eds) 2013. *Multilingualism and the Periphery*. Oxford, New York: Oxford University Press.

Pimienta, Daniel, Daniel Prado and Álvaro Blanco. 2009. Twelve years of measuring linguistic diversity in the Internet: Balance and perspectives. Paris: Unesco. http://unesdoc.unesco.org/images/0018/001870/187016e.pdf (accessed July 2017).

Pohl, Heinz-Dieter. 2007. *Kleines Kärntner Wörterbuch*. Klagenfurt: Heyn.

Polenz, Peter von. 1967. Fremdwort und Lehnwort sprachwissenschaftlich betrachtet. *Muttersprache* 77: 65–80.

Pool, Jonathan. 1972. National development and language diversity. In: J. A. Fishman (ed.), *Advances in the Sociology of Language*, vol. 2. The Hague: Mouton, 213–30.

Pool, Jonathan. 1991. The world language problem. *Rationality and Society* 3: 78–105.

Poplack, Shana. 2009. Quelle langue parlons-nous? [What language do we speak?] In *Les Cahiers de la Fondation Trudeau*. Montréal: Fondation Trudeau, 117–39, 125–47.

Poplack, Shana, David Sankoff, and Christopher Miller. 1988. The social correlates and linguistic processes of lexical borrowing and assimilation. *Linguistics* 26: 47–104.

Poston, Jr., Dudley L. and Leon F. Bouvier. 2010. *Population and Society*. Cambridge, New York: Cambridge University Press.

Poulisse, Nanda. 1999. *Slips of the Tongue. Speech Errors in First and Second Language Production.* Amsterdam: John Benjamins.

Pupavac, Vanessa. 2006. Discriminating language rights and politics in post-Yugoslav states. *Patterns of Prejudice* 40: 112–28.

PuruShotam, Nirmala Srirekam. 1998. *Negotiating Language, Constructing Race. Disciplining Difference in Singapore.* Berlin, New York: Mouton de Gruyter.

Pym, Anthony et al. 2016. MIME. Mobility and Inclusion in a Multilingual Europe. European Union Grant Report 613344, version 31-01-2016.

Quast, Pia. 2008. Sociolinguistic approaches to multiethnolect: Language variety and stylistic practice. *International Journal of Bilingualism* 12: 43–61.

Rahman, Tariq. 2011. *From Hindi to Urdu: A Social and Political History.* Oxford: Oxford University Press.

Rahman, Zia Haider. 2014. *In the Light of What We Know.* New York: Farrar, Straus and Giroux.

Rampton, Ben. 1995. *Crossing. Language and Ethnicity among Adolescents.* London, New York: Longman.

Redder, Angelika et al. 2013. *Mehrsprachige Kommunikation in der Stadt. Das Beispiel Hamburg.* Münster: Waxmann.

Reh, Mechthild. 2004. Multilingual writing: A reader-oriented typology—with examples from Lira Municipality (Uganda). *International Journal of the Sociology of Language* 170: 1–41.

Richards, Jack C. 1997. *Error Analysis: Perspectives on Second Language Acquisition.* Abingdon: Routledge.

Roca, Ana and M. Cecilia Colombi (eds) 2003. *Spanish as a Heritage Language in the United States. Research and Practice.* Washington, DC: Georgetown University Press.

Romaine, Suzanne and Daniel Nettle. 2000. *Vanishing Voices. The Extinction of the World's Languages.* Oxford: Oxford University Press.

Rubdy, Rani. 2001. 'Creative destruction': Singapore's Speak Good English Movement. *World Englishes* 20: 341–55.

Rubdy, Rani and Selim Ben Said (eds) 2015. *Conflict, Exclusion and Dissent in the Linguistic Landscape.* Basingstoke: Palgrave Macmillan.

Rubinstein, Ariel. 2000. *Economics of Language.* Cambridge: Cambridge University Press.

Ruhi, Şükriye, Michael Haugh, and Thomas Schmidt (eds) 2014. *Best Practice for Spoken Corpora in Linguistic Analysis.* Newcastle upon Tyne: Cambridge Scholars Publishing.

Ruhlen, Merritt. 1994. *The Origin of Language: Tracing the Evolution of the Mother Tongue.* New York: Wiley.

Russ, Charles V. J. (ed.) 1990. *The Dialects of Modern German.* Abingdon: Routledge.

Ryan, Camille. 2013. *Language Use in the United States 2011*. U.S. Department of Commerce, Economics and Statistics Administration. U.S. Census Bureau.

Saussure, Ferdinand de. 1985 [1916]. *Cours de linguistique générale. Édition préparé par Tullio de Mauro*. Paris: Payot.

Sawyer, Caroline and Brad K. Blitz (eds) 2011. *Statelessness in the European Union: Displaced, Undocumented, Unwanted*. Cambridge: Cambridge University Press.

Scheinfeldt, Laura B., Sameer Soi, and Sarah Tishoff. 2010. Working toward a synthesis of archaeological, linguistic, and genetic data for inferring African population history. *Proceedings of the National Academy of Science USA*. 107(Suppl 2): 8931–8.

Schilling-Estes, Natalie. 2006. Dialect variation. In R. W. Fasold and J. Connor-Linton (eds), *An Introduction to Language and Linguistics*. Cambridge: Cambridge University Press, 311–41.

Schmid, Monika S. 2011. *Language Attrition*. Cambridge: Cambridge University Press.

Schmidt, Thomas and Kai Wörner (eds) 2012. *Multilingual Corpora and Multilingual Corpus Analysis*. Amsterdam: John Benjamins.

Seferis, Giorgos. 1974. *Essays I, Erotokritos*. Athens: Ermis.

Sekerina, Irina, Eva M. Fernández, and Harald Clahsen (eds) 2008. *Developmental Psycholinguistics: On-line Methods in Children's Language Processing*. Amsterdam: Benjamins.

Sen, Amartya. 1992. *Inequality Reexamined*. Cambridge, MA: Harvard University Press.

Shin, Sarah J. 2005. *Developing in Two Languages. Korean Children in America*. Clevedon, Buffalo, Toronto: Multilingual Matters.

Shohamy, Elana and Durk Gorter (eds) 2009. *Linguistic Landscape. Expanding the Scenery*. New York, London: Routledge.

Siebenhaar, Beat. 2006. Code choice and code-switching in Swiss-German Internet chat rooms. *Journal of Sociolinguistics* 10: 481–506.

Sierp, Aline. 2008. Minority Language Protection in Italy: Linguistic Minorities and the Media. *Journal of Contemporary European Research* 4: 303–21.

Silva-Corvalán, Carmen. 2014. *Bilingual Language Acquisition. Spanish and English in the First Six Years*. Cambridge: Cambridge University Press.

Simmel, Georg. 1903. Die Großstädte und das Geistesleben. Dresden: *Jahrbuch der Gehe-Stiftung* 9, 185–206 [English translation: The metropolis and mental life, in: Gary Bridge and Sophie Watson (eds), *The Blackwell City Reader*. Oxford and Malden, MA: Wiley-Blackwell, 2002, 11–19].

Simonite, Tom. 2012. Translation tools could save less-used languages. *MIT Technology Review*. https://www.technologyreview.com/s/428093/translation-tools-could-save-less-used-languages/ (accessed July 2017).

Singstat. 2015. Population Trends. http://www.singstat.gov.sg/docs/default-source/default-document-library/publications/publications_and_papers/population_and_population_structure/population2016.pdf (accessed January 2017).

Skutnabb-Kangas, Tove and Robert Phillipson (eds) 1995. *Linguistic Human Rights. Overcoming Linguistic Discrimination.* Berlin: Mouton de Gruyter.

Smakman, Dick and Patrick Heinrich (eds) 2015. *Globalising Sociolinguistics. Challenging and Expanding Theory.* London: Routledge.

Smart, Alan and Josephine Smart. 2003. Urbanization and the global perspective. *Annual Review of Anthropology* 32: 263–85.

Snow, Don. 2004. *Cantonese as Written Language. The growth of a Written Chinese Vernacular.* Hong Kong: Hong Kong University Press.

Sokal, Richard R., Neal L. Oden, Pierre Legendre, Marie-Josée Fortin, Junhyong Kim, and Alain Vaudor. 1989. Genetic differences among languages families in Europe. *American Journal of Physical Anthropology* 79: 489–502.

Solèr, Clau. 2008. Rätoromanisch erhalten—die Quadratur des Kreises? *Bündner Monatsblatt* 2: 141–59.

Sorolla Vidal, Natxo. 2016. *Tria de llengües i roles sociolingüístics a la Franja des de la perspectiva de l'anàlisi de xarxes socials* [Language choice and social roles on The Strip (a Catalan-speaking area in Aragon, F.C.) from the perspective of social network analysis]. Universitat de Barcelona: http://www.tdx.cat/handle/10803/373905 (accessed July 2017).

South, Ashley and Marie Lall. 2016. Language, education and the peace process in Myanmar. *Contemporary Southeast Asia* 38: 128–53.

Special Eurobarometer 386. 2012. Europeans and their Languages. Report. http://ec.europa.eu/public_opinion/archives/ebs/ebs_386_en.pdf.

Sperlich, Wolfgang B. 2005. Will cyberforums save endangered languages? A Niuean case study. *International Journal of the Sociology of Language* 172: 51–77.

Spolsky, Bernard and Robert L. Cooper. 1991. *The Languages of Jerusalem.* Oxford: Clarendon Press.

Spotti, Massimiliano. 2011. Modernist language ideologies, indexicalities and identities: Looking at the multilingual classroom through a post-Fishmanian lens. *Applied Linguistics Review* 2: 29–50.

Sreevastan, Ajai. 2014. Where are the Sanskrit speakers? *The Hindu*, August 10.

Srivastava, R. N. 1984. Linguistic minorities and national language. In: F. Coulmas (ed.), *Linguistic Minorities and Literacy: Language Policy Issues in Developing Countries.* Berlin, New York: Mouton, 99–114.

Statistik Schweiz. 2014. Sprachen, Religionen, Daten. http://www.bfs.admin.ch/bfs/portal/de/index/themen/01/05/blank/key/sprachen.html (accessed January 2017).

Strubell, Miquel. 2007. The political discourse on multilingualism in the European Union. In: Darion Castiglione and Chris Longman (eds), *The Language Question in Europe and Diverse Societies*. Oxford: Hart Publishing, 149–83.

Sullivan, Nancy and Robert T. Schatz. 1999. When cultures collide: The official language debate. *Language and Communication* 19: 261–75.

Sun Hechuan and Keli Jiang. 2000. A study of recent borrowings in Mandarin. *American Speech* 75: 98–106.

Sun Hongkai and Florian Coulmas (eds) 1992. News from China: Minority languages in perspective. Special issue: *International Journal of the Sociology of Language* #97.

Swift, Jonathan S. 1991. Foreign language ability and international marketing. *European Journal of Marketing* 25: 39–49.

Tagg, Caroline. 2015. *Exploring Digital Communication: Language in Action*. New York: Routledge.

Tan, Mely G. 2005. Ethnic Chinese in Indonesia. In Melvin Ember, Carol Ember, and Ian Skoggard (eds), *Encyclopedia of Diasporas: Immigrant and Refugee Cultures Around the World*. New York: Springer.

Tang, Zhixiang. 2016. Language choice and language attitude among different social segments in Shenzhen. *Journal of Asian Pacific Communication* 26/1: 143–60.

Tessarolo, Mariselda. 1990. *Minoranze linguistiche e immagine della lingua*. Milan: Franco Angeli.

Thomas, George. 1991. *Linguistic Purism*. London & New York: Longman.

Thomason, Sarah G. 1997. A typology of contact languages. In: Arthur K. Spears and Donald Winford (eds), *Pidgins and Creoles: Structure and Status*. Amsterdam, Philadelphia: John Benjamins, 71–88.

Thomason, Sarah G. and Terrence Kaufman. 1988. *Language Contact, Creolization and Genetic Linguistics*. Berkeley: University of California Press.

Thornberry, Patrick. 1997. *International Law and the Rights of Minorities*. Oxford: Oxford University Press.

Tileagă, Christian. 2016. *The Nature of Prejudice: Society, Discrimination and Moral Exclusion*. Hove: Routledge.

Trifonas, Peter P. and Themistoklis Aravossitas (eds) 2014. *Rethinking Heritage Language Education*. Cambridge: Cambridge University Press

Trim, John L. M. 2002. Foreign language policies in Europe, with special reference to the roles of the Council of Europe and the European Union. In: Steven J. Baker (ed.), *Language Policy: Lessons from Global Models*. Monterey: Monterey Institute of International Studies, 182–93.

UN. 2014. *World Urbanization Prospects: The 2014 Revision, Highlights*. New York: United Nations, Department of Economic and Social Affairs, Population Division.

UN. 2016. *International Migration and Development. Report of the Secretary General*. http://www.un.org/en/development/desa/population/migration/generalassembly/docs/A_71_296_E.pdf.

UNESCO. 1953. *The Use of Vernacular Languages in Education*. Paris: United Nations Scientific and Cultural Organization.

UNESCO. 2003. *Education in a Multilingual World*. Education Position Paper. http://unesdoc.unesco.org/images/0012/001297/129728e.pdf.

UNESCO. 2008. *Mother Tongue Instruction in Early Childhood Education: A Selected Bibliography*. Paris: UNESCO.

UNESCO Atlas of the World's Languages in Danger. http://www.unesco.org/languages-atlas/ updated version February 2006.

Unger, Johan W., Michł Krzyżanowski, and Ruth Wodak (eds) 2014. *Multilingual Encounters in Europe's Institutional Spaces*. London: Bloomsbury.

Van der Horst, Joop. 2009. *Het einde van de standaardtaal*. Amsterdam: Meulenhoff.

Van Deusen-Scholl, Nelleke. 2003. Toward a definition of heritage language: Sociopolitical and pedagogical considerations. *Journal of Language, Identity, and Education* 2: 211–30.

Van Parijs, Philippe. 2007. Europe's linguistic challenge. In: Darion Castiglione and Chris Longman (eds), *The Language Question in Europe and Diverse Societies*. Oxford: Hart Publishing, 217–53.

Van Rooy, Bertus and Rias van den Doel. 2011. Dutch and Afrikaans as post-pluricentric languages. *International Journal of the Sociology of Language* 212: 1–22.

Vaughan, Liwen and Mike Thelwall. N.d. *Search Engine Coverage Bias: Evidence and Possible Causes*. http://citeseerx.ist.psu.edu/viewdoc/download?doi=10.1.1.65.5130&rep=rep1&type=pdf (accessed January 2017).

Verlot, Marc, Kaat Delrue, Guus Extra, and Kutlay Yağmur. 2003. *Meertaligheid in Brussel. De status van allochtone talan thuis en op school*. Amsterdam: European Cultural Foundation.

Vermeij, Lotte. 2002. De sociale betekenis van straattaal. Interetnisch taalgebruik onder scholieren in Nederland. *Pedagogiek* 22: 260–73.

Vertovec, Steven. 2004. Cheap calls: The social glue of migrant transnationalism. *Global Networks* 4: 219–24.

Vertovec, Steven. 2007. Super-diversity and its implications. *Ethnic and Racial Studies* 30: 1024–54.

Vigouroux, Cécile B. 2011. Magic marketing: Performing grassroots literacy. *Diversities*, 13/2: 53–69. www.unesco.org/shs/diversities/vol13/issue2/art4 (accessed July 2017).

Vogl, Ulrike and Matthias Hüning. 2010. One nation, one language? The case of Belgium. *Dutch Crossing* 34: 228–47.

Wallerstein, Immanuel. 2006. *European Universalism. The Rhetoric of Power.* New York: The New Press.

Wang, Xuan, Kasper Juffermans, and Caixia Du. 2016. Harmony as language policy in China: an Internet perspective. *Language Policy* 15: 299–321.

Wardhaugh, Ronald. 1987. *Languages in Competition.* Oxford: Basil Blackwell.

Warschauer, Mark, Ghada R. El Said, and Ayman G. Zohry. 2007. Language choice online: Globalization and identity in Egypt. In: B. Danet and S. Herring (eds), *The Multilingual Internet: Language, Culture, and Communication Online.* Oxford: Oxford University Press, 303–18.

Watts, Richard J. and Heather Murray (eds) 2001. *Die fünfte Landessprache? Englisch in der Schweiz.* Zurich: vdf Hochschulverlag.

Weber, Max. 1978 [1922]. *Wirtschaft und Gesellschaft. Grundrisse der verstehenden Soziologie.* Tübingen: Mohr Siebeck. [Trans. *Economy and Society: An Outline of Interpretive Sociology.* ed. G. Roth and C. Wittich. Berkeley: University of California Press, 1978. https:// archive.org/ details/ MaxWeber EconomyAndSociety.]

Wegerif, Rupert. 2013. *Dialogic: Education for the Internet age.* London: Routledge.

Weinstein, Brian. 1983. *The Civic Tongue. Political Consequences of Language Choices.* London: Longman.

Wellman, Carl. 1995. *Real Rights.* Oxford: Oxford University Press.

Wichmann, Søren and Anthony Grant (eds) 2012. *Quantitative Approaches to Linguistic Diversity. Commemorating the Centenary of the Birth of Morris Swadesh.* Amsterdam: John Benjamins.

Wiese, Harald. 2015. Language competition: An economic theory of language learning and production. *International Journal of the Sociology of Language* 236: 295–329.

Wiese, Heike. 2012. *Kietzdeutsch. Ein neuer Dialekt entsteht.* Munich: C.H. Beck.

Williams, Colin. 1994. *Called unto Liberty: Our Language and Nationalism.* Clevedon: Multilingual Matters.

Williams, Colin. 2014. The lightening veil: Language revitalization in Wales. *Review of Research in Education* 38: 242–72.

Willmott, Donald E. 1961. *The National Status of the Chinese in Indonesia 1900–1958.* Ithaca, NY: Cornell University Press.

Wodak, Ruth. 2014. The European Parliament: Multilingual experience in the everyday life of MEPs. In: Johan W. Unger, Michł Krzyżanowski, and Ruth Wodak (eds), *Multilingual Encounters in Europe's Institutional Spaces.* London: Bloomsbury, 125–69.

Wright, Sue (ed.) 2004. Multilingualism on the Internet. International Journal of Multicultural Studies 6/1. http://www.unesco.org/new/en/communication-and-information/access-to-knowledge/linguistic-diversity-and-multilingualism-on-internet/ (accessed July 2017).

Wright, Sue and Helen Kelly-Holmes (eds) 1998. *Managing Language Diversity.* Clevedon: Multilingual Matters.

Wunderlich, Dieter. 2015. *Sprachen der Welt. Warum sie so verschieden sind und doch alle gleichen.* Darmstadt: Wissenschaftliche Buchgesellschaft.

Xu Daming. 2015. Speech community and linguistic urbanization: Sociolinguistic theories developed in China. In: Dick Smakman and Patrick Heinrich (eds), *Globalising Sociolinguistics. Challenging and Expanding Theory.* London: Routledge, 95–106.

Yagmur, Kutlay. 2016. The differences between policy and practice of multilingualism in the European context. In: Almut Küppers, Barbara Pusch, and Pinar Uyan Semerci (eds), *Bildung in Trans-nationalen Räumen: Education in Transnational Spaces.* Wiesbaden: Springer VS, 91–107.

Yildiz, Yasemin. 2012. *Beyond the Mother Tongue. The Postmonolingual Condition.* New York: Fordham University Press.

Zartman, I. William (ed.). 1995. *Collapsed States. The Disintegration and Restoration of Legitimate Authority.* Boulder, London: Lynne Rienner.

Zhao Shouhui and Liu Yongbing. 2010. Home language shift and its implications for language planning in Singapore: From the perspective of prestige planning. *The Asia-Pacific Education Researcher* 16/2: 111–26.

Zhou Minglang. 2003. *Multilingualism in China. The Politics of Writing Reforms for Minority Languages 1949–2002.* Berlin, New York: Mouton de Gruyter.

Zsiga, Elizabeth C., One Tlale Boyer, and Ruth Kramer. 2014. *Languages in Africa: Multilingualism, Language Policy, and Education.* Washington, DC: Georgetown University Press.

Zuckerman, Ethan. 2013. *Rewire: Digital Cosmopolitans in the Age of Connection.* New York, London: W.W. Norton.

Zustand und Zukunft der viersprachigen Schweiz. 1989. *Abklärungen, Vorschläge und Empfehlungen einer Arbeitsgruppe des Eidgenössischen Departementes des Innern.* [State and future of quatrolingual Switzerland: clarifications, suggestions and recommendations of a working group of the Federal Department of the Interior]. Bern: Schweizerische Bundeskanzlei.

Index of Names

Index of Subjects